THE WHIG PARTY IN PENNSYLVANIA

STUDIES IN HISTORY, ECONOMICS AND PUBLIC LAW

EDITED BY THE FACULTY OF POLITICAL SCIENCE
OF COLUMBIA UNIVERSITY

Volume CI]   [Number 2

Whole Number 230

THE WHIG PARTY IN PENNSYLVANIA

BY

HENRY R. MUELLER

AMS PRESS
NEW YORK

COLUMBIA UNIVERSITY
STUDIES IN THE
SOCIAL SCIENCES

230

This Series was formerly known as
Studies in History, Economics and Public Law.

Reprinted with the permission of Columbia University Press
From the edition of 1922, New York
First AMS EDITION published 1969
Manufactured in the United States of America

Library of Congress Catalogue Card Number: 74-82233

AMS PRESS, INC.
NEW YORK, N. Y. 10003

To

MY MOTHER

PREFACE

THE study was undertaken as the result of a suggestion from Professor William A. Dunning of Columbia University. The original intention of the author was to confine the investigation to the last decade of the existence of the Whig party in Pennsylvania. As the work proceeded, it became necessary to examine portions of the early period of the party. It was soon evident that for the sake of unity and continuity the history of the Whig party in Pennsylvania should be presented from the time of its formation until its disappearance. The late Charles McCarthy in his excellent *The Anti-Masonic Party* and Miss Marguerite G. Bartlett in *The Chief Phases of Pennsylvania Politics in the Jacksonian Period* have covered the period in which the Whig party was formed but not with the Whig party as the main interest. Consequently, despite the previous work in the field, the author felt justified in including this material.

Pennsylvania during the period of the Whig party was undergoing an extensive expansion in manufacturing and mining, which tended to draw her to the policy desired by the New England states. On the other hand, conditions similar to those existing on the frontier persisted in the mountain districts of the state until the close of the period. The relation of certain sections of the state to the South through the mercantile interest was close, causing the adoption of a kindly attitude toward the slave holder. As a result of these conditions, the state, in a measure at least, reflected the sentiments of the different sections of the country. Consequently, the varied and varying political arguments all find expression in one or the other of the political groups within the state. During the period under study, as went Pennsylvania, so went the Union. In the majority of the elections, Pennsylvania was the determining factor.

Many kindnesses were shown the author in the prosecution of his work. A debt of especial gratitude is due to Professors William A. Dunning and D. R. Fox for numerous suggestions, which saved the author from many a pitfall. The author wishes gratefully to acknowledge the readiness with which the Historical Society of Pennsylvania and the Library of Congress placed the resources of their manuscript department at his disposal. Chief reliance for newspaper material was placed upon the excellent collection of the Pennsylvania State Library, where innumerable favors were extended by the librarians. The maps were prepared under the author's direction by Mr. Howard L. Weiss, one of his students.

CONTENTS

MAPS

CHAPTER I

THE PERIOD OF SUBORDINATION

1834-1838.

A marked characteristic of the American people has been their tendency to form combinations for the purpose of attaining a particular end.   In no phase of their social activities has this tendency been more noticeable than in the conduct of political affairs.   Political agitation never has failed to attract attention, but after the disappearance of the Federalist party interest in the maintenance of party organization waned.   For a short period of time organized national political parties ceased to exist.   Gradually in national politics new leaders with large personal followings appeared; from these groups new political parties were to come.   Of these leaders Andrew Jackson appealed particularly to the untutored laboring man, mechanic and farmer. In the presidential election of 1824 opposition to him in Pennsylvania was hardly worth the name.[1]   In the election of 1828 he carried the state by an overwhelming majority. Prior to the election of 1832 two political organizations opposed to Andrew Jackson had been formed with branches in the state.   In 1829 the Anti-Masonic party developed strength in the counties of the interior.   In Philadelphia

---

[1] In 1824 Jackson had been nominated by two conventions in Pennsylvania, the one said to be Federalist and the other Democratic; Sargent, *Public Men and Events*, vol. i, p. 41.

the commercial element, refusing to respond to the movement, supported Henry Clay for the next presidential election. In the rest of the state this movement for Clay, soon assuming the name of National Republican, made little headway. Unlike the situation elsewhere, no cooperation between these two parties existed, for the Anti-Masons were just as proscriptive of the National Republicans as they were of the Jackson party.

In preparation for the election of 1832 Clay urged his followers to assume an independent but conciliatory attitude towards the other elements of Jacksonian opposition.[1] So far as the state elections were concerned, they acquiesced, making no nominations of their own. The Anti-Masons, not being eager for this cooperation, viewed it with distrust. Amos Ellmaker, Anti-Masonic candidate for the vice-presidency, voiced it in a letter to Thaddeus Stevens, saying that "the remotest suspicion of Anti-Masons combining with any other party, or fragment of party, would be and ought to be injurious, if not fatal to the election of Ritner."[2] After the gubernatorial election, the electoral ticket for Clay and Sergeant was withdrawn; the National Republicans, in the main, voted for Wirt and Ellmaker, the Anti-Masonic nominees, who nevertheless, did not carry the

[1] Henry Clay to Thomas I. Wharton, July 25, 1831; Miscellaneous Mss. Collection of the New York Historical Society.

[2] Letter of August 16, 1832; *Publications of the Lancaster County Historical Society,* vol. viii, pp. 38-44. Ritner was the Anti-Masonic candidate for governor. For the presidential election the Clay supporters proposed a joint electoral ticket, allowing the voters to cast their ballot for either Clay or Wirt. General R. Rosebury, member of the Anti-Masonic state committee, on July 24, 1832, wrote the chairman, Joseph Wallace, "I should view defeat under present circumstances as less likely to prove prejudicial to the cause we are engaged in advocating than success that arises from a union with a party that has nothing in common with us." Wm. McPherson Mss.

state.[1] Although the Anti-Masons did not desire this support, yet they could not deny its existence; the way was thus open for future joint action, based on their consent.

Jackson's determination to ruin the Bank of the United States furnished the two opposition parties within the state the incentive and the opportunity for combining. The withdrawal of funds from the bank by the government caused the officers of the bank to curtail their loans and to draw bills of exchange for short periods only.[2] The financial flurry and business depression which followed were attributed by the bank to the policy of the government. Instructions came from Clay, showing how the indignation of the state, in which the bank had a fair degree of popularity, might be used to political advantage.[3] Following his instructions mass meetings at Philadelphia, Chambersburg, Pittsburgh, York, Easton, Huntingdon, Beaver, Williamsport, Gettysburg, and Chester adopted resolutions, sent committees to Washington to present them to Congress, and, much to his disgust and annoyance, to interview the President on the restoration of the deposits.[4]

The merchants of Philadelphia in openly directing the agitation acted in unison so that on the day of one of the mass meetings " nine-tenths of the mercantile houses were closed." [5] Pressure was brought to bear on the directors

---

[1] *Niles' Register,* vol. xlii, p. 273; vol. xliii, pp. 134, 136. Wirt had been unsuccessful in an endeavor to have the Anti-Masons endorse Clay; Kennedy, *Memoirs of the Life of William Wirt,* vol. ii, pp. 356, 359, 366, 380, 381.

[2] Catterall, *Second Bank of the United States,* pp. 314, *et seq.*

[3] Clay to Nicholas Biddle, December 21, 1833; McGrane, *Correspondence of Nicholas Biddle,* p. 218.

[4] *National Gazette,* January 3, February 4, 5, 6, 8, 10, 13, 24, March 10, 11; *United States Gazette,* January 4, 28, 29, February 4, 5, 26, March 5, 12, 1834. Some of the memorials and reports can be found in Hazard, *Register of Pennsylvania,* vol. xiii.

[5] *National Gazette,* March 21, 1834; *cf.* also Sargent, *op. cit.,* vol. i, p. 262.

of the Girard Bank of Philadelphia, one of the government depositories, because of their contract. A referendum to the stockholders voided the contract, which the directors had made with the government.[1] The agitation against the course pursued by Jackson was apparently so effective that the *National Gazette,* a bank organ, was led to exclaim, " The anti-Jackson sensation extends rapidly. The Stamp Act did not produce more excitement than the Dictatorship does now. President Jackson took a ' responsibility ' much more weighty than he supposed." [2]

Within the state the bank supporters looked longingly on the strength of the Anti-Masons. A small anti-bank section of this party endeavored to throw its support to Jackson in his fight against the bank. Richard Rush, leader of this group, in an open letter claimed that

if antimasons object to the *Lodge* that it makes the press *dumb,* if this be the cornerstone of their cause, can they look with other feelings than those of reprobation on the unwarrantable acts of another powerful institution for stimulating it to NOISE? I would fain persuade myself not.[3]

When his effort to have the Anti-Masonic party oppose the bank failed, Rush led his wing into the ranks of the Jackson supporters. From this failure it was evident that the bank partisans might, if they handled the situation astutely, win the support of the rest of the Anti-Masonic party. It was also evident that the bank question was too limited for any determined and continued agitation. Therefore opposition

---

[1] Hazard, *Register of Pennsylvania,* vol. xiii, pp. 108, 191, 304. The cancellation of this contract was revoked at a later referendum; the bank continued to act as a government depository, *ibid.,* vol. xiv, p. 143.

[2] March 15, 1834.

[3] *Pennsylvanian,* November 30, 1833.

to "executive usurpation" was stressed as the bond of union for all those unfriendly to the occupant of the White House. The cue for the politicians was again furnished by Clay.[1]

On February 22, 1834, a mass meeting at Philadelphia gave definiteness to the agitation when it resolved that all those opposed to the policy of the President should assemble in convention at Harrisburg. To clear up the confusion, resulting from the failure to select a date for the convention, "the Democratic members of the Legislature," on March 25, set May 27 as the time of meeting. At a later meeting they requested that double representation be sent in order to impress the public with the significance of the movement; it was thus possible to seat delegations from the two anti-Jackson parties, if they chanced to be sent from any one county.[2]

In the early part of April a portion of the Jackson opposition, adopting the name from the nearby states, began to call themselves Whigs.[3] They endeavored to have it accepted as a generic name for all the political opponents of Jackson, saying that "the great mass of the opponents of

[1] McGrane, *op. cit.*, p. 220, letter of February 2, 1834, to Nicholas Biddle.

[2] *United States Gazette*, February 26, April 2; *Pennsylvania Intelligencer*, April 10, 1834. The use of the term, "the Democratic members of the Legislature," by those who favored the Bank was declared to be deceitful by "the Democratic members of the Legislature" who opposed the bank; *Pennsylvania Reporter*, April 4, 1834.

[3] *Pennsylvania Intelligencer*, April 17; *United States Gazette*, April 5, 16; *National Gazette*, April 11, 16, 17, 24, 1834. Apparently the use of the word "Whig" was suggested by the editor of the *New York Courier;* it was immediately used to describe the anti-Jackson movement in New York, and a little later in Pennsylvania. *Pennsylvania Inquirer*, April 3, 5, 1834. Sargent, *op. cit.*, vol. i, p. 261, relying on his memory, incorrectly states that the term was used independently in Pennsylvania.

Federal usurpation, whether Masons or Anti-Masons, are Democratic Whigs; a man may be an Anti-Mason and at the same time a Whig."[1]   They strove to identify the policy of the federal executive with the despised Federalism, and theirs with the policy of those who struggled for freedom. One of their county meetings

Resolved, that we recognize the Democratic doctrines of 1798 and the Democratic Whig principles of 1834, as the resuscitated Whig doctrines of 1776 having for their object the fixing of the boundaries of the various departments of the government, and the deliverance of the people from the usurpations of Royal and Federal power. . . . [2]

The National Republicans were not unwilling to accept the new descriptive title of Whig, but the Anti-Masons, although willing to have the National Republicans act with them, were not ready to abandon their own party name or organization.   Inasmuch as the Anti-Masons were stronger than the National Republicans and had shown remarkable power in the interior counties of the state because of their sectarian appeal, the situation required careful handling. Therefore, when the convention assembled on May 27, precautions were taken not to offend the Anti-Masons, who were present in goodly numbers.   It was " Resolved, that this Convention be styled a Convention of Delegates from the Citizens of Pennsylvania opposed to executive usurpation and abuse." [3]   It is impossible to classify the delegates

[1] *Pennsylvania Intelligencer,* June 12, 1834.

[2] *Ibid.,* April 24, 1834, for Dauphin county mass convention of April 22.   On May 25, at Doylestown, there was formed a " Jefferson Democratic Association " of those who opposed Jackson; *ibid.,* June 12, 1834.

[3] *National Gazette,* June 3, 1834.   For the Anti-Masonic party in Pennsylvania, see McCarthy, " The Antimasonic Party," *Report of the American Historical Association,* 1902, vol. i, pp. 427-503.

according to previous political affiliation, but it was claimed that seventy-five of the two hundred and eight in attendance were former supporters of Jackson.[1] Thaddeus Stevens, Neville B. Craig, Ner Middleswarth, and Joseph Lawrence were prominent Anti-Masons in attendance, the last named being chosen president of the convention. Due to the opposition of this group no new political organization could be attempted, and therefore it was

Resolved, that it be earnestly recommended to our fellow-citizens, throughout this commonwealth, along with zeal and energy in the great and good cause, to cultivate a spirit of conciliation and mutual respect; and that it be further earnestly recommended to them, to distinguish with their high approbation and confidence, every member of Congress or of the Legislature, by whatever name he may have been chosen, who in his station has faithfully resisted Executive usurpation and abuse, and firmly maintained the rights of the people.[2]

Inasmuch as there were no general officers to be chosen, the question of joint action assumed only local importance. In the districts where the National Republicans had developed strength, particularly in Philadelphia and its environs, the Whigs directed the contest. In the balance of the state control rested with the Anti-Masons, excepting in a few counties, such as Allegheny, where cooperation was refused.[3]

The election failed to disclose any unusual movement away from the Democratic party despite the strenuous efforts, made in Philadelphia, to stir up enthusiasm for the new party. The Whig city convention had urged

the mechanics, manufacturers, merchants, and all others en-

[1] *Pennsylvania Intelligencer,* May 29, 1834.

[2] Proceedings of the convention in *Niles' Register,* vol. xlvi, p. 243.

[3] *Pennsylvanian,* May 22, 1834; Konkle, *Life and Speeches of Thomas Williams,* vol. i, p. 97.

gaged in trade, who are opposed to the odious tyranny of
Andrew Jackson, to close their workshops, stores and places
of business, on the days of the ward and general elections, at
12 o'clock noon, for the remainder of the day, so that all who
are disposed may be enabled to lend their aid in support of the
constitution and the law.[1]

Despite these efforts the Democrats retained control of the
legislature, although they carried several districts through
the failure of their opponents to cooperate, and they likewise elected a majority of the Congressmen. The Whigs,
in the main, attributed their defeat to the superior organization of the Democrats, but one Whig editor claimed, " The
Jackson men succeeded in some parts of the State in making
the question Bank or no Bank, instead of usurpation and
Van Buren on the one side, and Democracy and the Constitution on the other." [2]   Though thoroughgoing cooperation had not been attained in this election, yet a breach had
been made in the isolating wall of Anti-Masonry.

The Anti-Masons were not yet, however, ready to join a
fusion with the Whigs. This they made evident when
" the Democratic Convention opposed to secret societies and
political intrigue," meeting at Harrisburg on March 4, 1835,
nominated Joseph Ritner for governor.[3] Ritner was the
logical candidate; for, although defeated in the elections
of 1829 and of 1832, he had shown remarkable strength.
He was a Pennsylvania German, with all their characteristic
traits and could count on the support of that group
within the state. As a young man he had left his native
county, Berks, had crossed the mountains, and settled as

---

[1] *National Gazette,* September 27, 1834.

[2] *Pennsylvania Intelligencer,* October 17, 1834. The situation in Philadelphia was tense. Biddle, in fear of personal violence, sent his
family out of the city. Catterall, *op. cit.,* p. 356.

[3] *Pennsylvania Intelligencer,* March 5, 9, 13, 1835.

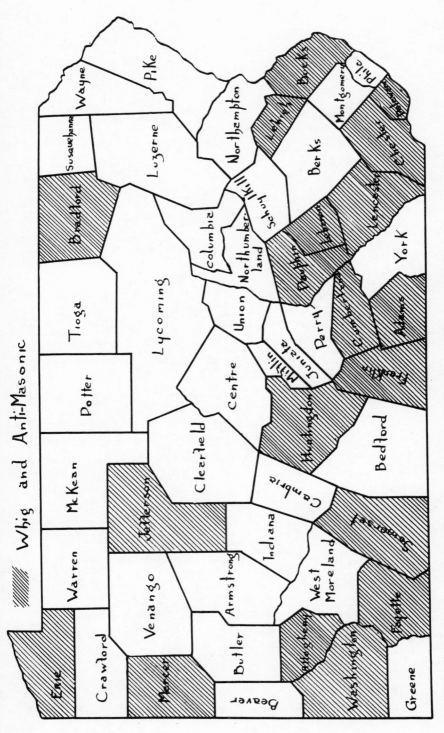

Whig and Anti-Masonic

CONGRESSIONAL ELECTION OF 1834 (PHILADELPHIA CITY, WHIG; PHILADELPHIA COUNTY, DEMOCRATIC)

a farmer in Washington county. For six years, from 1820 to 1825, he had been returned in the annual elections to the house of representatives, over which he presided in 1824 and in 1825, being chosen without opposition in the latter year. Although his views on the bank question were not considered by the Anti-Masons when they nominated him, yet they were of such a nature as to prove attractive to the Whigs. During his campaign of 1832 he had written,

It is impossible to forget the deplorable· condition of the Government, during the late war, for want of such a Bank, and the wretched state of the currency up to the time the Bank commenced operations was no less so. I can scarcely persuade myself, that the man *who can oppose re-chartering the Bank*, with all these facts staring him in the face, *possesses either a sound head, or a good heart.*[1]

With such an opinion on the value of the bank, he was in this respect well-nigh all the Whigs hoped for. Consequently demands for a Whig state convention were rebuffed by county conventions, which endorsed the candidacy of Ritner.[2] The Whigs were fully conscious of their numerical weakness, and one of them stated, " There are not five counties in the State, in which they can poll a larger vote than the Anti-Masons." [3] The Whigs were all the more willing to submit to this disdainful attitude of the

[1] *Democratic State Journal,* June 20, 1835, reprint of letter, dated July 7, 1832.

[2] *Pennsylvania Intelligencer,* March 13, 30, April 23, June 11, August 27; *United States Gazette,* March 14, 18, April 25, May 23, June 20, 24, 1835.

[3] *Carlisle Herald,* quoted in the *Pennsylvania Intelligencer,* March 13, 1835. The editor estimated the Whig strength to be 30,000, and the Anti-Masonic 60,0000. On the other hand, the *United States Gazette* claimed the Whig vote totaled 50,000; quoted in the *Pennsylvania Intelligencer,* March 5, 1835.

Anti-Masons, for the Democratic party had split into two factions, the one nominating George Wolf for reelection, and the other supporting Henry A. Muhlenberg. This factional fight boded well for the opposition.

The struggle in the Democratic ranks had been developing for some years. Fundamentally it was an effort to oust Governor Wolf and his supporters from the offices, which they had been holding for two terms, and to fill them with other Democrats. Involved with this were other issues. In December, 1833, Samuel McKean, a close friend of the governor, was chosen to represent the state in the United States Senate. Shortly after his election, the newspapers reported that he favored a presidential nominating convention to select the candidates for 1836. To clear up all doubts on this question, in an open letter of December 15, 1833, he stated,

I am, and always have been, decidedly and unequivocally opposed to this singular innovation upon the established usages of the democratic party, and adverse to the consummation of the *single* and *especial* object intended to be accomplished by it.[1]

His friendship with Governor Wolf was so close that the opinion, expressed in the letter, was accepted as that of the governor. On December 16, before the letter was published, certain of the Democratic members of the legislature resolved in favor of a national nominating convention.[2] The issue was thus sharply drawn by the " Convention Democrats," who were inevitably led by their declaration into opposition to the governor. During 1834 the sentiment of the " Convention Democrats " concentrated on Henry A. Muhlenberg.

Muhlenberg came from a powerful family with traditions

---

[1] *Niles' Register,* vol. xlv, p. 295.

[2] *Ibid.,* vol. xlv, p. 295.

of leadership among the Pennsylvania Germans and with a penchant for the governorship.[1] For twenty-seven years he had been the pastor of a large church at Reading, and consequently had a strong following. Failing health made him resign his charge and retire to a farm. Immediately he was induced to stand for Congress. After his election, in 1829, he resigned from the ministry. In Congress Muhlenberg heartily endorsed the views of Jackson on the bank, declaring that he was " opposed to the present or any other National Bank." [2] On the other hand, although Wolf had not opposed Jackson in his struggle with the bank, yet his views and those of Jackson did not coincide, for Wolf, in 1831 and in 1832, had signed resolutions of the legislature favoring the rechartering of the Bank of the United States.[3] On the question of calling a convention to amend the state constitution, Muhlenberg took a positive, favorable stand, but Wolf was evasively non-committal. Both factions were forced to admit that they favored Van Buren for the presidency. On March 4, 1835, the Democratic convention of the state assembled at Harrisburg with the factions of equal strength and with a large number of contesting delegations. After a struggle of several days the Muhlenberg supporters won a tactical victory in having resolutions adopted, calling for the choice of new delegates to meet in state convention at Lewistown on May 6. Thereupon the Muhlenberg men returned home. The Wolf

[1] His uncle, the Rev. Frederick A. Muhlenberg, was the Federal candidate in 1793 and in 1796; his cousin, John A. Schulze, was elected governor in 1823 and in 1826; his father-in-law, Joseph Hiester, defeated in 1817, was elected in 1820.

[2] Letter of January 26, 1835; *Democratic State Journal,* April 11, 1835.

[3] Resolutions of April 2, 1831, *Session Laws,* 1830-31, p. 505; resolutions of February 10, 1832, *ibid.,* 1831-32, p. 625; resolutions of June 6, 1832, *ibid.,* 1831-32, p. 644.

supporters met the following day, filled up their body as
well as they could, and placed Wolf in nomination. When
the Lewistown convention assembled, there was no opposition to the nomination of Muhlenberg.[1]

Feeling between the Democratic factions ran high; the
Muhlenberg supporters constantly sneered at Wolf as " the
caucus nominee." As was to be expected, the election resulted in defeat for the Democrats with Ritner receiving a
plurality of the votes cast.[2] " There has been not only a
Ritner current but a Ritner flood," wrote the defeated governor.[3] Control of the legislature was also wrested from
the Democrats. The lower house contained twenty-eight
Whigs, forty-six Anti-Masons, and twenty-six Democrats;
it chose Ner Middleswarth, an Anti-Mason, as its speaker.[4].
The senate remained under the control of the Democrats,
who were, however, divided by their factional fight. Taking advantage of this situation, the Whigs and Anti-Masons
threw their support to Thomas S. Cunningham, a Muhlenberg man, and elected him speaker.[5] This proved to be an
extremely wise move, for he and some of the other Muhlenberg men were later won away from the Democratic party.

[1] *Niles' Register,* vol. xlviii, pp. 21, 65, 190. Both the national convention and President Jackson carefully avoided acting as arbiters
between the factions; *ibid.,* vol. xlviii, pp. 227-29, 344, 378; vol. xlix,
p. 27.

[2] The vote was Ritner 94,023; Wolf 65,804; Muhlenberg 40,586;
Smull's Legislative Hand-Book, 1919, p. 719. A Democratic editor
estimated that the Anti-Masons cast between 40,000 and 50,000 of
Ritner's vote; *The Keystone,* October 4, 1837.

[3] Governor George Wolf to Lewis S. Coryell, October 16, 1835;
Coryell Papers, vol. iii.

[4] *National Gazette,* March 16, 1836.

[5] *Pennsylvania Intelligencer,* October 22, 1835, states the following as
the constituency of the Senate: anti-Van Buren 14; Wolf-Van Buren
11; Muhlenberg-Van Buren 8. For the election of the speakers see
United States Gazette, December 4, 1835.

Whether the Whigs were promised a state charter for the Bank of the United States in return for their support of Ritner is not clear, but such a measure was discussed immediately after the election.[1] Although the national charter of the bank was to expire on March 4, 1836, yet the bank did not proceed to wind up its affairs and the price of its stock rose considerably.[2] When the legislature assembled, the speaker of the house appointed committees favorable to the bank, notifying Nicholas Biddle, president of the bank, of their constituency before publicly announcing them.[3] John H. Walker, chairman of the Committee on Ways and Means, and E. F. Pennypacker, chairman of the Committee on Banks, sent Biddle a joint letter inquiring under what conditions he would accept a state charter.[4] The reply of Biddle on January 7, 1836, outlined the conditions which, with a few alterations, were later incorporated in the act. He urged that action be taken before February 17, on which date the stockholders were scheduled to take action on the expected charter.[5]

Absolute secrecy on the proposed action was maintained until January 19, 1836, when Thaddeus Stevens, a member of the Committee on Inland Navigation and Internal Improvements, introduced a bill, which amongst other things

[1] *National Gazette,* October 19, 20, 21, 1835. Biddle had been contemplating a state charter for over a year; McGrane, *op. cit.,* pp. 245, 257.

[2] *United States Gazette,* November 5, 1835. On January 4, 1836, the price quoted was $113½ and on February 19, 1836, it was $131½; *National Gazette,* January 4, February 19, 1836.

[3] McGrane, *op. cit.,* p. 257.

[4] *House Journal,* 1836-37, vol. ii, pp. 745, 757; an investigating committee established the fact of the correspondence but did not obtain the letter.

[5] McGrane, *op. cit.,* p. 246; the date of the letter is erroneously given as 1835.

provided for a charter for the bank.[1]   The chairman of this committee, William B. Reed, a Philadelphia lawyer, acting as one of the agents of the bank, had written Biddle that to secure votes, " The temptation of a turnpike, or a few miles of canal and railroad, as a beginning on a favorite route is nearly irresistible." [2]   Stevens claimed credit for evolving the scheme, whereby the state works might be extended and the state debt not increased, a policy to which he thought Ritner was pledged.   This was to be accomplished by securing a bonus for the charter from the bank.   This bonus could also be used to warrant the repeal of the tax laws.   The sections of the act relating to the repeal of the tax laws were drafted by Stevens, while Reed framed the portions dealing with the extension of the public works and the charter of the bank.[3]   On January 29, ten days after its introduction, this important measure passed the house.[4] Its passage in the senate was temporarily postponed until a committee investigated charges of bribery.   The majority of the committee reported that they

believe that a deliberate plan was concocted beyond the limits of Pennsylvania, to control the deliberations of the legislature by the pressure of the people acting under an excitement created by incendiary falsehoods, sent forth upon responsible authority, charging the bank with bribery, and the senate with interested treachery.[5]

---

[1] *House Journal,* 1835-36, vol. i, p. 279.

[2] McGrane, *op. cit.,* p. 258, letter of December 12, 1835.

[3] *House Journal,* 1836-37, vol. ii, pp. 769, *et seq.*

[4] *Ibid.,* 1835-36, vol. i, p. 407; the vote was 57 to 30; the votes in the negative came from 26 Democrats, 3 Whigs and 1 Anti-Mason, *Pennsylvania Reporter,* February 12, 1836.

[5] *Senate Journal,* 1835-36, vol. ii, p. 650.

After this report had been made, the bill was again taken up, passed, and approved on February 18, 1836.[1]

The title of this measure was, " An act to repeal the state tax on real and personal property, and to continue and extend the improvements of the state by railroads and canals, and to charter a state bank, to be called the United States Bank." It repealed the law of March 25, 1831, which had levied a tax on certain classes of property for the use of the state.[2] This act, which was temporary in nature, would have expired on March 25, 1836, but taxation was to cease as of October 1, 1835.[3] Direct taxation was abominated in the state and its repeal was an effort to win support for the coalition.

For its charter of thirty years and exemption from taxation on its dividends, the bank was to pay a bonus of $2,000,000. It was also to pay $500,000 in 1837, and $100,000 annually thereafter for twenty years, to be used by the newly established public school system. The bank could be called on for a permanent loan up to $6,000,000 and for a temporary loan up to $1,000,000 in any one year, both loans to carry a low rate of interest. The bank was also required to subscribe $675,000 to various designated railroads and turnpike companies. Of the $2,000,000, which the state received, all but about $50,000 was immediately appropriated; $600,000 were to be devoted to the payment of the interest on the public debt; $139,000 were

[1] *Session Laws,* 1835-36, p. 36. At a meeting on February 20, 1836, the stockholders of the Bank of the United States, incorporated by the United States, transferred all its property and rights to the state chartered bank of the same name. There was no change in the stockholders, excepting the elimination of the United States. *National Gazette,* February 23, 1836; *Niles' Register,* vol. 1, p. 23.

[2] *Session Laws,* 1830-31, p. 206.

[3] This was accomplished by a proclamation of the governor dated March 11, 1836; *Pennsylvania Intelligencer,* March 17, 1836.

granted to turnpike companies; extensions of the state
works, including the notorious Gettysburg railroad on which
work was ordered to be begun, were to receive $550,000;
there were set aside for surveys $12,000, and for repairs
and for new equipment on the old works a little over $650,-
000. These various "temptations" had proven "irresistible."

The bill had been supported in the senate by the anti-Van
Buren members and by eight Van Buren men, chiefly
Muhlenberg partisans. The support of the Muhlenberg
men seems distinctly strange, for in the last campaign they
had accused Governor Wolf of being anti-Jackson in sign-
ing the bank rechartering resolutions. The views of some
of the eight had been decidedly anti-bank. Charles B.
Penrose, one of them, had, on March 19, 1834, declared,
"I can never lend my aid to a recharter of the present bank,
under any circumstance." Another one of them, John
Dickey, had, at the same time, stated that he was opposed
to a recharter because the bank involved "a dangerous con-
centration of the monied power of the country." [1] After
the passage of the bill, both Penrose and Dickey tried to
justify their vote for the state charter by claiming that they
had not changed their views, for the corporation was now
not a national but a "new state bank," by no means having
the power of the expired national institution. [2] Criticisms
by the Washington organ of Van Buren led Penrose to
declare that this is

not a party question, it is a Pennsylvania question, and nothing
but an interference in that question, which belongs exclusively

---

[1] *Pennsylvania Reporter,* February 4, 1836.

[2] *Ibid.,* February 16, for letters of Charles B. Penrose and Jesse R.
Burden; letters of John Dickey, *Pennsylvania Intelligencer,* March 3,
September 8, 1836.

to us as Pennsylvanians to consider, by the candidate of the National Convention for the Presidency, would induce me to believe that the large mass of Pennsylvania Democracy, which will be found in support of this great State measure, were absolved from their party obligation to support him.[1]

In a letter of February 22, 1836, addressed to followers in Cincinnati, Van Buren sharply criticized the state legislature for passing the act.[2] The letter more deeply offended the eight senators; they placed themselves in opposition to Van Buren and from this time forward identified themselves with the Whigs and Anti-Masons. On March 4 the eight were given a banquet by the opponents of Van Buren and welcomed into the ranks of those who saw " that the only safety for constitutional freedom, is a maintenance of the reserved rights of the states." [3]

The legislature, elated by this simple method of procuring funds, proceeded to deal with other banks in a similar manner. The Girard Bank desired to increase its capital from $1,500,000 to $5,000,000 in order that it might receive a larger portion of the deposits of the government. Despite a veto by the governor the measure became law; the bank was to have its charter for twenty years, pay a bonus of $250,000, but was not to be exempt from dividend taxation.[4] The veto by the governor of a measure to increase the capital stock of other banks was effective.[5] The bonuses, paid by the banks, coupled with the repeal of the tax laws, and the distribution of the surplus by the national

[1] *Pennsylvania Intelligencer,* February 22, 1836.

[2] *Niles' Register,* vol. l, p. 135.

[3] *Pennsylvania Intelligencer,* March 8, 1836.

[4] *United States Commercial and Statistical Register,* vol. i, p. 346; *Session Laws,* 1835-36, p. 133.

[5] *House Journal,* 1835-36, vol. i, p. 1443.

government, completely unbalanced the financial sense of
the commonwealth. From its dementia the state was to
recover only after a long and painful period of impotence.[1]
The odium for this condition rests squarely upon the coalition.

In the meantime, agitation for the presidential nomination had been in progress. In Pennsylvania William H.
Harrison seemed to be the favorite candidate of those in
opposition to the Democrats. He had been suggested in
the newspapers immediately after the election of 1834.[2]
Newspaper agitation alone would accomplish nothing; so

[1] Bishop, "The State Works of Pennsylvania," in *Transactions of
the Connecticut Academy of Arts and Sciences*, vol. xiii, pp. 214, *et seq.*
The intimate connection of the state and the banks is shown by the
following figures. From May, 1814, to May 1, 1837, the state received as premiums on bank charters $3,302,586.18 with $2,185,916.67
still receivable; the tax on bank dividends during the same period was
$785,804.89; and the dividends, paid on state-owned bank stock,
amounted to $5,684,067.00. *Proceedings and Debates of the Constitu-
tional Convention*, 1837-38, vol. i, pp. 495-501. The following table
shows how little reliance was placed on taxation:

	Tax on real and personal property	Licenses and land fees; dividends on state-owned stock; tax on bank dividends
1832	$94,592.34	$422,623.56
1833	226,043.15	540,211.63
1834	219,501.12	294,134.59
1835	208,400.96	299,831.85
1836	224,310.31	356,973.48
1837	54,310.00	395,119.58
1838	10,101.28	397,638.67
1839	18,283.29	397,089.79
1840	2,697.86	352,980.01

For the years listed the sums represent the income of the state, with
the exception that the bonuses from the banks and the sums received
from the national government through the distribution of the surplus
are not included; *House Journal*, 1844, vol. ii, p. 420.

[2] *Pennsylvania Intelligencer*, December 14, 1834.

a call, signed by eleven men, who styled themselves the
"Democratic Republican Committee," was issued. The
call summoned those favoring General Harrison to meet at
Harrisburg on December 14, 1835, in order to place him in
nomination, to frame an electoral ticket, and to begin the
work necessary to secure his election. It was stated that
"the Democratic supporters of the present chief magistrate,
the Democratic Whigs, and the Democratic Anti-Masons
may, without losing their party names, or giving up their
party organization, be cordially invited to participate." [1]
This convention was not intended to interfere with the
Anti-Masonic convention, which met at the same time and
at the same place. In fact, when the two conventions met,
the Harrison convention waited for the Anti-Masonic body
to act; it adjourned from day to day, watched the proceedings of the other body, followed it in nominating Harrison
and Granger, and adjourned *sine die* after adopting the
electoral ticket formed by the Anti-Masons. It resolved
against calling a national convention as "it is a powerful
engine, not only in the hands of unprincipled demagogues,
to defeat the will of the people, but to enable the Federal
Executive to appoint his successor." [2]

In the resolution against the national convention the
members of the Harrison body reflected the attitude of the
majority of the Anti-Masons within the state with whom
they wished to cooperate. When the Anti-Masonic convention decided to place a candidate for the presidency in
nomination and not to choose delegates to a national convention, the organization was split. The presiding officer
of the convention, Harmar Denny, along with Thaddeus
Stevens and seven other delegates, left the convention.

---

[1] *Pennsylvania Intelligencer*, October 29, 1835.

[2] *Ibid.*, December 17, 21, 1835.

They saw the trend toward fusion with the newer organization and were endeavoring to prevent it.[1] In the address calling a national convention of the Anti-Masons, the seceders condemned the attempted amalgamation, in their hour of triumph, with the " Masonic Whiggery." [2] One of the

[1] There is much truth to the comment of the *Harrisburg Chronicle* (Van Buren paper), December 21, 1835, that it " was as much intended to put down Thaddeus S. and a few others, as it was to put up General Harrison." Ritner at this time did not fully trust Stevens, and was evidently bent on placing himself at the head of the Anti-Masonic organization. Stevens had opposed Ritner's nomination for the preceding gubernatorial election; Hood, " Thaddeus Stevens," in Harris, *Biographical History of Lancaster County*, p. 578. The struggle broke out in the convention over the seating of James Todd, Ritner's nominee for the attorney-generalship. Todd was applying for the seat of his son, who had resigned. The vote on the question of seating the elder Todd indicated clearly that the governor controlled the convention. Nor did close relations exist between the governor and Stevens over legislative matters, inasmuch as the bank bills favored by Stevens had received vetoes. In fact, Stevens had been so much disgusted with the nomination of Ritner that he had not intended to be a candidate for the legislature in the elections of 1835. His friends insisted that the party needed experienced guides and he yielded to this pressure; Thomas Elder to Joseph Wallace, August 3, 1835; Wm. McPherson Mss.

[2] *Pennsylvania Reporter*, January 5, 1836. Stevens' organ, the *Gettysburg Star*, April 11, 1836, quoted in the *Pennsylvania Intelligencer*, April 14, 1836, said that the national convention would " attempt to survive and sustain *pure unmixed* Anti-Masonry—not to daub over the foul treacherous doings of the ' base compound' Harrisburg Convention;" it would avoid " alike the insidious Masonic Van Buren and the unblushing Masonic Harrison.' For their alleged distrust of Harrison's Anti-Masonry, *cf.* McCarthy, " The Anti-Masonic Party," in the *Annual Report of the American Historical Association* 1902, vol. i, pp. 480, *et seq.; Memoirs of John Quincy Adams*, vol. ix, p. 273. The seceders were supporters of Webster; for a portion of the correspondence with him, *cf., The Writings and Speeches of Daniel Webster*, vol. xvi, p. 259; vol. xviii, p. 12. After Harrison's election in 1840, this group of the Anti-Masons claimed that even in 1836 they had been working to secure his nomination by a national convention; Joseph Wallace to William H. Harrison, January —, 1841; Wm. McPherson Mss.

seceding nine editorially described the Anti-Masonic state
convention as

a set of political resurrectionists, having dug up the body of old
Whiggism, as the devil wanted to get that of Moses; like vam-
pires disturbing the habitations of the living with the odorous
remains of the departed—as a last resort to draw a house for
the benefit of Mr. Clay. White is to be the Punch of the
puppets and Harrison to be Harlequin of the pantomine; and
poor Antimasonry, unwilling to miss the show but excluded
from all the rest of the house, begs for a ticket in the slips
among the women of the town.[1]

The seceders and their supporters met in a so-called national
convention in Philadelphia in May, passed strong condemnatory resolutions against the Whigs, but adjourned without endorsing Harrison and Granger or placing their own
candidates in nomination.[2]

The Whigs were not a unit in endorsing the work of the
Harrisburg convention. For a time the Clay supporters
held aloof, declaring that it was not a Whig convention and
that consequently they were not bound by its action.[3] The
prospect of the state being carried by Harrison and the pos-
siblity of the election then being thrown into the House of
Representatives reconciled them. Stevens was, however,
doing everything in his power to make cooperation between
the two parties difficult, if not actually impossible. As
chairman of the legislative committee to investigate

[1] *Pittsburgh Times*, quoted in the *Pennsylvania Intelligencer*, April
14, 1836.

[2] *National Gazette*, May 6, 1836.

[3] *United States Gazette*, December 30, 1835; the leaders in this group
were Horace Binney, John Price Wetherill, Nathan Sargent, and
David Paul Brown.

Masonry, he took keen delight in vexing the Whigs.[1] The
result was that many of the Whigs, filled with disgust, ab-
sented themselves from the polls in the October election and
thus helped encompass the defeat of some of the Anti-
Masonic candidates for the legislature.[2]

Although the coalition was defeated in the state election
of 1836, it entered the national campaign with increased
determination to carry the state through cooperation.[3]
Van Buren, who had never been a favorite in Pennsylvania,
was attacked " as the correspondent of the Pope of Rome—
as the fawning sycophantic flatterer of a foreign tyrant—
for the base purpose of arraying one religious denomina-
tion against the other." [4] He was further attacked for having

declared in the New York Convention, that a poor man ought
not to have a vote. He despises the American mechanics [they

---

[1] McCarthy, *op. cit.,* p. 473; *cf.* also the debate on the resolutions instructing the United States Senators on the expunging resolution,
Pennsylvania Intelligencer, March 8, 1836.

[2] *United States Gazette,* October 17, 1836, declared that "the proscriptive course of the Antimasons, particularly the unfortunate affair
at Harrisburg," led to their defeat in Adams, Lebanon, Dauphin, Allegheny, and Union counties. It stated that a total of twenty-three
seats in the house had been lost by only twelve hundred and fifty-four
votes; *ibid.,* October 18, 1836. Stevens was defeated, but by only
fourteen votes; *American Volunteer,* October 14, 1836. Joseph Lawrence, now state treasurer, on October 20, 1836, wrote Lewis S. Coryell,
"The abuse heaped upon the Whigs last winter by Stevens cannot be
easily swallowed by them." Coryell Papers.

[3] *United States Gazette,* October 22, 1836.

[4] *Pennsylvania Intelligencer,* September 15, 1836; the basis of this
accusation was a letter of July 20, 1830, written by Van Buren when
he was Secretary of State, in which our consul at Rome was authorized
to congratulate the Pope on his recent elevation, and to assure him
in reply to his inquiry that the Catholics in the United States had the
same privileges which those citizens professing another religious belief
had.

said] for he rides in a British coach, made in England, and is accompanied by British servants dressed in livery! What says the Democracy? Will they support the Federal Dandy of New York? Or the plain farmer—the veteran Harrison of Ohio? [1]

It was felt that the state held the balance in the national election; consequently the contest was keen.

In November, on the same day as the presidential election, members of a state constitutional convention were to be chosen. One of the Democratic candidates, George M. Dallas, thus outlined the powers of the convention.

It may re-organize our entire system of social existence, terminating and proscribing what is deemed injurious, and establishing what is preferred. It might restore the institution of slavery amongst us; it might make a penal code as bloody as that of Draco; it might withdraw the charters of the cities; it might supersede a standing judiciary, by a scheme of occasional arbitration and umpirage; it might prohibit particular professions or trades; it might permanently suspend the privilege of the writ of Habeas Corpus, and take from us (as our late General Assembly made the entering wedge to do) the trial by jury.[2]

In the western part of the state another Democratic candidate, Judge William Wilkins, declared that the power of the convention was " unlimited and illimitable." [3] These statements, used with telling effect against the Democrats as indicating their radicalism, led several of their nominees to the convention to abandon the party.[4]

[1] *Pennsylvania Intelligencer,* July 28, 1836,; *cf.* also *ibid.,* November 3, 1836.

[2] *United States Gazette,* November 2, 1836; letter to the Bradford county committee.

[3] *Pennsylvania Intelligencer,* November 3, 1836.

[4] Walter Forward came out openly against these contentions and was elected to the convention; *United States Gazette,* October 28, November 1, 1836. He worked with the Whigs until they broke with Tyler.

The election resulted in a victory for Van Buren and his supporters. Of the one hundred and thirty-three members of the constitutional convention, the Democrats secured a majority of only one. The Whigs derived comfort from this fact, as it was felt that with so small a majority the Democrats could do little towards putting their radical doctrines into effect.[1] The defeat of Harrison was attributed by the Whigs to the disorganized condition of the parties in the October election; they claimed that some of the leading Anti-Masons had openly opposed Harrison and Granger until after the state election.[2]

On May 2, 1837, the constitutional convention assembled at Harrisburg with the Whigs and Anti-Masons now having a majority of one because of a special election, necessitated by the death of a Democratic member-elect. An occupational analysis of the members shows little, if any, difference between the Democrats and their opponents.[3] Nor, on the other hand, did the Democrats possess any less wealth.[4] These facts had their effect on the work of the

[1] *Pennsylvania Intelligencer,* November 14, 1836.

[2] *Ibid.,* November 14; *United States Gazette,* November 15, 1836.

[3] *United States Gazette,* June 2, 1837, furnishes a list of the members from which the following was compiled.

	Dem.	Opp.		Dem.	Opp.
Farmers	27	29	Surveyors	4	0
Lawyers	16	24	Artisans	5	1
Physicians	6	4	Editor	0	1
Merchants	4	5	Gentlemen	1	0
Manufacturers	3	3	Total	66	67

It is well nigh impossible in some cases to discover whether an individual was an Anti-Mason or a Whig. As nearly as can be ascertained, there were fifty-two Anti-Masons and fifteen Whigs in the convention.

[4] C. J. Ingersoll, Democratic member from the county of Philadelphia, said on the floor of the convention, "Now, I will venture another guess, that, setting aside the large fortunes of two individual members of this

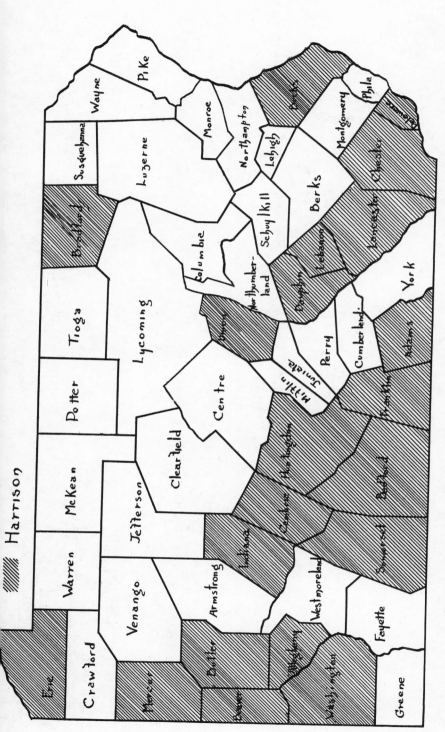

PRESIDENTIAL ELECTION OF 1836 (PHILADELPHIA CITY, HARRISON PHILADELPHIA COUNTY, VAN BUREN)

convention, and in the beginning of the sessions a Whig member wrote that little was heard " of radicalism, with reference to vested rights, the resumption of private charters and the violation of the compacts of the state with individuals." [1]

In organizing the convention the Whigs and the Anti-Masons closely cooperated, having previously gone into caucus together on the question of organization. John Sergeant, a prominent lawyer and politician of Philadelphia, was chosen president of the convention. [2] The refusal of the Whigs to follow Stevens in his proposition to adopt an amendment forbidding the existence of oath-bound societies irritated him. [3] Although, in the main, the Whigs and the Anti-Masons worked harmoniously together, yet Stevens at times took great pleasure in attacking the Whigs in order that the cooperation might not be too pronounced. [4] The small majority of the combined Whigs and Anti-Masons made their control of the convention pre-

body—one from the city of Philadelphia and one from Pittsburg—if, the property of the members of this convention were all to be valued, and divided according to the agrarian law, the greater part would be found among those who are called levellers. I am inclined to think, that if a fair valuation of property was made through this convention, the agrarians, as they are termed, would be found to possess more unencumbered real estate, than those who are in such terror lest there should be a division of property." *Proceedings and Debates of the Constitutional Convention,* 1837-38, vol. vii, pp. 84-85.

[1] *United States Gazette,* May 9, 1837. For a severe criticism of the Democratic members see *National Gazette,* February 26, 1838.

[2] *Proceedings and Debates of the Constitutional Convention,* 1837-38, vol. i, p. 12.

[3] *Journal of the Constitutional Convention,* 1837-38, vol. ii, pp. 489, 550.

[4] *Proceedings and Debates,* vol. ii, pp. 65, *et seq.;* a particularly acrimonious verbal clash occurred between Stevens and Wm. M. Meredith, in which the latter temporarily non-plussed Stevens by the sharpness of his attack. Stevens was amongst other things referred to as " the Great Unchained of Adams" county; *ibid,* pp. 108, *et seq.*

carious. Slight defections occurred from both wings. They were caused by personal predilections, professional pursuits, sectional interest, or previous political sympathy, but nevertheless, in the main, the policies of the opposing parties are shown by their votes in the convention.

The Democrats favored taking the power of appointing to the numerous state offices away from the governor, and making elevation to these offices depend on the will of the electorate. The Whigs and Anti-Masons did not oppose the election of justices of the peace, aldermen, coroners, prothonotaries, sheriffs and minor officials, but sternly opposed the proposition to make judges elective in the districts. The judges of the courts of record under the existing constitution were appointed by the governor and held office during good behavior. A compromise was eventually reached whereby the judges were to hold office for a term of years after appointment by the governor with the consent of the senate, which was to act on nominations in open executive session.[1]

The Democrats endeavored to have the restrictions on the suffrage decreased. They succeeded in having the residence requirement lowered, but failed to have the tax-paying qualification removed.[2] Their opponents inserted

[1] The vote in the committee of the whole was 63 in the affirmative, of which only 10 were Democrats, to 51 in the negative, 46 of which were Democrats; *Journal of the Committee of the Whole*, p. 181. The report of the committee of the whole was adopted by a vote of 60, of which 6 were Democrats, to 48, only 1 of which was Whig; *Proceedings and Debates*, vol. v, p. 138. The proposition to have the judges elected by the voters in the districts was defeated by a vote of 62 in the affirmative, in which number were found 12 Whigs and Anti-Masons (consisting of 8 farmers and 4 lawyers), to 64, in which were 13 Democrats (consisting of 4 farmers, 8 lawyers and 1 mechanic); *Journal of the Constitutional Convention*, vol. ii, p. 367.

[2] *Proceedings and Debates,* vol. ii, pp. 470, *et seq.*; vol. iii, pp. 159, *et seq.*

a clause requiring residence within the district for at least ten days preceding the election. To this provision the Democrats objected on the ground that it would bear heavily on the wandering mechanic; the delegates from the mountain districts feared that it would tend to check immigration to those sections.[1] The early efforts of the Democrats to insert the word " white " in the constitutional phrase " every freeman of the age of twenty-one," who had the other qualifications, should have the right to vote, failed through the efforts of the Whigs and the Anti-Masons, aided by a few Democrats.[2] In the closing days of the convention party lines were forgotten, prejudice was appealed to, and the clause was altered by the insertion of the word " white " by a large non-partisan vote.[3]

It was natural that the question of the banks should come to the fore, as the election in many of the districts had been fought exclusively on that issue.[4] The effort of the Democrats to have the constitution declare that the stockholders of a bank were individually and severally responsible for the obligations of the bank failed.[5] The passage of a resolution expressing the opinion that a charter is

[1] *Proceedings and Debates,* vol. ix, pp. 320, *et seq.* The vote was 64 in the affirmative, 6 of which were Democratic, to 60 in the negative, 5 of which were Whig.

[2] *Journal of the Committee of the Whole,* p. 85; 49 votes, 6 of which were not Democratic, were cast in the affirmative, and 61 in the negative, 12 of which came from Democratic members.

[3] *Journal of the Constitutional Convention,* vol. ii, p. 326; the vote on January 20, 1838, was 77 to 45; 19 Whigs and Anti-Masons voted aye and 3 Democrats no. For an excellent summary of the debates on negro suffrage, with no attention, however, paid to political alignment, cf. Olbrich, *The Development of Sentiment and Negro Suffrage to 1860,* pp. 51-70.

[4] *Harrisburg Chronicle,* November 9, 16, 1836.

[5] *Journal of the Committee of the Whole,* p. 217; the vote was 48 to 55; 1 Whig voted in the affirmative and 6 Democrats in the negative.

a " contract with the parties to whom the grant is made "
led the *United States Gazette* to exclaim,

Agrarianism has this day been most signally rebuked, after
one of the warmest contests that has yet been witnessed in
this convention. The friends of order, good government and
conservative principles, have nobly triumphed, Radicalism has
been fairly beaten. It selected the battle ground—it commenced the conflict—it rallied for the fight, and it now lies
bleeding and prostrate! [1]

After a lengthy debate and parliamentary struggle, in which
the Whigs and Anti-Masons on one occasion were saved
from defeat by a tie vote,[2] a compromise was made whereby
six months' notice of application for renewal or extension
of a charter was required, whereby the life of a charter was
limited to twenty years, with power to revoke and to alter it
resting with the legislature, provided that no injustice would
be done thereby to the stockholders.[3] The Whigs and the
Anti-Masons were more immediately concerned by this
legislation than were the Democrats, for they controlled
most of the banks within the state.[4]

[1] November 24, 1837. The vote on the resolution was 59 to 41, with
2 Democrats in the affirmative and no Whigs in the negative; *Journal
of the Constitutional Convention,* vol. i, pp. 804, *et seq.*

[2] The debate on this proposition began in November, 1837, and continued into January, 1838. The contest was keen on January 12, 1838,
when the balloting took place. The vote which saved the coalition was
62 to 62; 5 of the Whigs abandoned their party, while 2 of the Democrats did the same thing; *ibid.,* vol. ii, p. 254.

[3] The vote on the compromise was 86, of which 26 were Whig and
Anti-Masonic, to 29; *Proceedings and Debates,* vol. ix, p. 218.

[4] *The Keystone* (Democratic), September 7, 13, 1837, maintained that
the bankers were "Federalists," i. e. Whigs and Anti-Masons. From
an analysis of the politics of the directors and of the employees of
more than half of the banks in the commonwealth, it concluded that
there were fourteen politically doubtful, forty-six Democrats, and
two hundred and ninety "Federalists" connected with these institutions.

A mild contest developed over the question of the future amendment of the constitution. A proposed article of amendment was required to have a majority in two successive legislatures, and then to be confirmed by the electorate before it would be effective. Efforts to have the majority in the legislature raised to one of two thirds failed.[1] By a non-partisan vote, a provision prohibiting the submission of a particular proposed amendment more than once in any five-year period was inserted.[2]

The Whigs and Anti-Masons, though they had a small majority in the convention, had not been able to control its proceedings, but they had been able to check the more radical tendencies of their opponents. Incensed at the refusal of the convention to insert a clause in the constitution prohibiting the existence of oath-bound societies and at the provision limiting the suffrage to " white " males, Stevens and a few other members refused to sign the statement that " the foregoing is the amended Constitution of Pennsylvania, as agreed to in the Convention." [3] The Democratic members of the convention signed an appeal to the electorate, urging support of the amended constitution.[4] As an organization, neither the Whigs nor the Anti-Masons took action for or against the amended constitution; but they acted as individuals in condemning it. John Sergeant, president of the convention, stated in an open letter of

[1] *Journal of the Constitutional Convention,* vol. ii, p. 488. The first effort to require a two-third majority vote failed by 44 to 60, *ibid.,* vol. ii, p. 495; the second effort failed by a tie vote of 60 to 60, 2 Anti-Mason farmers voted in the negative and 2 Democratic lawyers in the affirmative, *ibid.,* vol. ii, p. 544.

[2] The vote was 76, composed of 55 Anti-Masons and Whigs and of 19 Democrats, to 45, all Democratic save 2 Anti-Masonic farmers, *ibid.,* vol. ii, p. 516.

[3] Harris, *Political Conflict,* p. 41.

[4] *Pennsylvania Intelligencer,* March 7, 1838.

September 10, 1838, that he would oppose its adoption by his vote, and that the same course would be pursued by the other six Whig members in the convention from Philadelphia.[1] Anti-Masonic members of the convention from the interior of the state came out in opposition to ratification.[2] Ex-Governor John A. Schulze, a former Democrat, declared that "the work of the good men of the Revolution will not be laid aside, to take up and adopt the piece of patch-work which was put together by the late generally condemned convention. The Germans of Pennsylvania will hold fast to what they know to be good."[3] Opposition was aimed at the provision limiting the tenure of the judiciary and at the process of amendment. The *National Gazette,* the organ of the Philadelphia merchants and financiers, was particularly sharp in its criticisms, saying,

If radicalism does not falter, but boldly marches on as it has done, we may all live to see every principal town in the State with its Tammany Hall, where the divine founder of the Christian dispensation will be represented as having been a living impostor, or at best an allegory; and where the tenets of pure agrarianism will be asserted, commanding that estates be cut up and parcelled out, according to the clearest definition of equal rights. Mr. Dallas's doctrines will be the text-book for every future attack against the Constitution. That instrument, amended, leaves itself open, to the consummation of any and every political atrocity on its face, and when the public mind is the better inured to the horrible doctrines of the Bradford County Letter, then let us look out for amendments. Amendments! Draughts according to Frances Wright. Legislative speeches on heads from Skidmore Parallels, in reports of com-

[1] *United States Gazette,* September 21, 1838.
[2] *Chambersburg Whig,* September 28, 1838.
[3] *United States Gazette,* September 7, 1838, letter of August 20, 1838.

mittees between the tottering condition of the duplicate curse
" banks and Christianity." Once open a sluice in the Constitution and the very dregs of Radicalism will flow through
it, and the embankment will be washed away.[1]

Despite this vigorous, unorganized opposition the constitution, as amended, was ratified in the fall election of 1838,
but by a small majority.[2]

A portion of the Whigs were no less eager than Stevens
to prevent their party from cooperating with the Anti-
Masons. They claimed that the defeat of Harrison in the
presidential election of 1836 had been due to the head-
strong Stevens and his followers, who, they asserted, had
worked openly for Van Buren.[3] Early in 1837 an effort
was made to form an independent Whig organization in
Chester county, where the Anti-Masons were particularly
strong, and at the same time to start a movement for an
independent state organization; but nothing came of this
premature movement.[4]

The Democrats, who in 1837 controlled the lower house
of the legislature, investigated the granting of the charter
to the Bank of the United States. They could find no
evidence of bribery, but they concluded that the bank had
violated its charter in several instances. The investigating

---

[1] October 11, 1838.

[2] The governor proclaimed that the constitution had been ratified by
a vote of 113,971 to 112,759; *Pennsylvania Archives*, series iv, vol. vi,
p. 440. The corrected returns should be 119,228 for, and 116,076
against; *Senate Journal*, 1838-39, vol. i, p. 1012.

[3] *Pennsylvania Intelligencer*, January 26, February 13, March 2, 1837.

[4] *Ibid.*, February 13; *Pennsylvania Telegraph*, March 7, 1837. A considerable portion of the dissatisfaction arose over the question of
appointment to office. The *Pennsylvania Intelligencer*, February 2,
1837, claimed, " To be a Ritner man would not do—to be a liberal
Anti-Mason would not do—to be a warm Harrison man was heresy,
but to bow the knee to Stevens, was the passport to office."

committee, however, made no recommendations on the ground that the constitutional convention was soon to assemble and that there the question of the banks and their charters would receive proper treatment. The minority of the committee contended that if the charter had been violated, such violations should be referred to the legal authorities of the state for action.[1]

During this session of the legislature an improvement bill received the veto of Governor Ritner, which proved to be effective. The governor regretted that he was forced to withhold "the Executive approbation from an act which involves no question of constitutional right." He claimed that the bill would squander the funds of the state among privately owned companies and would thus delay the completion of the state-owned improvements.[2] The legislature, incensed at the veto, refused to make provision for the continuation of the work on the public improvements. The Democrats declared that the veto message displayed "the consummate ignorance" of the governor.[3] Ritner's supporters, on the other hand, claimed that nothing saved the commonwealth

from the sack and pillage by the plunder party—rescued it from bankruptcy, and preserved the means of completing the public improvements now progressing, but the bold and independent stand taken by the Executive. . . . The State would again, as it did a few years ago, truly represent the public goose, plucked as bare as an acorn; and the people would have the satisfaction of being ground down with taxes ten-fold more odious than before.[4]

[1] *Pennsylvania Telegraph*, March 17, April 3, 1837.
[2] *House Journal*, 1836-37, vol i, p. 1053.
[3] *The Keystone*, April 6, 1837.
[4] *Pennsylvania Telegraph*, April 5, 1837.

Financial pressure, due to the approaching panic of 1837, was causing commercial uneasiness and distress, which, it was asserted, the veto would prevent from being aggravated.[1] With the suspension of specie payment in May, pressure was brought to bear on the governor to have him call a special session of the legislature. In a proclamation of May 20, 1837, the governor called on the banks to do everything in their power to better financial conditions, warning them against violating their charters by increasing the volume of their notes. The governor, however, refused to call an extra session, declaring that the financial evils of the country were due to the acts of the federal authorities, and that nothing, which the state could do, would lessen the distress.[2] This proclamation was declared by one of his supporters to be " a state paper, which for manliness of tone and soundness of doctrine, is worthy the independent chief magistrate of this great commonwealth." [3]

The politicial campaign of 1837 was listless and colorless. Appeals were made to elect men to the legislature who would support the financial policy of the governor.[4] Endorsement of the veto of the " Mammoth Improvement Bill " was sought. Van Buren's motto was declared to be, " Gold for the office-holders—shinplasters for the people! " [5] The election left the upper house in the control of the Whigs and Anti-Masons, but the Democrats secured fifty-six of the one hundred members in the lower house.[6]

---

[1] *United States Gazette*, April 12, 1837.

[2] *Pennsylvania Archives*, series iv, vol. vi, p. 346.

[3] *National Gazette*, May 23, 1837; *cf.* also *ibid.*, May 24, 25, 26, 27, 29, 30; *Pennsylvania Telegraph*, May 23, June 1, 8; *Pennsylvania Intelligencer*, May 22, 1837.

[4] *National Gazette*, October 5, 7, 10; *United States Gazette*, September 20, October 2; *Pennsylvania Telegraph*, October 2, 1837.

[5] *Pennsylvania Intelligencer*, October 5, 1837.

[6] *Pennsylvania Telegraph*, October 19, 1837.

Despite this defeat, the Anti-Masons in the Stevens faction were determined to ignore the Whigs and to continue their independent state and national organization. On May 22, 1837, there had assembled at Harrisburg a state "Democratic Anti-Masonic Convention." It called a national convention to meet at Washington on the second Monday in September for the purpose of nominating candidates for the presidency and vice-presidency.[1] On November 7, 1837, the state committee, which had been appointed at this convention, called a state convention to meet on March 5, 1838, for the purpose of nominating a gubernatorial candidate.[2] At the time appointed the convention assembled, and, since Stevens and Ritner were reconciled, without difficulty nominated the governor for reelection.[3] Assertions that the Whigs of Philadelphia were hostile to the reelection of Ritner were vigorously denied by them.[4] The Whig convention of Philadelphia city and county, endorsing the nomination, asserted in the resolutions that

his policy of retaining capital within the state, his resistance to schemes of improvident expenditure, and dangerous speculation, his statesmanlike admonition in an hour of panic neither to fear nor to hope too much, his spirited defense of the credit of the Commonwealth when assiduously assailed abroad and of the high character of her merchants when calumniated at home, give him a claim to which Philadelphia is not insensible.[5]

[1] *Pennsylvania Telegraph*, May 27, 1837.

[2] *Ibid.*, November 15, 1837.

[3] *Ibid.*, March 9, 1838.

[4] *United States Gazette*, February 10; *National Gazette*, March 9, 15, 22, 1838.

[5] *United States Gazette*, March 21, 1838.

Ritner was endorsed elsewhere by Whig county conventions, which pledged party support to him.[1]

With the approach of the election, the governor determined to win the support of the Whigs through a more conciliatory policy than heretofore pursued. Therefore, he appointed William B. Reed, a Mason and a Whig of Philadelphia, attorney-general of the state.[2] In the first years of his administration the governor had distrusted Thaddeus Stevens, hitherto the well-nigh undisputed leader of the Anti-Masonic forces within the state. The governor intended to break the control of the Gettysburg ironmaster and lawyer. The task of party leadership in the face of the opposition of Stevens was, however, beyond the capacity of the " Pennsylvania Dutch " farmer, who occupied the highest administrative office in the commonwealth. The elections in the fall of 1836 had been disastrous to the coalition, and the defeat in 1837 was a bad omen for Ritner's reelection. Fear of defeat made the governor place his political fortunes in the hands of Stevens. In May, 1838, Stevens was appointed a canal commissioner, and at the first meeting of the new board was elected its president. Immediately he extended the policy of using the public works as the basis of a powerful political machine. According to his political opponents, the " moral character or religious principles " of bidders for contracts on the public works were investigated before the bid was considered. " A missionary fund " was collected from the successful bidders " for the purpose of diffusing useful knowledge among the people." Colonization along the extensions of the public works, more thorough than anything previously attempted,

[1] *United States Gazette,* June 27, 1838.

[2] *Ibid.,* March 30, 1838.

was resorted to in order to carry doubtful districts in the coming election.¹

The national question of the Sub-Treasury Bill was, in the meantime, attracting considerable attention in the state. A resolution, instructing the Senators and requesting the Representatives to oppose this measure and to " vote for such a mode of receiving, keeping, and disbursing the public moneys, as will separate, as far as practicable, the Banks from the Government," was adopted.² This resolution, introduced into the legislature by a Democrat, was supported by a number of them.³ The two Senators from Pennsylvania, mindful of their pledge to obey instructions, voted against the bill.⁴ When the bill was defeated in the House, the Democratic Representatives from Pennsylvania supported the measure.⁵ Their vote gave point to the criticisms directed against David R. Porter, gubernatorial candidate of the reunited Democratic party.

He is a bitter politician of the Sub-Treasury school, with just such a fringe of Conservative pretension on his Radical garments as will enable dexterous friends and anxious relatives to try to cajole the credulous into the hope that he is not in heart as destructive as might be inferred from his acts and expressed opinions. The game by which at the last Governor's election some of our friends were imposed upon cannot succeed again.⁶

¹ *House Journal*, 1838-1839, vol. ii, pt. ii, pp. 1, *et seq.*, pp. 372, *et seq.; ibid.*, 1840, vol. ii, pp. 225, *et seq.*

² *Session Laws*, 1837-38, p. 674, resolutions of February 16, 1838.

³ *National Gazette*, February 20, 1838.

⁴ *Ibid.*, March 27, 1838.

⁵ *United States Gazette*, July 4, 1838, for an analysis of the vote.

⁶ *National Gazette*, March 8, 1838; *cf.* also *United States Gazette*, September 25, 29, 1838.

Due to the opposition of the Whigs and Anti-Masons, the attempt of the Democrats to pass a bill requiring the resumption of specie payment within the state by a fixed date failed.[1] In the meantime, the financial situation was improving. Representatives of the banks of Philadelphia city and county met on June 1, 1838, and, after declaring that the repeal of the specie circular by Congress made resumption possible, suggested August 1 as the date for full resumption of specie payment.[2] The defeat of the Sub-Treasury Bill on June 25 gave the governor his opportunity; so, on July 10, he issued a proclamation requiring the resumption of specie payment on August 13.[3] On July 23 delegates from banks in Massachusetts, Rhode Island, Delaware, Virginia, Connecticut, Maryland, Kentucky, and Pennsylvania were represented in a convention at Philadelphia. They selected the date set by the governor for the resumption of specie payment.[4] When the banks resumed on the day agreed upon, it was declared that this might " be considered as the victory of the people over the ' bars, bolts, and strong boxes ' of the Sub-Treasuryites, and as the crowning sheaf of Whig triumphs." [5]

[1] *Chambersburg Whig,* March 9; *United States Gazette,* February 13, 1838.

[2] *National Gazette,* June 4, July 19, 1838.

[3] *Ibid.,* July 14, 1838. *The Democratic Press,* July 17, 1838, characterized the proclamation as " one of the most impudent pieces of political humbug, which even these times, so pregnant in charlatanism, have produced." *The Upland Union,* August 7, 1838, said the proclamation proved the governor to be " the poor dupe of Biddle, Stevens, and Co."

[4] *National Gazette,* July 26, 1838; the editorial comment was, " After all the jesuitical attacks made in New York on our banks, the grand difference between resumption there and here is, that with the one party it was forced on them to the injury of their debtors and the embarrassment of their mercantile community, and with the other it comes with comparative ease some few months later."

[5] *United States Gazette,* August 13, 1838.

Progress in bringing the two factions of the Democratic party together had been made. Ex-Governor Wolf was holding a lucrative federal office. Henry A. Muhlenberg had gone to Europe as the first American ambassador to Austria. With the leaders thus disposed of, their followers were willing to coöperate.. When the Democratic convention assembled at Harrisburg on March 5, 1838, without difficulty it nominated David R. Porter, of Huntingdon county, for governor. Porter came from an eminent family of Scotch-Irish descent. His political activities had been confined to the holding of appointive county offices, to two terms in the house and to one term in the state senate. At one time he had been engaged in the production of iron but the panic of 1819 had caused his firm to fail. As the result of his experience, he was distinctly favorable to the principles of a protective tariff. The campaign for governor proved to be one of the most virulent ever waged in the state. Ritner, nominated by the Anti-Masons for reelection, was assured of the support of the financial interests of Philadelphia. The struggle therefore developed into an effort to secure control of the interior counties of the state. Vicious attacks, buttressed with affidavits, were made against the personal morality of Porter.[1] The Democrats sneered at Ritner as " the old Dutch Farmer Governor," and this sneering was used by the Whigs and the Anti-Masons in an endeavor to capture the vote of the " Pennsylvania Dutch." [2] Ex-Governor Schulze, who had

---

[1] *Pennsylvania Telegraph*, August 1, September 5, 12, 19, October 3, 1838. A trial for libel in Lehigh county after the election, in which the affidavit makers were present as witnesses, vindicated Porter; *Pennsylvania Reporter*, May 10, 1839.

[2] *Pennsylvania Intelligencer*, June 1, 8, July 20, September 21; *Harrisburg Chronicle*, May 30, 1838, began printing at the head of its editorial column, "Der Joseph Ritner ist der Mann, Der unsern Staat regieren kann." *Die Harrisburg Morgenröthe*, not to be outdone, carried at its

been reelected as a Democrat in 1826 with practically no opposition, opposed Porter because he was supported by those favoring Van Buren.[1] The true issue, the Whigs and the Anti-Masons declared, was Ritner *versus* Van Buren- ism.[2]

It is not surprising that this campaign of bitter denun- ciation and vile calumniation should have its aftermath of disorder. In order to accomplish the election of C. J. Ingersoll in the third congressional district, consisting of a portion of Philadelphia county, the election judges by a vote of ten to six rejected the returns from the entire Incor- porated Northern Liberties, although fraud was alleged to have been committed in only one of the seven wards. By rejecting the returns from all the wards of the Incorporated Northern Liberties, Ingersoll was assured of a majority. The Whig judges, incensed at this procedure, refused to sign the returns with the vote of the Incorporated Northern Liberties omitted. They met at a later hour, made out re- turns, which were based on the districts carried by the Whigs and which showed that the Whig candidates to the state senate and house had been elected.[3] The Whig re-

head, "Für Gouvernör David Rittenhaus Porter, der praktische Bauer von Huntingdon County." *The Harrisburg Chronicle,* July 23, 1838, declared, "The Germans are decidedly partial to Germans, and dis- like the English particularly when known to be haughty, and aristo- cratic in feeling."

[1] *National Gazette,* September 5, 1838. The Democrats later claimed that Schulze had been influenced by the handsome award for damages he had received from the board of canal commissioners, of which Ste- vens was president; *House Journal,* 1838-39, vol. ii, part ii, pp. 12, 376. Schulze had, however, broken with the Jackson party on the bank question and had presided at a bank meeting which chose delegates to the Harrisburg convention of May 27, 1834; *Pennsylvania Inquirer,* April 9, 1834.

[2] *United States Gazette,* June 1, 1838.

[3] *House Journal,* 1838-39, vol. ii, part ii, pp. 96, *et seq.*

turns, hastened to Harrisburg by special courier, were filed
in the office of the secretary of the commonwealth before
those of the Democratic judges. When the returns of the
Whig judges were delivered to the secretary, Thaddeus
Stevens was present.[1]

Up to this point the struggle had been between the Whigs
and the Democrats of Philadelphia county. The course of
events, now directed by Stevens, resolved itself into a contest for control of the state. If the returns of the Whig
judges were accepted, Ritner might have a majority, and
thus be governor for another term. Furthermore, the
amended constitution, hated by Stevens, might be defeated.
In addition, although the senate would be controlled by the
Whigs and Anti-Masons with or without the two senators
from Philadelphia, yet the eight representatives from the
county were needed to prevent the Democrats from having
a majority in the house. These eight representatives were
also needed in the joint session of the two houses when they
met for the election of a state treasurer and a United States
Senator.

Thomas H. Burrowes, secretary of the commonwealth,
was also chairman of the " State Committee of Correspondence and Vigilance," which was responsible for the conduct of the governor's campaign. Over his signature, on
October 15, there was issued an address to " The Friends
of Joseph Ritner." Intimating that extensive frauds had
been committed in the election, he urged an immediate investigation, and "until this investigation is fully made and
fully determined, let us treat the election of the ninth inst.
as if we had not been defeated and in that attitude abide the
result." [2] Following the publication of this pronuncia-

---

[1] *House Journal,* 1838-39, vol. ii, part ii, pp. 143-44.
[2] *Niles' Register,* vol. lv, p. 205.

mento, denunciations and threats were loudly and violently made by both sides. Great fears were entertained by the Democrats of the determination of their opponents to deprive them of their victory.[1]

When the legislature assembled on December 4, the situation was tense. On the basis of either the Whig or Democratic returns, Ritner was defeated and the amended constitution adopted. The struggle, therefore, was resolved into one for control of the legislature. Large numbers of the partisans of both sides crowded to Harrisburg. In the lower house, which organized in the morning, two bodies each claiming to be legal were formed. The Cunningham house, named after its speaker, was composed of fifty-two Whigs and Anti-Masons, including the eight contestants from Philadelphia. The Hopkins house had fifty-six members, including the eight from Philadelphia. Neither house had uncontested seats sufficient to constitute a majority of the full house. The Democrats feared that the Cunningham house might be recognized by the Whig senate, which would make it the legal body. Therefore, when, in the afternoon, the senate proceeded to organize itself, the Democrats disturbed its sessions. Their threats of violence caused Charles B. Penrose, speaker of the senate, Thomas H. Burrowes, and Thaddeus Stevens, the last two being present as spectators, to make their escape through a window in a small room in the rear of the speaker's desk.[2] The three men made their way to the

---

[1] *Gettysburg Compiler*, quoted in *Pennsylvania Reporter*, November 9, 1838. The fears of the Democrats were well-founded, as Stevens later acknowledged that his group practically intended to do what the Democrats claimed they intended to do; *Senate Journal*, 1838-39, vol. ii, pp. 801-2, 813-15.

[2] *Public Ledger, United States Gazette, National Gazette, Pennsylvanian*, December 6, 7, 1838. Stevens' overdrawn account of the affair is in the *Pennsylvania Telegraph*, January 17, 1839, and in the *Senate*

residence of the governor, who was formally notified by
Penrose of the disturbance in the senate chamber.[1]   A proclamation was issued, which, amongst other things, called
on the militia to hold itself " in instant readiness to repair
to the seat of government." [2]

It is not necessary to go into the details of the disorder
at the capital, but this disorder led the governor to call out
the militia after he had been refused assistance by Captain
E. V. Sumner, in command of the federal troops at Carlisle,
who claimed that the disturbance appeared " to proceed
from political differences alone." [3]   The order of Major-
General Robert Patterson of the Pennsylvania militia that
the troops should " assemble in winter uniform, with knap-
sacks, provided with thirteen rounds of buckshot cartridges
and seventeen rounds of ball cartridges " gave the entire
episode the sobriquet of " The Buckshot War." [4]   With
the arrival of the troops on the ninth of December, the
senate resumed its sessions.   The question of the recognition of one or the other of the two houses pressed for attention.   After the Hopkins house had once been refused
recognition by the senate, it received it on December 25,
after three members of the Cunningham house had gone
over to the rival organization, which then had a majority of
the full house consisting of undisputed seats.[5]   For all prac-

---

Journal, 1838-1839, vol. ii, pp. 799-802. For the details of the disorder
at Harrisburg see, McCarthy, *op. cit.*, pp. 495-501; McMaster, *History
of the People of the United States*, vol. vi, pp. 501-508.

[1] The formal notification by Penrose is dated December 4, but internal
evidence indicates that it was not written until the following day;
Niles' Register, vol. lv, p. 295.

[2] *Ibid.*, vol. lv, p. 240.

[3] Correspondence in *ibid.*, vol. lv, pp. 295-97.

[4] The various orders are found in *House Journal*, 1838-39, vol. ii,
part ii, pp. 245, *et seq*.

[5] *Senate Journal*, 1838-39, vol. i, pp. 123, 149.

tical purposes this ended the dispute for control of the state.[1]

The contest had its judicial phase. A number of the Democrats had been arrested and indicted for rioting, conspiracy, and treason. On April 18, 1839, these cases were on trial, but were withdrawn because of defective indictments.[2] When they came up again in the August term, the president judge, James M. Porter, brother of the governor, quashed the proceedings because of a defect in form.[3]

When the Twenty-sixth Congress assembled in December 1839, the last phase of the struggle was disposed of. Charles Naylor, relying on the proclamation of election issued on October 31, 1838, which was based on the Whig returns, was present as the Whig claimant. C. J. Ingersoll, armed with a proclamation of election, signed by Governor Porter on November 25, 1839, was also claiming the seat. The struggle for control of the House was sharp and keen, as the two parties were evenly balanced. In the preliminary organization, the claim of Naylor to the seat was recognized as valid. Later he was given an undisputed title to the seat.[4]

---

[1] Stevens for a long time refused to join the house. On May 4, 1839, he wrote, "I have (with great reluctance) determined to go into that den of thieves—the 'Hopkins House.'" Letter to Joseph Wallace, Wm. McPherson Mss. When he appeared in order to be sworn in, the house decided that he had resigned and it ordered a new election, which resulted in Stevens' favor. *House Journal*, 1838-39, vol. i, pp. 922, *et seq; National Gazette*, May 11, 14, 18, 28; *Harrisburg Chronicle*, June 19, 29, 1839; Harris, *Political Conflict*, pp. 59, *et seq.*

[2] *Pennsylvania Reporter*, April 19, 1839; Harris, *op. cit.*, p. 63.

[3] *Pennsylvania Reporter*, August 30; *National Gazette*, August 24, 29, 31, September 7, 1839.

[4] *National Gazette*, December 5, 7, 14, 17, 19, 1839; *House Journal*, 26th Cong. 1st sess, p. 1300; *Reports of the House of Representatives*, 26th Cong., 1st sess., no. 588. For the challenging of Naylor to a duel by Charles Ingersoll, son of C. J. Ingersoll, because of his statements in

The political effects of this struggle were long enduring. The consistent efforts, made by the Whigs and Anti-Masons to have the Democrats appear as rebels, had culminated in calling out the militia to quell " the insurrection." The outcome of these efforts had, however, been the reverse of what had been hoped for by Stevens and his followers, for their candidates had not been seated. This gave point to the contention of the Democrats that the militia had been called out to seat the Whig claimants at the point of the bayonet, but that only the stout and determined resistance of the Democrats, fortunately without bloodshed, had prevented the accomplishing of this unholy purpose. Thus it was quite possible to condemn the coalition as the party of disorder and violence, and the disappearance of the Anti-Masonic member of the coalition did not free the Whigs from odium. The immediate effect of the struggle on the Democrats was to make them more solidly united than they had been previously.[1] The effect on the coalition was that the Whigs were now no longer willing to entrust their political fortunes to the direction of the remnant of the Anti-Masonic party. In particular they shunned the extremist Stevens, who never rose to great influence in the

the press during the congressional hearing, and for the fight between Colonel Pleasonton, bearer of the challenge, and Naylor, and for the subsequent binding of all, by the police, to keep the peace, see *National Gazette,* March 21, 24, 26, 1840.

[1] There is much truth to the comment of John K. Kane, a leading Democrat of Philadelphia, who on December 27, 1838, wrote Lewis S. Coryell, " Whiggery is I presume an inmate of the tomb of the Capulets from this time forward in Pennsylvania. It has become *ridiculous,* a worse epithet for a party even than *wicked,* for men are more cheerfully accounted knaves than fools. Our party has been concentrated, harmonized, confirmed. We shall hear no more of our old domestic squabbles, and more than one excellent man too long estranged from his fellows, has resumed his natural position among our counsellors and guards."—Coryell Papers, vol. iii, p. 80.

Whig party.   The Whigs did not hesitate to coalesce with
the Anti-Masons, but control from this time rested in the
hands of the Whigs.   The result of the adoption of this
policy was the creation of an independent Whig state organization and the ultimate absorption of the Anti-Masonic
party.

CHAPTER II

YEARS OF TRIUMPH AND TRIBULATION

1839-1843.

EVEN before the debacle of the bizarre "Buckshot War," the Whigs had become weary of Anti-Masonic leadership. Prior to the election of 1838 the Whigs in Chester county had resented the treatment received from the Anti-Masons in the distribution of the offices. Their mass meeting endorsed Ritner for governor, declared for Clay as the next presidential candidate, and determined to support the local coalition nominees for this election. The Whigs were, however, resolved

to loose the chains which bind us to the fortunes of anti-masonry, asserting our rights as citizens and organizing as a political party. . . . It is too plain that the Whigs are used to give effect to principles which they do not recognize. If it could be conceded that there was, in truth, no difference in principle between the Whigs and Anti-Masons, then indeed we might with propriety rally under the Anti-Masonic banner.[1]

Circumstances, however, forbade the immediate execution of the desire for independent organization.

The Anti-Masons started their presidential campaign of 1840 early. On May 22, 1837, the state Anti-Masonic convention called a national convention to meet at Washington in September of the same year to make nominations for the presidency and vice-presidency.[2] An address of

---

[1] *United States Gazette*, September 17, 1838.

[2] *Pennsylvania Telegraph*, May 27, 1837.

56

the state convention urged the Anti-Masons of other states
to send delegates.[1] When the convention assembled, it
was poorly attended; twenty-seven of the fifty-three delegates came from Pennsylvania and the balance came from
Ohio, New York, Massachusets, and Rhode Island. On
account of the poor attendance it was decided not to make
nominations, but to call another convention to meet at
Philadelphia in November, 1838, with the stipulation that
no one from an unrepresented state would be nominated.[2]
When this nominating convention assembled on November
13, 1838, delegates from six states were in attendance.
William H. Harrison and Daniel Webster were unanimously
nominated.[3] A small portion of the Whig press gave these
nominations a half-hearted endorsement.[4] The Clay supporters recommended that no action be taken by the Whigs,
even as individuals, until after the Whig national convention had acted. The editor of the *United States Gazette,* a
Mason, felt that the " Whigs will no longer consent to be
mere hewers of wood and drawers of water for a party
that turns all victories to its own advantage, and dictates
with arrogance to those who number twenty in its ranks
to one which the other can muster." [5] Harrison in acknow-
ledging the notification of his nomination stated what he
considered to be the principles of his candidacy.[6] His

---

[1] *Pennsylvania Telegraph,* June 20, 1837.

[2] *Ibid.,* September 21, 1837.

[3] *National Gazette,* November 14, 1838. After the nomination of Harrison and Tyler by the Whigs, Webster withdrew his name.

[4] *Ibid.,* November 15, 17, 1838.

[5] *United States Gazette,* November 30, 1838.

[6] *Niles' Register,* vol. lv, p. 360. Webster thought that the only
chance of success for the Whigs, and that not a very good one, was
in supporting Harrison; *The Writings and Speeches of Daniel Webster,*
vol. xviii, p. 45. Clay claimed that " The mock nomination of the

nomination indicated that he, and he alone, would be acceptable to the Pennsylvania Anti-Masons, who had controlled the " national " convention.

A caucus of the Whig members of Congress had issued a call for a national nominating convention of Whigs to meet in Harrisburg in December, 1839.[1] The call for this convention met with a hearty response from those who were agitating for an independent Whig organization. Plans were made to perfect a state organization of the Whigs before the assembling of the national convention.[2] When the Whigs of Philadelphia city and county met in convention on November 30, 1838, they urged a " thorough Whig organization throughout this commonwealth " and recommended that a state convention assemble at Chambersburg on June 13, 1839.[3] When this convention assembled, it was soon evident that it was under the control of the supporters of Henry Clay. They advised the ubiquitous Anti-Masons to depart and perfect their own organization. The latter, seventeen in number, then withdrew and issued a call for a convention of all anti-Van Buren men to meet at Harrisburg on September 4, 1839.[4] The convention at Chambersburg claimed that the seceders had withdrawn because of a difference over candidates for the presidency. It stated that the delegates had been selected "to organize the Whig party of the state " which they had done. It asserted that the seceders, on the other hand, had

Anti-Masons has fallen still-born, and has produced no material effect even in the Anti-Masonic portion of the state" of New York; Colton (editor), *The Private Correspondence of Henry Clay*, p. 432.

[1] *Pennsylvania Intelligencer*, May 4, 1838, quoting the *Boston Atlas*.

[2] *National Gazette*, February 22, November 28, 1838.

[3] *United States Gazette*, December 1, 1838.

[4] *National Gazette*, June 18, 20, 27, 1839; in some places the calls for the preliminary conventions had been to Clay men; *Chambersburg Whig*, June 28, 1839.

desired to prevent this organization by having the convention adjourn *sine die,* without declaring a preference for any one for the presidency, and by having it issue a call for an anti-Van Buren convention for that special purpose.[1]

With a break in the opposition to Van Buren, the state would be carried by the Democrats. To prevent this, the anti-Van Buren members of the legislature, led by Charles B. Penrose, speaker of the senate and one of the seceders from the Chambersburg convention, endorsed the call for a convention to meet at Harrisburg on September 4, 1839. The call stated that " the interests of the country imperatively require that the two branches of the anti-Van Buren or Democratic Whig party in this state should be united to reestablish the ascendancy of the Constitution." Nothing was to be done to " interfere in any way with the distinct or independent organization of either of the two great divisions " into which the friends of the constitution were divided.[2] This movement was endorsed in various counties through " Union and Harmony " conventions.[3] In the meantime, the supporters of Harrison were stressing the statement that he was the only candidate who could secure the Anti-Masonic vote, thereby preventing the Democrats from carrying the state.[4] When the state Harrisburg convention met on September 4, it was composed of Harrison men. Clay was lauded as a great leader, but it was asserted that Harrison alone would satisfy all the political elements in the state opposed to the Democrats.[5] The same cry was

[1] Address in the *National Gazette,* August 3, 1839.

[2] *Harrisburg Chronicle,* June 26, 1839.

[3] *Chambersburg Whig,* August 2, 23; *National Gazette,* July 11, September 7, 10, 1839.

[4] *National Gazette,* April 25; *Chambersburg Whig,* June 14, 28, August 2, 23, 1839.

[5] *Niles' Register,* vol. lvii, p. 46; address in *ibid.,* vol. lvii, p. 190.

eagerly caught up in Ohio and Indiana, where Anti-Masonry had made some progress.[1]

When the Whig national convention assembled on December 4, 1839, at Harrisburg, Pennsylvania was represented by delegates from both of the state conventions. The compromise which was effected gave control of the state delegation to the Anti-Masons. Before the assembling of the convention, Penrose, who was working with the Anti-Masons in favoring Harrison, assured political leaders in other states that no one else could carry Pennsylvania.[2] On the floor of the convention Penrose was the capable and active leader of the Harrison men. Sprague of Massachusetts proposed a cumbersome method of balloting and reporting through committees. On the motion of Penrose the plan after being amended to provide for the unit rule of voting the state delegations was adopted. The scheme gave ample opportunity to exert pressure on the delegates. The result of the manipulation of the delegations was the nomination of William H. Harrison and John Tyler, without the formulation of any political principles.[3] The result, all the Anti-Masons had hoped for, had been attained largely through the clever leadership of Penrose.[4]

[1] Greeley, *Recollections of a Busy Life*, p. 130; Weed, *Autobiography and Memoirs*, vol. i, p. 480.

[2] Seward, *Life of Seward*, vol. i, p. 447.

[3] *Niles' Register*, vol. lvii, pp. 248-252, for the proceedings of the convention; Stanwood, *History of the Presidency*, vol. i, p. 194.

[4] Sargent, *Public Men and Events*, vol. ii, pp. 75-96. The Anti-Masons "were adroit enough to get a majority of the Pennsylvania delegation of the wolf-in-sheep's-clothing stripe, and thus cast the vote of the state for Harrison;" *ibid.*, p. 92. The method of voting he characterized as "an ingenious *contrivance*—unknown till then to the most skillful political engineers, and never resorted to since;" *ibid.*, p. 90. Penrose is called "the chief engineer"; *ibid.*, p. 75. Weed has claimed great credit for himself in securing the nomination of Harrison; Weed, *Autobiography and Memoirs*, vol. i, p. 480, vol. ii, p. 76. For an ac-

In the formation of the electoral ticket, which at this time was considered of great importance, the Anti-Masons of the state made another gain. Twenty-three of the thirty electoral candidates, as eventually selected through the county conventions, had been named in May by the Anti-Masons.[1]

In the meantime, the election of 1839, in which the effect of the " Buckshot War " was felt, had resulted favorably for the Democrats. In Philadelphia county, where the dispute had originated, the Democratic candidates were triumphantly elected by a large majority.[2] The same chastisement of the Whigs and Anti-Masons was administered in the rest of the state, with the result that the legislature was fully given into the control of their opponents.[3] Consequently during the sessions of the legislature the Whigs and Anti-Masons could do little save try to block some of the measures of their opponents and criticize those which were adopted.[4]

When the term of Governor Ritner expired in January 1839, the treasury of the state was empty. It had been the policy of the coalition to avoid taxation. The bonuses

count of the "triangular correspondence" in New York, *cf.* Wise, *Seven Decades of the Union,* pp. 165, *et seq.* For the activities of Thaddeus Stevens, who was not a delegate, in preventing the nomination of Scott, *cf.* McClure, *Our Presidents and How We Make Them* p. 68.

[1] The electoral tickets can be found in *Chambersburg Whig,* June 14, 1839, and in the *United States Gazette,* September 18, 1840. For the method of forming the electoral ticket see *National Gazette,* February 25; *Daily Telegraph,* January 29; *United States Gazette,* April 16, 1840.

[2] *National Gazette,* October 15, 1839.

[3] *Ibid.,* October 22, 1839, credits the Democrats with sixty-nine of the one hundred members in the lower house.

[4] *United States Gazette,* January 3, February 5, April 3, 18, 20, June 1, 3, 4, 10; *Daily Telegraph,* February 13, March 4, April 7; *National Gazette,* January 14, 18, March 12, 1840.

received from the Bank of the United States and from the Girard Bank and the share of the state in the surplus funds of the federal government had been expended on internal improvements and for current expenses. The incoming administration of Porter made no immediate effort to settle the financial problem; it resorted to borrowing to procure funds for the needs of the state.[1] The embarrassment of the Bank of the United States in 1839 led the governor, in his message of 1840, to recommend far-reaching legislation to control the banks, to free the state from its dependence on borrowing by returning to some system of taxation to procure funds for current expenses, and to dispose of the public works.[2] On his recommendation an act was passed which levied a tax on bank stocks, according to the dividend which was declared, on mortgages, on judgment notes, on household furniture above a certain value, on pleasure carriages, on watches, and finally a one per cent tax was placed on all salaries received from the commonwealth.[3] Drastic as this measure seemed at the time, it was entirely inadequate and loans were resorted to even in the year of the passage of the act.[4] Although the amount of money col-

[1] Worthington, *Finances of Pennsylvania*, p. 46.

[2] *Pennsylvania Archives*, series iv, vol. vi, pp. 600, *et seq.*

[3] *Session Laws*, 1840, p. 612; Act of June 11, 1840. The bill passed the house by 47 to 41, and the senate by 17 to 15; *House Journal*, 1840, vol. i, p. 1230; *Senate Journal*, 1840, vol. i, p. 817.

[4] Worthington, *op. cit.*, p. 54. For the amounts of money raised from 1832 to 1840, *cf. supra*, p. 28n. The following amounts were raised after the resort to taxation; *House Journal*, 1844, vol. ii, p. 420.

	Tax on real and personal property	Receipts from all other sources
1841	$35,224.69	$363,920.52
1842	487,536.56	355,276.63
1843	554,921.26	250,989.62

lected was inadequate, yet a return to taxation had been effected—a policy never again to be abandoned. By subsequent increases in the rates, the financial rehabilitation of the state was ultimately secured.

At the close of the sessions of the legislature the Whig and Anti-Masonic members, or as they chose to call themselves "The Democratic Republican members of the Legislature," issued an address in which they criticized the policy of their opponents, on whom they tried to fasten the opprobrious name of "Federalists." Their opponents, they declared, were

breathing nothing but destruction to the banking and credit systems of the Commonwealth. . . . Men of no practical experience in the affairs of life—beardless enthusiasts, full of crude and chimerical notions of reform, and with no better idea of a banking institution than such as might be picked up in the various but unmeaning vocabulary of a village newspaper —tyros in political science whose whole knowledge was confined to the noisy inanities of a town meeting—such were the master spirits whom the fermentation of the political cauldron, and the chances and changes of political life had thrown upon the surface, and invested with the power of legislating upon the rights and property of their fellowmen.

The governor had intervened, they claimed, in the struggle over the banks and with him they had cooperated. The result was the adoption of resolutions whereby the suspension of specie payment, which had begun on October 9, 1839, was to be legal until January 15, 1841, but the suspending banks were to be called on for a loan to the state. They, as usual, charged extravagance and corruption in the administration of the public works. "Some potent and mysterious influence" was brought to bear on the question with the result that it " was supported by the natural enemies

of the system and opposed by many of its warmest friends."
The value of the state stocks had decreased. Two remedies
for this evil were available, but the Democrats had adopted
the worse. They had refused to adopt resolutions asking for
a distribution of the proceeds of the public lands to all the
states, their rightful proprietors; by this plan of distribution
the commonwealth would ultimately have received one hundred and twenty-five millions of dollars. They had, however, adopted a scheme of burdening the people with taxation, which they preferred to "the cheap declaration even
of an *opinion* which might be considered offensive at Washington." Their refusal to consider resolutions on the tariff,
was mentioned, but was not stressed.[1]

The national administration was held responsible by the
Whigs and Anti-Masons for the business depression which
had begun in 1837.[2] The continuance of the hard times
and the low prices obtained for agricultural products was
working for Harrison's success. The return of prosperity,
it was proclaimed, would follow his election, but no hope
was to be placed in the Democrats as was shown by a statement of Senator Buchanan, who because of the wage he was
alleged to favor was dubbed "Ten-Cent Jimmie."[3] The
passage of the Sub-Treasury Bill, it was stated, could not
make business conditions worse, for it merely proposed to
legalize a system already illegally applied.[4]

[1] For the address in full, *National Gazette*, July 2, 4, 1840.

[2] *Ibid.*, October 1, 1839, said, "Figures and facts fix upon the federal
administration, beginning with Jackson's veto of the United States
Bank, every calamity of the mercantile community. Before that event,
the credit system, although obnoxious to certain exceptions, was com-
paratively sure and regular." *Cf.* also *ibid.*, October 5, 10, 1839;
United States Gazette, March 19, October 10, 1840.

[3] *United States Gazette*, June 9; *Daily Telegraph*, February 20, 24,
25, 1840.

[4] *United States Gazette*, July 3, 9, 1840.

Inasmuch as Harrison had been nominated without a platform, reliance was placed on his letter of acceptance of the Anti-Masonic nomination in 1838 for a statement of his political principles.[1]   The campaign, however, was primarily one of personalities and not one of principles.[2]   The Whigs, endeavoring to fasten the term " Federalist " on their opponents,[3] claimed that they themselves were the true supporters of the Jeffersonian doctrines.[4]   The sneer of the Democrats at Harrison's rusticity was eagerly seized and employed with telling effect against them by the Whigs. At the numerous meetings of the Whigs the " log cabin," the " barrel of hard cider," and the " same old 'coon " were constantly in evidence;[5] indeed, it was a Harrisburg politician who is said to have been the first to see the possibilities of the " log-cabin " cry.[6]   The cry that the nomination

[1] *Niles' Register,* vol. lv, p. 360.

[2] Some felt that the bank question was still paramount. Francis R. Shunk, secretary of the commonwealth, on October 5, 1840, wrote Lewis S. Coryell, " Stripped of all its clothes the naked question for decision at the next Presidential election is whether the bank aristocracy partly American and partly British, or the people shall be sovereign in these States—Antimasons, abolitionists, hard-ciderites, democratic Whigs flourish upon the Stage but the Bank and Stock gamblers are the life of the opposition and if success could attend them they would rule. They care not for the offices.   A splendid bank and national debt by assumption of state debt fill their imaginations, they are grasping for that power by which her Kings have ruled England since the Stuarts lost the right of governing by prerogative." Coryell Papers, vol. iii, p. 106.

[3] *Daily Telegraph,* January 30, February 20, March 12, July 2; *United States Gazette,* June 20, 1840.

[4] *National Gazette,* January 20, 30, July 4, September 1; *Daily Telegraph,* January 21, April 4, 1840.

[5] *United States Gazette,* March 18, May 8, June 16, 20, August 22, September 21, 30, 1840.

[6] R. S. Elliott, *Notes taken from Sixty Years,* p. 120.

of Harrison was the "appeal military" was declared to
come with poor grace from the party of Andrew Jackson.[1]
The use of bloodhounds to track Seminoles in the swamps
of Florida was proclaimed a shocking military barbarity,
authorized by the Van Buren administration.[2]

The state elections, held on October 13, did not indicate
a political upheaval in the commonwealth. The official returns for Congressmen indicated a Democratic majority of
forty-six hundred. Fifteen of the twenty-eight Congressmen-elect were Democrats. The Whigs, however, by small
majorities secured control of the legislature.[3] Both sides
after the election campaigned more vigorously than before
in order to secure the choice of their electoral ticket. Van
Buren, never popular in Pennsylvania, was held responsible
for the accumulated financial ills of the country. The
people of the interior were attracted more by the personality
of the frontiersman Harrison than by that of the suave politician from New York. In the election Harrison carried
the state by a small majority of about three hundred and
fifty.[4]

With the election of Harrison to the presidency it was
only natural that Pennsylvania, which had been so largely

[1] *National Gazette*, February 15, 1840.

[2] *Daily Telegraph*, January 30, April 3; *United States Gazette*, February 3, 1840.

[3] *National Gazette*, December 5, 1840. There had been no opposition
to the Democrats in Berks county.

[4] *Smull's Legislative Hand-Book*, 1919, p. 715. For a time a split
between the Anti-Masons and Whigs seemed imminent. The Anti-
Masonic state committee of seven, which had been appointed at their
convention of May 22, 1839, had been expanded at the Harrison State
Convention of February 22, 1840, to a committee of fourteen. The
question of the acceptance of Josiah Randall, a Mason, as an elector
puzzled the expanded committee, for his name on the ticket threatened
to drive Anti-Masonic votes away. Thomas H. Burrowes, July 19,
1840, to Joseph Wallace; Wm. McPherson Mss.

instrumental in securing this result, should be anxious for
representation in his cabinet. Amongst the many claims
advanced for consideration were those of John Sergeant
for the Treasury, and Thaddeus Stevens for the Post-
Office.[1] Intimations were made that pressure had been
brought to bear by Stevens, Ritner, and Burrowes on the
members of the electoral college to secure signatures to a
recommendation of Stevens for the postmaster-generalship.
The recommendation, it was alleged, had been signed by
all the members of the college save ten, all the Whigs and a
few Anti-Masons spurning it.[2] Opposition to Stevens was
also manifested in the state senate, where, according to
report, a statement condemning his appointment was prepared.[3] It was quite evident that Harrison could make no
cabinet appointment from either of the two branches of his
supporters within the state without giving offense to the
other; consequently when his cabinet was announced no one
from Pennsylvania was on the list. The Anti-Masons
found what comfort they could in the presence of Francis

[1] The statement is made that Harrison had promised the postmaster-
generalship to Stevens, but that he did not fulfill his promise because of the pressure exerted by Webster and Clay, who thereby incurred the undying hostility of Stevens; Hood, " Thaddeus Stevens,"
in Harris, *Biographical History of Lancaster County;* McClure, *Our
Presidents and How We Make Them,* p. 68; Adams, *Memoirs of John
Quincy Adams,* vol x, p. 388; Tyler, *Letters and Times of the Tylers*
vol. iii, p. 87; *Daily Telegraph and Intelligencer,* January 20, 28, 30;
Lancaster Examiner, quoted in *ibid.,* January 19; *Pennsylvania Telegraph,* January 20, 30; February 3, 6, 1841.

[2] *United States Gazette,* January 23; *Keystone,* January 12, quoting
" Wyoming " in the *United States Gazette; Pennsylvania Telegraph,*
March 6, 1841. Letter of December 28, 1840, from Samuel Parke to
Joseph Wallace; Wm. McPherson Mss.

[3] *Daily Telegraph,* February 5, 8; *Pennsylvania Telegraph,* January 27,
February 6, 17, 1841.

Granger of New York, and refrained from condemning Harrison.[1]

The attacks of the Whigs on Stevens, when his name was suggested for the cabinet, offended the Anti-Masons. The charge was made that the *Gettysburg Star and Banner,* the mouthpiece of Stevens, was " stirring up the old, stale, and offensive matter of anti-masonry, dead, effete, and turned out of all decent society long since. . . . *The Banner* will find itself just two years too late in its attempt to rake up such feelings." [2]   Such insults led some of the Anti-Masons to consider the revival of an independent state organization for the gubernatorial contest, which was then impending.[3] Failing in this endeavor, they succeeded, however, in continuing the organization in some of the counties.[4]   The joint

---

[1] *Pennsylvania Telegraph,* February 17, 20; *National Gazette,* February 16; *Daily Telegraph,* February 16, 1841. The Anti-Masons complained that they were being discriminated against in the distribution of the offices. Stevens, on March 27, 1841, wrote Webster urging the appointment of Ritner as collector of the port of Philadelphia. " What offence has the interior of Penna. committed against the administration; what crime have the anti-Masonic counties, every majority county of ours save one, perpetrated, that the rule is to be reversed to their prejudice? What high merit has the city and county of Philadelphia lately exhibited which is to command or to justify their elevation over all Penna., and their monopoly of the two great offices in the State, contrary to uniform usage? You may not know the fact, which is nevertheless true, that not a single office at Washington or elsewhere has been given to a Penna. Antimason. And yet intelligent honesty will not deny that they form 4/5ths of the Harrison party of the State. This neglect I cannot suppose to be intentional. But if we are to be denied the collectorship, the *accidents* adverse to our friends would seem to accumulate with all the certainty of design." Webster Mss., Lib. of Cong.

[2] *United States Gazette,* January 14, 1841. Joseph R. Chandler, editor and owner of this journal, had recently been elected grand-master of the state Masonic organization; *Keystone,* January 30, 1841.

[3] *Pennsylvania Telegraph,* January 20, 30, February 3, 6, 1841.

[4] Particularly in Lancaster, Adams, and Allegheny counties. *Ibid.,* June 9; *Daily Telegraph,* February 27, March 3; *Keystone,* January 30, 1841.

state organization was largely under their control, and they endeavored to use it to advantage. On January 6, 1841, there went forth from the " Democratic Harrison State Committee," of which Thomas H. Burrowes was chairman, a call to " the friends of General Harrison in Pennsylvania " to elect delegates to a state convention to meet in Harrisburg on March 10, 1841, " for the purpose of selecting a candidate for the office of Governor, to be supported by the Democratic party of the State, at the approaching general election." [1]   When the convention assembled, it nominated John Banks, the competent, but little-known, president-judge of the Berks-Lehigh-Northampton district, and referred to itself as " the convention representing the great Democratic party which on the 30th of October last achieved a glorious victory in the election of Gen. William Henry Harrison." [2]

On January 15, 1841, the day set by the resolutions of April 3, 1840, the banks of the state resumed specie payment, which had been suspended since October 9, 1839. At the time it seemed quite possible that the banks might be able to continue meeting all demands for specie payment; but, on February 4, the Bank of the United States, after having paid out six million dollars in specie, was again forced to suspend. Most of the other banks were able to avoid taking this step. [3]   The banking situation was thus again forced on the attention of the legislature.

The Whigs, who, as a result of the election of 1840, were in full control of the legislature, determined to handle the situation in their own way. Without a roll-call a bill, entitled " An act relating to State Street, in the borough of

[1] *National Gazette,* January 11, 1841.
[2] *United States Gazette,* March 12, 1841.
[3] *Ibid.,* March 12, 1841.

Harrisburg," had, on February 1, passed the senate.[1] For more than two months, while their opponents tried various measures to secure action on the banking situation, the Whigs allowed this bill to slumber in a committee of the house. On April 16, by a strict party vote of fifty-four to forty-four, the bill was so amended by the house that it provided for the raising of revenue, the increasing of taxation, the making of many appropriations, the authorizing of a loan to the state, the issuance of " relief notes " by the banks which participated in the loan, and the possible resuscitation of the Bank of the United States.[2] The Democrats failed in their effort to have adopted a section requiring Nicholas Biddle to turn over to the assignees of the Bank of the United States the service of sterling silver " presented to him by the directors or self-styled majority of stock-holders of said Bank, as a reward for his alleged meritorious service in conducting the financial operations of said Bank," and compelling the directors personally to pay the difference between the cost of the service and its value as bullion.[3] The senate refused to accept all the amendments of the house. Efforts to hold the bank for the unpaid portions of its pledge to the public school fund were readily defeated.[4] On April 30 the report of the conference committee was accepted by strict party voting, in the senate by 17 to 14, in the house by 50 to 42. The bill was now entitled " An act to provide revenue to meet the demands on the treasury and for other purposes." [5] On

[1] *Senate Journal*, 1841, vol. i, p. 172.

[2] *House Journal*, 1841, vol. i, pp. 229, 804, 859.

[3] *Ibid.*, 1841, vol. i, p. 810.

[4] *Senate Journal*, 1841, vol. i, p. 869; the vote was 7 to 20.

[5] *Ibid.*, 1841, vol. i, pp. 908, 933; *House Journal*, 1841, vol. i, pp. 952, 971.

the following day the governor returned the bill with his
veto, declaring that " the boon extended to the banks is
not only greater than is necessary, but greater than has been
asked for by any of these institutions." [1] The day set for
the adjournment of the legislature was rapidly approaching.
The Whigs had declared their intention, in the event that
they would be unable to override the governor's veto, to
adjourn without taking any further action on the important
measures which were involved in the bill. The contractors
on the state works would then be left unpaid and disaster
would descend on many counties. Immediately after the
receipt of the vetoed bill, the senate passed the measure by
a vote of 17 to 8; the refusal of six Democrats to vote
assured success. [2] In the house victory for the Whigs did
not come so easily. After two failures to override the
veto, the Whigs, with the assistance of thirteen Democrats,
passed the bill, on May 4, by a vote of 62 to 28. The
thirteen Democrats asserted that they objected to the bill,
but since the suggestions of the governor would not be followed by the existing legislature they had reluctantly voted
for it rather than " behold our Commonwealth become a
by-word and reproach among the nations of the earth." [3]

The act provided for a further loan to the state up to
three million and one hundred thousand dollars, which, with
certain exceptions, could be subscribed for by the banks of
the state in bank-notes, authorized by the act and issued in
denominations of five dollars and less. These " relief
notes," redeemable in state stocks, were receivable for
debts due to the state. [4] Because of the failure to provide

---

[1] *Senate Journal,* 1841, vol. i, p. 965.

[2] *Ibid.,* 1841, vol. i, p. 969.

[3] *House Journal,* 1841, vol. i, pp. 971, 1011, 1047, 1055, 1059.

[4] *Session Laws,* 1841, vol. i, p. 307. Thirty-three banks accepted, and

for the redemption of these "relief notes" through taxation, their depreciation followed.[1] The act also provided for the possible resuscitation of the Bank of the United State, or for its liquidation, if revival should prove to be impossible. Liquidation proved to be necessary; consequently on September 4, 1841, an assignment of the resources of the bank was made.[2] The bank had been a Whig organization, and within the state its notes had been an important medium of exchange. Now that the notes were not accepted, the criticisms of the Whigs by the Democrats were convincing to the holders of the well-nigh worthless certificates.[3]

During the sessions of the legislature Governor Porter had vetoed a large number of bills. Following his nomination for reelection at the state Democratic convention of March 4, 1841, the "Harrison Democratic members of the State Legislature," adopting the plan of the year before, issued an address under date of May 5, in which they attacked the governor for his abuse of the veto power. They excoriated him for his veto of the bill to relieve the financial stringency, claiming that previous to the veto he had made no suggestions to them as to what would be acceptable. The passage of the bill over his veto had offered relief to a large number of men who would otherwise have been made destitute through the failure to provide funds for the

eighteen did not; "Report of the Auditor General," *House Journal,* 1842, vol. ii, p. 118. There were issued $2,220,264 in "relief notes." The auditor-general still annually reports the issues; for there are $40,806 of the old issue, and $55,287 of the new issue "in circulation"; *Report of the Auditor-General,* 1917, p. 12.

[1] Worthington, *Finances of Pennsylvania,* p. 56.

[2] *National Gazette,* November 30, 1841.

[3] *The Keystone,* May 18, June 2, 23, August 4, 11, September 8, 22, 27, 1841. The fact that "Ritner's and Stevens' Regulator" had eventually exploded was stressed.

continuance of construction and for the payment of labor already done on the public works of the state. They decried the use of the veto for other than constitutional reasons. Summing up their criticism, they said,

At least ten Executive vetoes disfigure the Journals of this session, and in but one of them has the Governor pretended to indicate other than considerations of local expediency, of which the Representatives of the people believed they were the best judges.[1]

Before election day national affairs attracted attention. The death of Harrison elevated Tyler, whose political views had not been fully ascertained when he was nominated for the vice-presidency. In accordance with the call of Harrison, Congress assembled in special session on May 31. Tyler's message, if not enthusiastically received, was considered at least favorably.[2] It seemed to indicate that he would not oppose the will of Congress, but his veto of the " Fiscal Bank Bill," followed by his veto of the " Fiscal Corporation Bill," disrupted the party, and the entire cabinet with the exception of Webster resigned. These vetoes by the Whig President took the edge off of the criticisms of the vetoes by the Democratic governor.

The governor was also subjected to criticism by the Whigs as the result of an incident growing out of the campaign of 1840. E. W. Hutter and John J. C. Cantine had been editors of a Democratic campaign paper called *The Magician*. During the heat of the campaign they had printed an article asserting that the Whigs engaged in sacrilegious and blasphemous rites at their political meetings. They stated that at the Gettysburg meetings Thaddeus Stevens, officiating as " High Priest," led the out-

[1] *Niles' Register,* vol. lx, p. 212.
[2] *United States Gazette,* June 3, 1841.

rageous ceremonies. After the election Stevens sued the
editors for libel in his home county, Adams. When the
case was on trial, the attorney for the defendants offered
as a bar to the proceedings a proclamation, signed January
23, 1841, by the governor, pardoning the defendants from
the charge of libel.[1] The issuance of a pardon before conviction was held by the Whigs to be a perversion of the
pardoning power.

The virulent attacks on the personal morality of Porter,
which had been so common in the election of 1838, were not
revived for this election. Charges of maladministration
were made instead. It was claimed that there had been an
unwarranted increase in the amount of the state debt and
that the public works were being mismanaged. Peculation
and bribery in the passage of the Bank Act of 1840 were
alleged. The sum of ninety-nine thousand dollars was
mentioned as having been used by the Bank of the United
States for some undeclared and unholy purpose.[2]

The returns showed the election of Porter by a large
majority.[3] In the legislature the Democrats gained control
of the house, but the senate, due to the large number of
hold-overs, remained in the power of the Whigs.[4] In endeavoring to account for their defeat the Whig editors
claimed that many who in 1840 had voted for Harrison had
left the party because of unfulfilled expectations, which they
had anticipated would be realized through a mere change

[1] The proclamation of pardon is in *Pennsylvania Telegraph*, February
3, 1841.

[2] *Ibid.*, September 18; *National Gazette*, September 21, 1841.

[3] *Smull's Legislative Hand-Book*, 1919, p. 720; David R. Porter (Dem.)
136,504; John Banks (Whig) 113,473; F. J. Lamoyne (Liberty) 763;
scattering 23.

[4] *Pennsylvania Telegraph*, December 29, 1841. The senate contained 17
Whigs and 16 Democrats; the house had 37 Whigs and 63 Democrats.

of administrations. Neglect of the former Anti-Masons in the distribution of the patronage accounted for a great deal of coolness in certain sections of the state.[1] The former Anti-Masonic press attributed the defeat, which they had been expecting, to slurs which had been made against them. They claimed that their party had redeemed the state, and that of the 140,000 votes, cast for Harrison, 120,000 had been Anti-Masonic. Despite their numerical strength they had not been appointed to office.

The anti-masons were represented as unpopular, vulgar, and inefficient. The *gentlemen* whigs and the 5 o'clock converts were the meritorious and able candidates for office. They found favor with the present administration; and were appointed to all offices from which locofocos could be spared.[2]

Both Whigs and Anti-Masons agreed in thus accounting for the heavy loss in the counties which had been strongholds of the latter.

The problem of the financial rehabilitation of the state was still unsolved. The governor therefore took up the question in his annual message recommending that in addition to disposing of the state-owned stocks the public works be sold, claiming that they could not be administered as economically under governmental as under private control.[3] Nothing came of his recommendation as attention was directed to other financial problems. Resolutions, from a mass meeting in Philadelphia, urging repudiation of the

[1] *National Gazette,* October 17; *United States Gazette,* October 15, 23, 1841.

[2] *Gettysburg Star* quoted in *Pennsylvania Telegraph,* November 3, 1841. Ex-Governor Ritner, one of the few Anti-Masons nominated, had been rejected by the Senate of the United States because of alleged "incurable blindness"; *Pennsylvania Telegraph,* September 22, 1841.

[3] *Pennsylvania Archives,* series iv, vol. vi, p. 831.

state debt met with immediate non-partisan condemnation.[1]
The state was, however, on the verge of bankruptcy, and
interest on the state debt was not met promptly when it fell
due on February 1, 1842. Beginning on January 29,
there had been a run on the Bank of Pennsylvania, the
state depository and disbursing agent. The run on the bank
had followed the closure of the Girard Bank a few days
previously. The other banks of Philadelphia had refused
to render either of them any assistance. The governor,
who chanced to be in Philadelphia at the time, had an in-
junction issued against the Bank of Pennsylvania forbidding it to pay out further moneys. This action guaranteed
the funds of the state, enabling the Bank of Pennsylvania
to begin paying the interest on the public debt on February
14, a delay of two weeks.[2] Thus the banking question
again assumed importance.

The Democrats brought in their bill to remedy the
banking ills, which to their mind consisted in the participation of the state as a partner in various private corporations.
They, therefore, called for a " total divorce between Bank
and State." [3] The bill readily passed the house, although
the section ordering immediate resumption under threat of
forfeiture of charter received considerable opposition.
The senate amended the bill slightly. A conference between
the two houses adjusted the differences, and the measure
received the signature of the governor on March 12, 1842.[4]
Although the act was not strictly a party measure, yet it

[1] *North American*, January 7, 8; *The Keystone*, January 15, 1842.

[2] *North American*, January 31, February 1, 2, 3, 4, 7, 12, 14, 15; 1842.
It was not until April 17, 1843, that resumption was effected; *ibid.*, April
18, 1843.

[3] *The Keystone*, February 5, 1842.

[4] *Session Laws*, 1842, p. 68.

received severe criticism from the Whigs, particularly from those in Philadelphia, one of whose editors exclaimed,

Some think our resumption bill should be called a bill to relieve our country banks, break down those of our city, and help the New York brokers; others think it should be called a bill to establish a state currency, with relief notes as a basis; others insist it should be called a bill to postpone indefinitely specie payment. Were we called upon ourselves to christen it, we should call it a bill to lose all the benefits which it sought, and realize all the evils it would shun; or, if that won't do, then call it a bill, composed of party springs, to catch political wood cock.[1]

In the meantime, the charges that the Bank of the United States had resorted to bribery to secure the passage of the resolutions of April 3, 1840, were being investigated.[2]   The Handy Investigation, as it was called because George Handy, one of the directors of the bank, had acted as its agent, began on February 14.   In order to relieve Handy from the danger of a criminal prosecution, which might be based on his testimony before the committee, the legislature adopted a joint resolution authorizing the attorney-general to issue a *nolle prosequi,* if such suit were brought against Handy.[3]   Handy claimed that Daniel M. Brodhead, " a constant borer at Harrisburg, for many years past, on behalf of Banks and other corporations," had acted as the intermediary between him and the governor.   A letter from J. Solms, president of the Moyamensing Bank of Phila-

---

[1] *North American,* March 11, 1842; *cf.* also *ibid.,* March 15, 18, 19; *United States Gazette,* March 9, 1842.

[2] " Report of the joint committee of investigation, appointed by the legislature of Pennsylvania, to investigate whether corrupt means had been used to procure legislation favorable to the banks from 1836 to 1841." *Senate Journal,* 1842, vol. ii.

[3] *Session Laws,* 1842, p. 479.

delphia, to George Handy was produced, stating that Solms would again pay his respects to the governor and would " talk in the Indian language." Many letters in code were submitted at the investigation. In one to an undisclosed addressee, possibly Handy, Solms wrote,

To-morrow, I expect to hear from you respecting business in the lumber way, which is plenty, cheap now, and will sell. People will build in hopes of better times, however you are more sanguine than I am in that business way.—They may not sell as low as you think. Persons in desperate circumstances take care of themselves when they are pressed; in obtaining time they believe to weather the storm.[1]

The letters furnished the political opponents of the governor the opportunity of lampooning him as an Indian chief, particularly as a " Kickapoo," and of manifesting great interest in the lumber market.[2]

The incomplete investigation failed to establish the fact that either the governor or any member of the legislature had received any of the $131,175, placed at the disposal of Handy.[3] The committee, both in the majority and in the

[1] *House Journal,* 1842, Appendix, pp. 461, *et seq.*

[2] *Pennsylvania Telegraph,* April 20, 27, May 4; *North American,* April 6, 8, August 4, 6, 1842. A portion only of the Democratic press defended the governor; *The Keystone,* April 13, May 10, June 22, July 13, 18, 1842. When charges were made against the governor, he ordered the attorney-general to commence a criminal prosecution of Handy so that the entire matter might be investigated, claiming that the resolution ordering a *nolle prosequi* would not be violated thereby; *Pennsylvania Archives* series iv, vol. vi, p. 900. The anti-administration papers claimed that he was trying to stifle the investigation. The governor did not appear before the committee, although it had resolved that " if he were desirous of appearing before them to testify they would have no objections to hear him;" *The Keystone,* July 13, 1842.

[3] *Miners' Journal,* March 11, 1843, thought it " but proper to infer that he shared the proceeds."

minority reports exonerated them, claiming that the money had been lavishly spent on "borers." Attacks on the governor were continued in the next legislature; but the efforts to impeach him were easily defeated.[1] M. B. Lowry, one of the Democratic members of the investigating committee, took a view of the situation, which reflected the opinion of many members of the party.

It is a striking fact, and one which strongly illustrates its enormous wickedness, that the very individuals who by fraud and corruption brought it [the Bank of the United States] into a Pennsylvania Institution after the Union had rejected it have turned abruptly round and charged their own high offences upon the Democratic Party which from principle and sound policy has uniformly contended in opposition to it. The undersigned however conceives this a fruitless task, and thinks that these men will have to share the responsibility of its rise and downfall among themselves, the verdict of an impartial posterity will say, the Whig party created it, its advocates and agents plundered its stockholders and creditors, and the Democratic party has had neither part nor lot therein.[2]

That the Whigs, in the main, were responsible for the evils in the banking system can not be denied. The final failure of the Bank of the United States and the passage of various bank acts by the Democrats during their long period of power removed the question from political strife. Furthermore, the tariff was rising to a position of great importance, directing attention away from state to national politics.

The question of the payment of the interest on the state debt required attention; for the legislature had adopted a

[1] *Public Ledger,* January 16; *United States Gazette,* January 9, 19; *North American,* March 8, 13, 1843.

[2] *House Journal,* 1842, Appendix, p. 187.

joint resolution to aid the contractors on the state works
by appropriating for their benefit the money which had
previously been set aside to pay the interest.[1]   To preserve
the remnant of the credit of the state, the act of July 27,
1842, was passed. The semi-annual payment of the interest was due on August 1, but no funds were available.
The act authorized the payment of the interest in six per
cent scrip due in one year. A certain percentage of the
claims of the contractors, some of which were dated before
May 11, 1841, was to be paid. The sale of the state-owned
stock in private corporations was authorized. The governor was given authority to receive bids for the sale of
the public works. Retirement of the scrip was provided
for by the levy of a small tax on real and personal property.[2] It was hoped that this measure would prove to be
a temporary expedient, but recourse had to be had to scrip
on the interest dates in 1843 and in 1844.[3]

Another matter of state importance was the veto by
the governor of the apportionment bill, which had been
passed as a result of the districting act of Congress, based
on the census of 1840. The governor claimed that the proportion in the districts was not equal and that the minority

[1] *Session Laws,* 1842, p. 486, resolutions of April 7, 1842.

[2] *Ibid.,* 1842, p. 441. *The Pennsylvania Telegraph,* August 17, 1842,
said, "No one voted for the tax bill but loco focos, the city Whigs
and a few western members, who were representing the interests of
the 'domestic creditors'. The bill was so log-rolled, that these latter
could not help voting as they did, although in every instance where
a tax was proposed by itself, without the condition annexed of a disposal of the public works, they opposed it." The state-owned stock
could not be sold because of restrictions in the act; no adequate bids
for the state works were received.

[3] Worthington, *Sketch of the Finances of Pennsylvania,* p. 57. A
total of $4,502,824.01 was issued in this scrip. Under the acts of April
29, 1844, and April 16, 1845, $4,360,494.39 were funded; *Report of the
Auditor-General,* 1882, p. 233.

party was favored; he said, "I assure the world, that no apportionment will ever receive my sanction, which in any degree, is designed to steal power from the many, and confer it upon the few." [1]   Due to the failure of the legislature to pass an act satisfactory to the governor, no election for Congressmen was held this year.

In December, 1841, interest was directed to national affairs by the assembling of Congress in its regular session. The reference by the President in his message to the banking question attracted slight attention. [2]   More concern was felt in the state over the disposal of the tariff question. On March 25, 1842, the President submitted a message to Congress relative to the funds at the disposal of the Treasury. [3]   His proposal to repeal the land-distribution act, passed at the recent extra session of Congress, and to apply the funds thus released to the payment of the interest and of the debt of the federal government was condemned.   It was declared,

The true question at issue is not whether the general government, or the States, shall have the avails of these lands, but whether the old States shall share them with the new; or whether the new shall have the whole; *that* is the question. For the old States to vote for a repeal of the Land Bill would be the most suicidal act that they could possibly commit. [4]

While the Whigs of the state condemned the proposal to repeal the distribution act, the proposal to increase the tariff

[1] *Pennsylvania Archives*, series iv, vol. vi, p. 944. In McClure, *Old Time Notes of Pennsylvania*, vol. i, p. 69, it is stated that Porter vetoed the bill because it made the election of two of his friends impossible.

[2] Richardson, *Messages and Papers of the Presidents*, vol. iv, p. 83.

[3] *Ibid.*, vol. iv, p. 106.

[4] *North American*, March 28, 1842.

rates was heralded gladly. "A tariff is sufficient, and *that* we must have, repeal or no repeal." [1]

A tariff bill, which proposed to raise the rates above twenty per cent and at the same time continue the provisions of the distribution act, was returned on June 29 with a presidential veto.[2] The President felt that a temporary revenue measure was overthrowing a permanent compromise. His use of the veto was condemned by the Whigs; for, although its exercise was constitutional, he had advanced no constitutional argument for its use.[3] It was pointed out that the President was now in full and complete harmony with the policy of the Democrats.[4] Another tariff bill, similar to the preceding one save in a few minor matters, was returned on August 9 with a veto message, which virtually repeated the previous arguments in its insistence on the non-inclusion of the distribution provisions in the tariff measure.[5] The veto was declared to be " an act of madness " on the part of " his Accidency," who cared little how much the country suffered.

The manufacturers of the country are crushed, our commerce broken up, our shipping rotting in the docks, and ruin and consternation spread abroad upon the land: and all this done in the mad hope of retaining a station which would never have been accorded to him at the hands of the people.[6]

An analysis of the vote on the bill, in its passage through the

[1] *United States Gazette,* March 29, 1842.

[2] Richardson, *op. cit.,* vol. iv, p. 180.

[3] *United States Gazette,* July 1; *North American,* July 1, 1842.

[4] *North American,* July 2, 1842.

[5] Richardson, *op. cit.,* vol. iv, p. 183; reference of this message to a committee, which reported condemnatory resolutions, led to a protest from the President; *ibid.,* vol. iv, p. 190.

[6] *United States Gazette,* August 11, 1842.

House, which was to receive the signature of the President, shows that it was primarily a Whig measure, but that more Whigs voted in the negative than Democrats voted in the affirmative. It was not distinctively a sectional measure, for as many votes south of the Mason and Dixon line were cast for it, as votes north of the line were cast against it. Ten Whigs and ten Democrats from Pennsylvania voted for it, while three Whigs and five Democrats did not vote.[1] In Pennsylvania the question of the tariff was not yet a party issue, although the Whigs were asserting that it was.[2] The act was generally received with favor although it was recognized that it lacked permanency. The tariff Whigs were urged to be conciliatory to the distribution Whigs, who were to be congratulated for yielding and sacrificing their provision.[3]

Before the adjournment of Congress, "Vetoes No. 5 and 6" were received. The former on the land-distribution bill had been expected, but the latter, coming unexpectedly, was condemned as an unwarranted interference in a matter which affected merely the organization of Congress.[4]

The supporters of Tyler, few in number though they were, were active in trying to get the aid of the Democrats for their leader. At Philadelphia, on the Fourth of July, 1842, a delegation was sent from the Tyler banqueters to carry a toast to Democratic banqueters. The Democrats replied in their toast that they "sought no alliance but look for the justice of our cause for success. Truth is mighty and will prevail." [5] At a Fourth of July dinner at the

---

[1] *North American*, August 26, 1842.

[2] *Pennsylvania Telegraph*, September 14, 1842.

[3] *Ibid.*, August 31; *North American*, August 25, 1842.

[4] *North American*, September 3, 1842.

[5] *Ibid.*, July 7; *United States Gazette*, July 6, 1842.

White House nearly forty Democrats were present. One of these, C. J. Ingersoll, a Philadelphia Congressman, was credited with the toast, " Veto and Ditto." [1]   The Democrats were making it evident that they were willing to encourage disaffection in the Whig party, willing to profit by the resulting split, but unwilling to follow Tyler. The patronage was also, of course, being used for the purpose of developing a Tyler following. Secretary of the Treasury Walter Forward had in April asked Jonathan Roberts, collector of the custom duties at Philadelphia, to remove a certain number of employees. Roberts asked for and was granted a conference on the question of the removals. His refusal to comply with the request was followed in September by his own removal.[2]

Following these events came the election of 1842, at which only members of the state legislature were to be chosen, and which in consequence failed to attract much attention, although the next legislature was to choose a United States Senator to succeed James Buchanan. The Whigs had no one for whom to work up enthusiasm, while the Democrats sneered at the possibility of the state being represented by " Thaddeus Stevens, Joseph Ritner, Thomas H. Burrowes or some other of the back window heroes of the Buckshot War." [3]   The tariff could not be used as an issue, for its effects were not yet felt and the state Democrats had supported the measure. The failure of the Democrats to support the distribution bill was condemned, as now the taxpayer would be forced to bear still heavier burdens.[4]   The ensuing election gave control of both houses

[1] *United States Gazette,* July 8, 1842.

[2] Correspondence in the *North American,* September 13, 15, 17, 1842.

[3] *The Keystone,* September 28, 1842.

[4] *United States Gazette,* October 7, 1842.

by safe majorities to the Democrats.[1] The *United States*
Gazette felt called upon gloomily to insist that the election
indicated that the people of the state had declared against
a tariff.[2]

Upon the assembling of the legislature the financial situation was reviewed by Governor Porter in his message. As
previously, so now, he urged greater recourse to taxation
in order that the state might have at its disposal adequate
funds to be used for the reduction of the state debt.
However, he now recommended a specific measure to con-
sist of a levy of a few cents a ton on the iron ore and coal
mined within the state, assuming that this would not be
heavy enough to cause increased importations.[3] The
Whigs directed their objections to this feature of the message. The *North American* contended that since the Pennsylvania delegation in Congress had exerted itself " to
have a duty laid upon foreign Coal and Iron, it seems hardly
consistent to tax these same articles so as to make foreign
competition the more easy." [4] The whole proposition met
with the hearty condemnation of the *Miners' Journal* which
held that coal and iron were already highly taxed as land.
Furthermore, the state debt was due to the construction
of the internal improvements, which were of little value
to the mining interests, for of the million tons of coal
shipped in 1842 from the Schuylkill, Lehigh and Lacka-
wanna regions only one fifth was carried on the state works.[5]

The efforts which were made to pass a bill laying a ton-

---

[1] *Ibid.*, January 4, 1843; the Democrats had nineteen of the thirty-
three senators and sixty-one of the one hundred representatives.

[2] *Ibid.*, October 31, 1842.

[3] *Pennsylvania Archives*, series iv, vol. vi, pp. 920, *et seq.*

[4] January 5, 1843.

[5] January 14, 1843.

nage tax on coal and iron ore met with insurmountable opposition. Consequently scrip, as in 1842, had to be relied
on to provide funds for the payment of the interest on the
public debt.[1] The governor recommended that the state
debt be decreased by the proceeds from the sale of the state-
owned stocks in various corporations. Without much difficulty, an act authorizing their sale was passed. Pur-
chasers were allowed to make payment with the certificates
of debt, which had been issue by the auditor-general. The
result was that little money found its way into the state
treasury, although the debt was somewhat reduced by the
redemption of the certificates.[2]

Within the state the Democratic party underwent the
same experience that the Whig party had undergone nation-
ally, in that the executive whom it had elected was not in
harmony with the Democratic legislature. Early in January, the sheriff of Philadelphia died. Governor Porter
appointed his own son to fill the vacancy, which appoint-

---

[1] Worthington, *Finances of Pennsylvania*, p. 57.

[2] In his message of 1842, Governor Porter stated that the par value
of the state-owned stock was $6,134,074.45. The market value of it
had been steadily decreasing. A share of stock in the Bank of Pennsylvania, par value $400, sold in 1839 for $496, in 1840 for $410, in
1841 for $412, and in 1842 for $160; in 1843 the state disposed of its
shares, for prices ranging from $140 to $187.25. From June to
October, 1843, sales of state-owned stocks were held. For the stocks,
which proved saleable, $1,319,730.65 were received; stocks with a
par value of $1,986,797.56 could not be sold. *Pennsylvania Archives*,
series iv, vol. vi, pp. 821-839; *House Journal*, 1844, pp. 28-46. Under
the authority of the act of June 12, 1878, the amount of state-owned
stock was reduced to a par value of $501,454.62; *Report of the Auditor-
General*, 1882, p. 238. The greater portion of this still remains un-
sold; the auditor-general today reports state-owned stock to a par
value of $432,884.62; *ibid.*, 1917, 9. 31. The state-constructed and state-
owned canals and railroads had cost $35,096,671.18. When they were
sold, under authority of the acts of May 16, 1857, and April 21, 1858,
only $10,981,500 were received for them; *ibid.*, 1860, p. 114.

ment openly started the breach between the governor and his party.[1] The rearrangement of his cabinet by President Tyler widened the breach when he appointed James M. Porter, a brother of the governor, *ad interim* Secretary of War. Of the sixty-nine Democratic papers in the state all save twelve, which were controlled either by his appointees or by his brother, abandoned the governor.[2] *The Pennsylvanian* was particularly sharp in its criticisms, saying,

Were the people to be purchased thus, they would sell themselves cheaply indeed. This junction of the two administrations, with all the influences they can bring to bear, will neither transfer the people on the one hand to sustain Mr. Tyler for the presidency nor governor Porter for the vice-presidency, nor will it serve to distract and divide the party in 1844. Such chaffering and peddling, first of the offices of the people themselves, for the benefit of *two families*, will create an emotion of just anger not easily to be tranquilized.[3]

Charges of an endeavor to establish Porterism as the equal and partner of Tylerism abounded.

A strong point of attack on Porter was his unabated use of the veto. An act dividing the state into congressional districts, which he approved, was secured after several vetoes.[4] His veto of the bill, providing for the election of the canal commissioners by the legislature, was effective

---

[1] *The Pennsylvanian*, which was attacking Porter, was answered by the *Spirit of the Times*, which on February 15, 1843, said "that this whole establishment with the Brokers, Auctioneers, Bullies, Pawnbrokers, Lawyers, Job Printers, and others who have control over it, are about to make one grand leap—to turn a complete somersault—and come down in the middle of the Whig Senate camp."

[2] *The Keystone*, May 10, 1843, quoted in *Niles' Register*, vol. lxiv, p. 179.

[3] Quoted in *Niles' Register*, vol. lxiv, p. 44.

[4] *Session Laws*, 1843, p. 115.

despite the fact that a number of the Democrats combined
with the Whigs in an effort to overcome it.   The governor
maintained that " the election or appointment of the Canal
Commissioners belongs only to the Executive or to the
people, and cannot be vested in the Legislature without a
gross usurpation of power." [1]   A bill providing for their
election by the people became effective despite the opposition
of the governor.[2]   Not only the governor but also the Democracy was condemned for beginning

the experiment of arraying the nominally poor against the
ostensibly rich.   The former being a majority in the American,
as in every other nation, it was prudently determined to win
their affections.   The hue and cry against aristocracy was successful, so far that the polity, stigmatized as aristocratic, was
abandoned for a succession of schemes, all opposite in their
nature, but all acceptable, under the name of democratic.[3]

The " temperate conservatism " of the Whigs was needed
to save the country " when innovation is stalking so fiercely
abroad." [4]

The elections to be held in the fall of 1843 were of unusual importance, for, in addition to members of the state
legislature, Congressmen and, for the first time, canal commissioners were to be chosen.   Into the election the Whigs
made efforts to prevent the presidential question from entering.   It was quite probable that Clay would be the choice
of the Whig national convention, called for May 3, 1844.
He had been endorsed as the preference of the state at a
mass convention held at Harrisburg on February 22, 1843.[5]

[1] *Pennsylvania Archives,* series iv, vol. vi, p. 979.

[2] *Session Laws,* 1843, p. 337.

[3] *North American,* April 15, 1843.

[4] *Ibid.,* March 16, 1843.

[5] *Public Ledger,* February 24, 1843.

There existed some fear that McLean might be used " by
the remnants of the New York clique, which made a stalking horse of the manly form of Scott " in 1839, and thus
Clay might be defeated.[1]   Tyler caused little concern, for
his attempts to control the Whig party had failed dismally,
and his advances to the Democrats were being scorned.[2]
Tyler was declared to stand in such poor favor that the
reception accorded him by the people in his journey to the
dedication of the Bunker Hill monument was characterized
as " cool and dignified." [3]

On the other hand, some of the former proscriptive
leaders of the Anti-Masonic party, who had not been admitted to a position of influence in the Whig ranks, threatened trouble.   They too had held a state mass convention
and had declared themselves favorable to Scott.   To use
the committee, appointed at this convention, would dis-
credit their movement.   They therefore resorted to the
committee, which in 1841 had had charge of the campaign
of Banks for governor and which was subject to their influence.   This committee on May 17, 1843, issued a call
for a convention of the " Democratic Harrison Party " to
assemble on September 6 to make nominations for canal
commissioners.[4]   This was an effort to block the endorsement of Clay by the Whigs and, at the same time, to disrupt
the organization which had been perfected at the Clay convention of February 22.[5]

---

[1] *United States Gazette,* May 12, 1843.

[2] *North American,* May 12, 1843.

[3] *Ibid.,* June 14, 1843.

[4] *Pennsylvania Telegraph,* July 4, 1843.

[5] Egle, *Notes and Queries,* 1896, p. 146; in a letter, dated May 20,
1843, to John Strohm, John A. Fisher condemned the movement " *in
toto,* and see in it, if assented to, or recognized by us, the virtual
triumph of that clique of bold, bad men whose motto is rule or ruin."

The directing genius of this movement to block the endorsement of Clay was Thaddeus Stevens, who in 1842 had moved to Lancaster from Gettysburg. In Lancaster and Allegheny counties, the proscriptive Anti-Masons had been maintaining an independent organization. On August 30, 1843, the "Anti-Masonic and Whig" convention for the county met at Lancaster to choose delegates for the state convention of September 6. The delegates chosen at this county convention were instructed to withdraw, if the Stevens delegation, which had been chosen at an "Anti-Masonic" county convention, received any recognition at the state convention.[1] At the state convention the committee on contested delegations rejected Stevens and his associates.[2] This faction, however, ran its own ticket in Lancaster county. The same thing was done also in Allegheny county, from which no contesting delegation had, however, been sent to the state convention.[3] In the other counties of the state the former Anti-Masons gave the Whig party their undivided allegiance, and the effort to revive political Anti-Masonry for the elections of this year failed.

In the election campaign no distinctive issue was raised The more effective organization of the Democrats gave them the three canal commissioners by a majority of over fourteen thousand in a total vote of two hundred and seven thousand.[4] The Democrats now held twenty-two of the thirty-three seats in the state senate, and fifty-eight of the one hundred in the house.[5] Sufficient importance had not

[1] *United States Gazette,* September 1; *Public Ledger,* September 2, 1843.

[2] *North American,* September 9, 1843.

[3] *Daily Forum,* quoted in *Niles' Register,* vol. lxv, p. 169, for the returns from these two counties.

[4] *North American,* October 24, 1843.

[5] *Public Ledger,* January 2, 1844.

been attached to the election by the Whigs, as was shown
by the fact that in some districts of Schuylkill county ballots for the Whig candidates had not been printed.[1]   The
Democrats secured only twelve of the twenty-four Congressmen, inasmuch as the Whigs had combined with dissatisfied
Democrats in some of the congressional districts and had
elected volunteer Democrats, who expressly declared for a
protective tariff.

[1] *Miners' Journal*, October 28, 1843.

CHAPTER III

TEXAS AND THE TARIFF

1844-1846.

As soon as the elections of 1843 were past, plans were made for the ensuing presidential campaign. The Democrats of the state, under the control of Buchanan, pledged their support to him. But on December 19, 1843, before the meeting of the state convention, Buchanan in a letter, published in the *Lancaster Intelligencer*, withdrew his name as a candidate for the presidency.[1] He did this because he received no support in other states, the majority of which were already pledged to Van Buren.[2] The sentiment of the Democracy in the state was by no means strongly in favor of Van Buren, nevertheless the Democratic state convention, at Harrisburg on March 4, 1844, pledged its delegates to him for the presidency and to R. M. Johnson for the vice-presidency. After a sharp contest the convention nominated Henry A. Muhlenberg, the anti-Wolf Democratic candidate in 1835, for governor.[3] On August 10, before the election, Muhlenberg died suddenly at his home in Reading. The Democratic state central committee reconvoked the convention, which, on September 2, nominated Francis R. Shunk, who had been the opponent of Muhlenberg at the first convention.[4] Shunk was the inevitable choice of

[1] Moore, *The Works of James Buchanan*, vol. v, p. 437.

[2] *Ibid.*, vol. vi, p. 1.

[3] *Public Ledger*, March 6, 7, 8; *North American*, March 8, 1844.

[4] *Public Ledger*, August 15, September 4, 1844.

the Democrats at their second convention. His friendship with the Porters tended to hold that faction to the party. Furthermore, the party owed him a debt of gratitude for the firmness displayed during the Buckshot War, when as clerk of the house he had been the chief instrument in thwarting the machinations of the Whigs and Anti-Masons. He was strongly opposed to special grants, and consequently would continue the policy of his predecessor. A contemporary eulogist stated,

The tendency of capital to accumulate in the hands of the few, the power which it always wields, the antagonism between it and labor, and the encroachment of the former on the just rights of the latter, even under the best administration of the most equitable laws, he regarded as one of the dangers of republics.[1]

Such views appealed particularly to the masses in the interior of the state. Shunk had, however, continuously held public office since early manhood. His opponents sharply contrasted his career with that of their non-office-holding candidate.

On December 8, 1843, there appeared a call, signed by the members of the Harrison state central committee, for a "Democratic Harrison Convention" to meet at Harrisburg on March 4, 1844.[2] The committee appointed in 1841 to conduct the election for governor was the only anti-Democratic state organization which had any regularity to its existence. Since that year, there had been no general state election save that for canal commissioners. The only other way in which a call for a state convention might come would be from the members of the legislature. As this

[1] DeWitt, *A Discourse on the Life and Character of Francis R. Shunk, late Governor of Pennsylvania, delivered August 9, 1848*, p. 23.

[2] *North American*, December 11, 1843.

body did not assemble until January, the call might have come too late for the convention to meet at the customary time. Furthermore, the name of Harrison still had an attraction for many former Anti-Masons. Some of them, led by Thomas H. Burrowes, were not reconciled to the disappearance of political Anti-Masonry, and were threatening trouble. In November, 1843, they questioned Clay about his views on Masonry and about his membership in that organization. Clay replied that he " became a mason in early life, from youthful curiosity and a social disposition," but that he never took any high degrees, that he was not a member at the time, and that he never voted for anyone because he was a Mason.[1] Nothing definite came from this agitation, but fear of the Anti-Masons led to the suggestion that inasmuch as " Harrisonism in Penna. . . . is *per se* strong " it would be well to identify the Whig cause in the state with it. Care should be taken to fill the Harrison counties with Whig almanacs and songs and to impress upon the voters " that if it is not for Harrison they are fighting, it is against Harrison's enemies. If we can even to a tolerable extent raise this feeling, and then add to it a personal enthusiasm for Mr. Clay, and tariff principles, our course is far from impropitious." It might be " expedient to take up the Harrison Electoral ticket defying our adversaries to do the same." [2] The Anti-Masonic irreconcilables made no headway with their movement, which practically marked the end of their efforts to form an independent party by breaking away from the Whigs.[3]

[1] *Niles' Register,* vol. lxv, p. 244.

[2] William B. Reed to John M. Clayton, December 18, 1843; Clayton Papers, Lib. of Cong.

[3] The decadence of the power of the Anti-Masons is illustrated in Allegheny county. In the congressional election of 1843, the straight Anti-Masonic candidate received over 2200 votes. In a special election

When the "Democratic Harrison State Convention," as some of the former Anti-Masons called it, or the "Whig" state convention, as the resolutions had it, met, no great opposition to the endorsement of Henry Clay as the next presidential candidate developed. It took twenty-two ballots, however, to select Joseph Markle, of Westmoreland

in March, 1844, the same individual received only 600 votes; *Niles' Register*, vol. lxvi, p. 80. Thomas H. Burrowes, who had been chairman of the Harrison state central committee in 1840 and who had been active in trying to keep Anti-Masonry alive, on March 1, 1844, wrote Joseph Wallace, "I never was—am not—and never will be a Whig. Ergo I must be and am a Locofoco, because antimasonry being now extinct even to the last spark, I have no other party to go to, and vote I will while possessed of strength to go to the polls." William McPherson Mss. Care was taken not to offend the former Anti-Masons. In the counties in which they had been strong, the conventions were called "Whig and Anti-Masonic" or ".Anti-Masonic and Whig," at times with the word "Democratic" prefixed to the phrase; *Lancaster Union and Tribune,* January 19, 1847; *Butler Whig,* September 9, 1846; *Pittsburgh Gazette,* September 20, 1849. This nomenclature was continued in Allegheny county as late as 1852; *Daily Commercial Journal,* December 11, 1852. This was not merely the survival of a name, but represented a strong sentiment. On June 3, 1846, for example, the "Anti-Masonic and Whig" convention of Allegheny county "Resolved, That we are utterly opposed to all secret oath-bound societies, believing their existence in our midst contrary to the spirit of and fraught with danger to our free institutions, and that we highly approve of the resistance made by our members of the Legislature last winter, to the chartering of Odd Fellows Associations." *Daily Commercial Journal,* June 5, 1846. It was deemed worthy of mention that in a Masonic parade, held later in the same month, many Democrats but few Whigs were seen marching; *ibid.,* June 25, 1846. In 1850, the Democrats asserted that the Whig candidate for Congress from this district was a Mason. To this charge the Whigs replied, "Mr. Howe, we are pleased to state, is not now, and never has been, a member of any secret society whatsoever." *Pittsburgh Gazette,* July 4, 1850. In this same election, it was contended that membership in Odd Fellows Associations caused the defeat of candidates in Allegheny and Indiana counties; *ibid.,* October 18, 1850. As late as 1876, there were cast 83 votes for the "Anti-Masonic Ticket"; *Smull's Legislative Hand-Book,* 1879, p. 311.

county, as the gubernatorial candidate. As Markle had never held public office, little was known of his political views. This was held to be offset by the fact that he "was fresh from the ranks of the people" and was "earning his bread by the sweat of his brow." He had volunteered for one of the Indian wars and since then been elected a major-general in the Pennsylvania militia. What military glory could be derived from the fact that "at the battle of Mississinewa, and at the sortie of Fort Meigs, he led the fight, and slew the enemy with his own hand" was derived.[1] One of the Democratic journals asserted that Markle "was taken up for a sort of Tippecanoe rusher—his services in the wars being considered sufficient to raise a strong breeze of patriotism in his favor."[2]

Political events were so shaping themselves that more interest was to be displayed in national than in state issues. Tyler, abominated by all loyal party men, was moving to secure the annexation of Texas to the United States, a plan which met with the hostility of the Whigs within the state. The *North American* asserted that the Whigs were ready to abide by the compromises of the Constitution on slavery, but that they would prefer to sacrifice the integrity of the Union rather than extend the power of the South. Continuing, it said,

In any aspect, the annexation of Texas would be a monstrous folly and fraud. Any alternative would be preferable. Were slavery out of the question, there is reason enough to oppose the scheme upon the simple ground that the territory of the United States is already sufficiently large and unwieldy— sufficiently varied in climate and products to make common legislation for the equal benefit of its whole extent extremely difficult, if not wholly impossible.[3]

[1] *Pennsylvania Telegraph,* March 6, 1844.

[2] *Spirit of the Times,* March 7, 1844.

[3] November 24, 1843.

The *United States Gazette* declared its opposition to the proposal because the slave area would be increased. The proposed plan was declared to be not a national, nor a Whig, nor a Democratic measure, but a mere Tyler scheme.[1]

When a treaty of annexation was submitted to the senate, the administration forces attempted to create a favorable public sentiment. Secreary of War Wilkins, in an open letter to his former constituents in the Allegheny county congressional district, pointed out what the loss to the industries in and around Pittsburgh would be, if the treaty failed.[2] Through the efforts of the Democrats a resolution against annexation was defeated in the house of the Pennsylvania legislature.[3] Wider publicity to the question was given by the letters of Clay and Van Buren.[4] The projection of the Texas question into the pre-convention cam-

---

[1] April 1, 1844. This attitude was reflected in some of the 1844 campaign songs. One of the "Annexation War Songs", to the tune of "Yankee Doodle" printed in the *Pennsylvania Telegraph*, July 3, 1844, from the *Whig Standard*, opens as follows:

> "Come one, come all! sound drum and fife—
>   The loud tin trumpet blowing;
> For Texas, plunder, and all that
>   Our martial band is going.
> Who cares for what the world may say?
>   John Tyler says we're right, sirs,
> We'll grab the land of Mexico,
>   Or else we'll have a fight, sirs.
>
> *Cho.* Then shoulder muskets, one and all,
>   Hurrah! for war and plunder,
>   We'll wave our bunting o'er their heads,
>   And give them Tyler thunder."

[2] Letter of April 13, 1844, *Niles' Register*, vol. lxvi, p. 118.

[3] *House Journal*, 1844, vol. i, pp. 536, *et seq.;* p. 869.

[4] Clay's letter of April 17, 1844; Van Buren's letter of April 20, 1844; *Niles' Register*, vol. lxvi, pp. 152-157.

paign resulted in the rejection of Van Buren and the nomination of Polk by the Democratic national convention at
Baltimore, which assembled on May 27, 1844.[1] Polk, immediately declared for " the re-annexation of Texas to
the territory and government of the United States." This
position was strengthened by a letter from ex-President
Jackson, whose opinion carried great weight in all parts of
Pennsylvania.[2] The leader of the Pennsylvania Democrats
in the lower House of Congress, C. J. Ingersoll, deemed
" it most peaceable and safe to declare at once, beyond the
Monroe and Adams position, not only that we shall not like,
but that we will not suffer, European encroachment in, at
any rate, the northern parts of the American hemisphere." [3]

The Whig convention, which assembled on May 1 at
Baltimore, nominated Clay and Frelinghuysen.[4] Meeting
at Baltimore at the same time as the regular Democratic
convention was a body calling itself the " Tyler Democratic
National Convention." This body had intended to await
the action of the regular Democratic convention, in the hope
that it might be induced to support Tyler. But as the sessions of the regular Democratic convention became protracted and no intention of nominating Tyler was evidenced,
the " Tyler Democratic National Convention " performed
its duty by placing Tyler in nomination, but adjourned
without naming a running mate.[5] The *North American*
sneered at this convention as the " Loaves' and Fishes' Con-

---

[1] *Niles' Register,* vol. lxvi, pp. 211-218.

[2] Polk's letter of April 23; Jackson's of May 13, 1844; *ibid.,* vol. lxvi,.
p. 228.

[3] Letter of September 4, 1844; *ibid.,* vol. lxvii, p. 167.

[4] *Ibid.,* vol. lxvi, p. 178.

[5] *Ibid.,* vol. lxvi, p. 221.

vention." [1] Tyler kept his name before the public until
August 20, when it was withdrawn. [2]

The Whigs of Pennsylvania heartily endorsed the position of Clay on the annexation question. Before the treaty
of annexation was defeated on June 8, 1844, their condemnation was reserved chiefly for Tyler, whose course was
characterized as a plot. The *North American* said,

If impeachment will reach the presumptuous demagogue, who
has dared, without consulting popular will, to place the
country in a warlike attitude towards a neighboring Republic,
with which we are or should be at peace, if impeachment will
reach the author of this outrage, we trust the process may
be instantly begun. What is this government coming to, if
its accidental head may upon his own responsibility, order
troops and vessels to be placed at the disposal of a foreign
power, and for the purpose of sustaining a war with a third
power, without the semblance of a rightful course! [3]

The campaign in the state was not, however, to be fought
on the question of the annexation of Texas, since the citizens
of the state were more deeply concerned over the maintenance of the tariff rates established by the act of 1842.

The business depression of 1837, followed by the banking problems within the state, by the dispute on the proper
method of liquidating the state debt and meeting the interest
thereon, was largely spent when the Tariff Act of 1842 was
passed. Following hard upon the passage of the act had

[1] June 4, 1844.

[2] *Niles' Register*, vol. lxvi, p. 416.

[3] May 17, 1844. Chancellor Kent of New York had "no doubt
that the enormous abuses and stretch of power by President Tyler
afford ample materials for the exercise of the power of impeachment,
and an imperative duty in the House of Representatives to put it in
practice." Letter of May 21, 1844, to H. J. Raymond; *North American*,
May 29, 1844.

come a business revival, noticeable particularly in the iron industry. Old furnaces were again put into blast and new ones erected. The first successful anthracite furnace was constructed in 1840 in Lehigh county.[1] This was followed by the construction of other furnaces of the same type in the eastern part of the state, chiefly in Luzerne and Columbia counties, which were strongholds of the Democracy.[2]

The attitude of the citizens of the state, regardless of party affiliation, on the tariff question is clearly reflected in a letter of Hendrick B. Wright, who was later chosen permanent chairman of the national Democratic convention of 1844. From his home at Wilkes-Barre, under date of January 23, 1844, he wrote Buchanan that the only objection to Van Buren is that

he is too ultra anti-tariff to suit the meridian of Penna. politicks. . . . There is, Sir, a revolution in Penna. on the question of protective & discriminating duties and the invasion of the doctrine on our old land marks of tariff for revenue—is signal—and our creed must be tempered to the times or we will find in the end our party in this State will be prostrated. It cannot be denied. And whether it be right or wrong—it is enough for us to know that such is the fact.[3]

Governor Porter, in his annual message of 1844, again

[1] Swank, *Progressive Pennsylvania*, p. 278. There had been constructed an anthracite furnace the year before at Pottsville; *United States Commercial and Statistical Register*, vol. i, pp. 335, 352.

[2] *Daily Chronicle*, May 14, 1844.

[3] Buchanan Mss. A state Democratic convention, favorable to R. M. Johnson, under the chairmanship of Simon Cameron had "Resolved, that the democratic party of Pennsylvania is in favor of a *Tariff*— that one of the cardinal principles of the democratic creed has been the protection of American industry, and that opposition to that principle of national policy will receive, as it merits, the unqualified condemnation of every Pennsylvania democrat." *Niles' Register*, vol. lxv, p. 371.

discussed the need of adequate protection to the industries
of the state.

If those entrusted with the guardianship of the public welfare,
[are] but true to their trust, the day is not far distant, when
Pennsylvania must become the great workshop of the American
Union, for the production of coal and iron, and the fabrics
constructed from these materials.   If these great interests are
surrendered to some imaginary, theoretic, Arcadian scheme of
free trade, we may still continue to serve as hewers of wood
and drawers of water to foreign capitalists and artizans, and
our incalculable mineral deposites may lie useless for ages.   I
trust, however, the people of this Commonwealth will never
be seduced into a sacrifice of their dearest rights.[1]

The legislature likewise reflected the same sentiment in
favor of a protective tariff.   By a vote of 81 to 0 in the
house and 30 to 1 in the senate, a resolution, with the yeas
and nays attached, instructed the United States Senators
and requested the Representatives

to oppose any change in the present tariff, which might prove
injurious to the manufacturing and agricultural interests of
this commonwealth, sternly to resist any reduction in the
present duties on iron, coal and wool, and to omit no effort
to sustain all the great interests of the Nation, calculated to
foster and promote American industry.[2]

Practical unanimity existed in the state that the rates of
the tariff of 1842 must be maintained.

Early in January, 1844, Congress made several attempts
to alter the tariff rates.   These attempts according to the
North American were " strangled by a cord of which the

---

[1] *Pennsylvania Archives*, series iv, vol. vi, pp. 1012-1013.   Porter both
before and after his two terms was extensively interested in the iron
industry, owning several furnaces.

[2] *Session Laws*, 1844, p. 601.

Whigs pull one end and Van Burenism the other." [1]   The continuation of the movement for alteration of the rates led the " Executive Committee of the Clay Association of the City and County of Philadelphia " to call for March 25 a mass meeting, which declared that the tariff of 1842 was a Whig measure. [2]   In the latter part of April, the national House of Representatives decided to go into the committee of the whole to take up the question of revising the tariff.   Not a vote from Pennsylvania was cast in favor of the motion. [3]   When in May a motion was adopted to table the tariff bill, the entire Pennsylvania delegation voted for the motion. [4]

No sooner had Polk been nominated by the Democrats than the Whigs in the state made the tariff the issue of the campaign.   The alternative for the manufacturers, mechanics, and farmers of Pennsylvania, it was declared, was " Texas and No Tariff, or Tariff and No Texas." [5]   Polk was immediately cautioned by Democratic leaders in the state to exercise great care in his utterances on the tariff. [6]   Acting on this advice, Polk wrote his famous letter of June 19, 1844, to John K. Kane of Philadelphia.   This letter received wide publicity during the campagn, particularly the statement that he was

in favor of a tariff for revenue, such a one as will yield a sufficient amount to the treasury to defray the expenses of the government, economically administered.   In adjusting the

---

[1] January 6, 1844.

[2] *United States Gazette*, March 26, 1844.

[3] Analysis of vote, *ibid.*, April 24, 1844.

[4] Analysis of vote, *Niles' Register*, vol. lxvi, p. 177.

[5] *North American*, June 3, 1844.

[6] J. Miller to Polk, May 31; J. M. Porter to Polk, June 5, 1844; Polk Papers, Lib. of Cong.

details of a revenue tariff, I have heretofore sanctioned such
moderate discriminating duties as would produce the amount
of revenue needed, and at the same time afford reasonable
incidental protection to our home industry. I am opposed
to a tariff for protection merely, and not for revenue.[1]

This letter was relied upon by the Democrats to refute the
Whig statements that Polk was a free trader and to prove
that he was in favor of a stronger protective tariff than
Clay. On August 8, 1844, Wilson McCandless, head of
the Democratic electoral ticket, in order to stop defections
from the Democratic ranks on account of the tariff issue,
wrote a letter to a Clarion county mass meeting. In it he
scored Clay for his vote on the Compromise Tariff Act, and
contended that if Clay were elected, he would

carry out the principles of that bill, and afford you a hori-
zontal duty, to enable you to contend with the pauper labor of
Sweden and Russia. In doing so, he would give you and the
Tariff the same *support* that the *rope* does the hanging man—
instant death, and " without benefit of clergy." Support him
if you can—for my own part, I shall go for POLK and
DALLAS, who have at heart the true interests of Pennsylvania.[2]

In addition to these letters, which were used extensively,
Buchanan was called upon to tour the northern counties of
the state to refute the claim that the tariff of 1842 was a
Whig measure.[3] In many parts of the state, the Democrats exhibited banners bearing the legend " Polk, Dallas,
and the Tariff of 1842." [4]

[1] *Niles' Register,* vol. lxvi, p. 295.

[2] Republished in the *Pittsburgh Gazette,* March 23, 1850.

[3] Wm. B. Foster to Buchanan, July 18, 1844; Buchanan Mss.

[4] *United States Gazette,* May 14, 1845; *Pennsylvania Telegraph,* December 18, 1844; Sargent, *Public Men and Events,* vol. ii, pp. 236, 239.

The nomination of G. M. Dallas to be Polk's running mate caused some of the Democrats concern because of his unorthodox position on the bank question.[1] The Democratic national convention resolved " that Congress has no power to charter a National Bank." [2] *The Forum* of Philadelphia pointed out the variance existing between the course of Dallas in Congress and this resolution of the party.[3] When the campaign was under way, this issue was eagerly accepted by the Democrats, who were anxious to keep the tariff question in the background.[4] The real issue of the campaign, however, remained the tariff.

In the meantime, a third party movement was spreading in Philadelphia. On November 14, 1842, the Roman Catholic Bishop of Philadelphia requested the school board to allow the use of the Roman Catholic version of the Bible in the public schools to those of his parishioners, who were attending them. On January 10, 1843, the school board adopted a resolution allowing those conscientiously objecting to the reading from the Bible to be excused from joining in the opening devotional exercises.[5] Inasmuch as the majority of the Catholics in and about Philadelphia were Irish, the Catholic religion appeared to be a non-American belief. Encouraged by the success of the Native American party in New York city, supporters of the movement planned in 1843 for the organization of the party in Phila-

[1] J. W. Forney, June 11, 1844, to Buchanan, " His course on the U. S. Bank question is very questionable, to say the least, and in proper hands may operate vastly to our injury. Nothing can save him but the union and enthusiasm which now pervade the party." Buchanan Mss.

[2] Stanwood, *History of the Presidency*, vol. i, pp. 200, 215.

[3] Quoted in *Niles' Register*, vol. lxvi, p. 266.

[4] George Plitt to Buchanan, September 22, 1844; Buchanan Mss.

[5] Correspondence in *North American*, January 14, 1843.

delphia.[1]   In the early part of December, the organization
of the " American Republican Association of Second Ward,
Spring Garden," was perfected.[2]   This movement was so
strong that in the municipal election in the following April
this ward was carried by the new party.   Organizations
in other wards also made respectable showings.   This year
also a local officer was elected in Moyamensing by the
Native Americans.[3]

These preliminary successes encouraged them to try for
wider organization.   On March 13, 1844, a large mass
meeting was held in Independence Square.[4]   The publication of several newspapers under Nativist support soon followed.[5]   In order to complete their organization in Kensington, a mass meeting was held there on May 3, 1844, but
this meeting was broken up by Irishmen of the neighborhood.[6]   A call for another meeting for May 6 was made.
The warning was, " Natives be punctual and resolve to
sustain your rights as Americans, firmly but moderately." [7]
The meeting led to rioting between the Natives and the
Irish, which continuing for several days resulted in the
destruction of several Catholic churches and other property

[1] The first Native American meeting in Philadelphia county had been
held at Germantown as early as 1837; but this movement soon died.
Scharf and Westcott, *History of Philadelphia,* vol. i, p. 663.

[2] *Native American,* May 25, 1844.

[3] *United States Gazette,* March 18, 1844.

[4] *North American,* March 14, 1844.

[5] *Native American, Daily Sun, American Advocate,* and *Native
Eagle and Advocate* were all daily papers, sold for a penny to large
numbers of workingmen.

[6] *Native American,* May 4, 1844.   Kensington had been the scene of
previous conflicts between the Irish and other members of the community.   The first clash came in 1828, and another in 1843; Scharf
and Westcott, *History of Piladelphia,* vol. i, pp. 623, 661.

[7] *Native American,* May 6, 1844.

and the loss of a number of lives. In the early part of July, rioting of several days' duration again occurred, but this time in Southwark. The animus of the rioters was directed against a Catholic church in which stored firearms were discovered.[1] The movement now became fully identified with anti-Catholicism, thus attracting support which it would not otherwise have secured.[2] The trials of the rioters, extending well into October, helped keep interest in Nativism alive. An organization in Philadelphia city and county was perfected; nominations for Congress, for the state legislature, and for county and city officers were made. It was deemed inexpedient to attempt the organization of the state this year for the election of governor and canal commissioner.[3]

Outside of Philadelphia, the only other county in the state in which the Native Americans perfected an organiza-

[1] An excellent account of the riots is given in Scharf and Westcott, *op. cit.*, vol. i, pp. 664, *et seq.; cf.* also *Public Ledger, Daily Chronicle, Spirit of the Times, North American, Native American, Daily Sun,* May 7-13, July 6-10, 1844. The various newspapers show their party affiliation as follows: the Native press exonerated their followers from all blame; the Democratic papers condemned the Natives for causing the riots; the Whig sheets attempted to distribute the onus for the disturbances but placed the greater portion of it on the Irish. After the Southwork riots, a large number of citizens, regardless of party affiliation, signed an address to the governor pledging their support to him in an endeavor to check all future disturbances; *Public Ledger,* July 12, 1844.

[2] "It will be seen that such a contest involves an issue purely *ROMAN CATHOLIC* on one side and *AMERICAN* on the other. . . . . There is no other question before the people. Let us decide it then, as becomes the descendants of George Washington," declared the *Daily Sun,* September 30, 1844.

[3] *Native American,* August 5, 16, 1844. The official title of the party was " The Native American Republican Party." The *American Advocate,* August 11, 1844, urged that the " half and half " principle be adopted in naming candidates from the old parties in order to attract voters from them.

tion, made nominations, and polled a respectable vote was Lancaster.[1] In this county, Anti-Masonry had been particularly strong because of its appeal to the numerous religious sectarians. Even after the abandoning of the state organization, Anti-Masonry had continued in this county. A new political movement with a religious appeal attracted some Anti-Masons who had not identified themselves with the " Anti-Masonic and Whig " party.[2] Little was accomplished in Allegheny county where an endeavor was also made to form a Native American party out of the unabsorbed Anti-Masons.[3] In the western portion of the state this element joined the newly formed Liberty party, which ran congressional candidates in the western districts.[4]

Although the Native Americans had no candidate of their own for governor, yet they did not fail to make themselves felt in the election. The Democratic candidate had written a letter, in which he intimated that he favored the

[1] *Native American*, June 10, July 18; *Daily Sun*, July 13, 1844. The Native vote polled in Lancaster county was 2,500 out of a total of more than 14,500; *North American*, October 28, 1844.

[2] The leaders in the movement in Lancaster county were E. C. Reigart, who in 1843 questioned Clay on his views on Masonry, and George Ford, one of the committee which called the " Democratic Harrison Convention " of 1844. Other Anti-Masons, Thomas H. Burrowes and his brothers, Samuel Parke, ex-member of the legislature, and John C. Van Camp, chairman of the county committee in 1840, joined the Democrats. Thaddeus Stevens for a time deliberated over the course he would pursue; the Anti-Masonic party had disappeared, the Democrats were impossible, the Natives at best problematical, and the newly formed Liberty party was considered temporarily too extreme, so he held aloof until September when he came out openly for Clay.

[3] *Native American*, August 10, 1844.

[4] No candidate was run in the 18th congressional district, composed of Fayette, Greene, and Somerset counties. Candidates were run in Philadelphia and Chester counties, where many Quakers lived, but the vote polled was not large. *Public Ledger*, September 26, October 2, 1844.

exclusion of the reading of the Bible from the public schools. His participation in the dedication of the Roman Catholic cathedral at Pittsburgh was also construed to his disadvantage. This agitation on the religious question was quickly adopted by the Whigs.[1]

The excitement displayed in this election, according to the *Public Ledger*, exceeded that in the election of 1840, when the Democrats had not been so active as the Whigs.[2] It was particularly evident in Philadelphia, where the October elections were based primarily on the Native American movement, but did not extend to other portions of the state. An address of the Whig state central committee declared that if the Democrats are successful,

the odious sub-Treasury scheme, dividing the offices from the people—taking care of one and letting the others take care of themselves, will be revived. The war is to be renewed against the currency—against commerce—against a protective tariff—against the distribution amongst the States of the proceeds of the public lands—against commercial credit —against manufactories, etc. In Pennsylvania no favorable change is proposed.

The Whigs proposed to better the financial condition of the state: 1. by the sale of the public works on advantageous terms, thereby lowering the indebtedness of the state; 2. by a change of men and measures, thereby stopping the cry of bribery and corruption; 3. by the distribution of the money from the sale of the public lands; 4. by retaining the present tariff, which was giving protection to home industries; 5. by fewer changes in legislation affecting commerce; 6. by

[1] *Pittsburgh Daily Morning Post,* October 1; *American Advocate,* October 5; *North American,* September 20, 25, October 5, 1844.

[2] September 2, 1844.

an equitable mode of taxation.[1] These were the points which the Whigs stressed during the campaign.

The elections on October 8 demonstrated that the state was controlled by the Democrats and that the Natives had developed unexpected strength in Philadelphia county. Shunk defeated Markle, the Whig candidate for governor, by a majority of four thousand votes.[2] Of the twenty-four Congressmen from the state, twelve were returned by the Democrats, ten by the Whigs, and two by the Natives. Encroachment on the Democratic majority in the state legislature came through the Natives, who secured one senator and seven representatives at the expense of the Democrats, and one representative at the expense of the Whigs.[3] The vote for Congressmen in Philadelphia city and county was much greater than in 1843, with the returns indicating that the Native American party was built up largely from Whig material.[4] The *Spirit of the Times,* the leading Democratic paper in Philadelphia, asserted that more than two-thirds of the new party consisted of Whigs, and that it was nothing but the Whig party in disguise.[5] Some of the Whig papers openly gloried in the triumph of the Native Americans.[6]

---

[1] Printed in the *United States Gazette,* July 17, 1844.

[2] *Smull's Legislative Hand-Book,* 1919, p. 720; Francis R. Shunk (Dem.) 160,322; Joseph Markle (Whig) 156,040; F. J. Lamoyne (Liberty) 2,566. The fact that Markle was a "fast friend of Stevens" lost him votes from the Clay men; Hood, "Thaddeus Stevens" in Harris, *Biographical History of Lancaster County.*

[3] *North American,* October 28, 1844. Lewis C. Levin and John H. Campbell were returned respectively from the first and third congressional districts. The total vote polled by the Natives in the congressional districts is given as 19,192. For a characterization of Levin *cf.* McClure, *Old Time Notes,* vol. i, p. 89.

[4] *Public Ledger,* October 10, 11, 12, 1844.

[5] October 10, 1844.

[6] On November 11, 1844, the *North American* openly endorsed the

The Whigs were not greatly discouraged by the defeat of
their gubernatorial candidate and entered the presidential
campaign with zeal.   They pointed out the fact that the
majority which Shunk received was less than that received
by Porter in 1841.   In 1840 the adverse total against the
Whigs in the congressional districts had been 11,000, yet
they had carried the state for Harrison.   These com-
parisons, unfavorable to the Democrats, were declared to
be an "omen for November."[1]   It was also stated that
Markle did not develop the anticipated strength because he
came from a strong opposition county and had been little
heard of previously.   The tariff, it was asserted, had not
been the issue for it had not been shown that Shunk was
opposed to the protective principle.   Concerning the hostility of Polk to a protective tariff, however, there could be
no doubt; consequently, the Whigs would carry the state.[2]
Assuming the aggressive on the tariff dispute, the Whigs
charged that large sums of gold were being raised in England, particularly in Manchester, to spread the doctrine of
free trade in the United States.[3]   The Democrats were accused of having called the tariff of 1842 "the Black Tariff,"
until they discovered that the object of their attack was held
in high favor in Pennsylvania.[4]   Indeed, the most difficult
thing to believe was declared to be the report that some
banners, flown in the interior of the state, bore the words
"Polk, Dallas and the Tariff of 1842."[5]

Native American cause. After the lapse of several months it again
supported the Whig party. The *Harrisburg Telegraph* advised "politicians who are looking to their own advancement to be cautious how
they make themselves obnoxious to this growing party." Quoted in
Native American, October 12, 1844.

[1] *North American*, October 14, 1844.

[2] *United States Gazette*, October 16, 1844.

[3] *Daily Forum*, October 9, 1844.

[4] *North American*, October 17, 1844.

[5] *Ibid.*, October 26, 1844.

The Democrats did not shrink now from the tariff as the campaign issue. They continued to use the letter from Polk to Kane contrasting, with telling effect, its statements with the utterances of Clay. The letter of McCandless to the Clarion county meeting was chiefly relied on in the western portion of the state. Since the contest would be close, efforts were made to capture the vote of abolitionists in the state. An alleged statement by Clay that he would not sign a bill abolishing slavery in the District of Columbia was used by the Democrats for this purpose. A letter from James G. Birney, the Liberty candidate, saying he preferred Polk to Clay was given due publicity.[1] This was soon followed by another letter, later proven to be a forgery, in which Birney stated that he had always been a Democrat.[2] The Catholics were held to the Democracy by a quotation from the *Tennessee Whig,* an authoritative Clay organ, to the effect that " There can be no peace until the Catholics are exterminated from this country." [3] Attacks on Frelinghuysen because of his prominent position in the Bible Society were frequently made.

The vote polled in the November election was much larger than the vote cast in October; both parties shared in the increase, but the Democrats retained their majority.[4] The Whigs carried Philadelphia county, normally a Democratic stronghold, through the addition of the Native American vote.[5] The only other county in which a change of political

---

[1] *Spirit of the Times,* October 16, 1844.

[2] *North American,* October 31, 1844.

[3] *Spirit of the Times,* October 26, 1844.

[4] *Smull's Legislative Hand-Book,* 1919, p. 715; James K. Polk (Dem.) 167,447; Henry Clay (Whig) 161,125; James G. Birney (Liberty) 3,100.

[5] Some felt that the Native Americans cost Clay the election. *Louisville Journal,* quoted in *Public Ledger,* October 20, 1845, " But for the

alignment took place was Mercer, which was carried by the Democrats because of the large number of votes cast for the Liberty party. The deciding issue in the campaign, however, had been the tariff. Governor Porter in his last annual message in 1845 put it:

I hazard nothing in asserting that neither of the presidential candidates could have hoped, for a moment, to get a majority of the votes in this state, had not his claims been based upon the assurance that he was friendly to the continuance of the present tariff laws, substantially as they stand.[1]

The Whigs had not proven to the electorate that Polk was opposed to the tariff of 1842.

On December 9, 1844, the " Committee on Organization of the Clay Club " issued an address on the recent elections. They charged that in the Whig counties the increase over 1840 was normal, but that in some of the Democratic counties, chiefly in the northern tier, there was an abnormal Democratic but only a normal Whig increase.

Is it by *accident* that the illegitimate increase in the vote of the State is ALL IN THE LOCOFOCO COUNTIES, and ALL ON THE LOCOFOCO SIDE? Is it by *accident* that the increase in the *Whig vote is the exact ratio of the increase of the population,* and that the *Locofoco vote* EXCEEDS THAT RATIO BY ALMOST TEN THOUSAND? Is it by *accident* that the Locofoco gain in the *Whig* counties is met by a corresponding loss in the Whig *vote*, and that a *Whig* gain in the *Locofoco* counties is answered by a STILL LARGER GAIN FOR THE LOCOFOCOS?

Native American movement, the Whigs would have been victorious in the Presidential elections of last fall." *Cf.* Barnes, *Memoir of Thurlow Weed,* p. 134; Colton, *Private Correspondence of Henry Clay,* pp. 495, 497.

[1] *Pennsylvania Archives,* series iv, vol. vi, p. 1072.

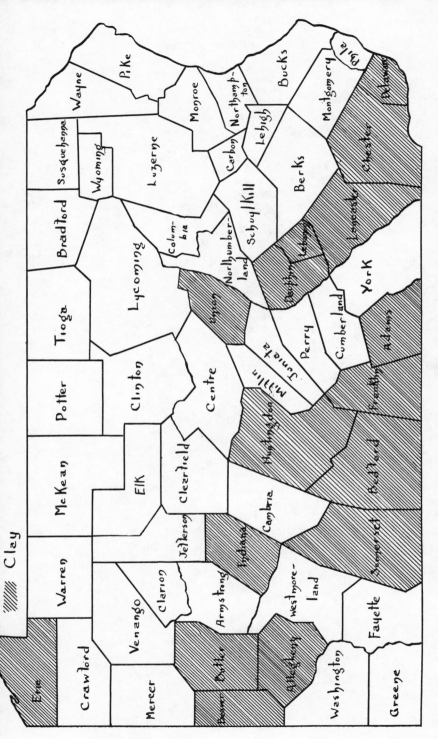

PRESIDENTIAL ELECTION OF 1844 (PHILADELPHIA CITY, CLAY; PHILADELPHIA COUNTY, POLK)

In Pike county, it was claimed, more votes were cast in 1844 than there had been male inhabitants of twenty-one years and over in 1840. The committee asserted that at least 10,000 illegal votes had been cast in the state. Clay was declared to have been elected President and Markle governor. The committee, however, departed from the precedent established in 1838 in not urging a course of action to secure the offices which they claimed.[1]

It is not difficult to account for the failure of Clay to carry the state. His personality, in the first place, did not appeal strongly to the rural voters, a thing which was necessary if the normal Democratic majority in the state was to be overcome. Furthermore, in the past he had been Jackson's opponent, and the name of Jackson was still one to conjure with in the commonwealth. In the Whig party itself, a large element, composed of former Anti-Masons, distrusted Clay. This element had controlled the opposition to the Democracy in 1836 and nominated Harrison as the candidate of the state. It had been particularly influential in 1839 in blocking the nomination of Clay by the Whig national convention. This element had, in large measure, opposed Masonry on religious grounds, and for the same reason it could well find cause for complaint in Clay's duelling and gambling. Politically organized, there was no such thing as Anti-Masonry, but the sentiment for the old principles still prevailed. The position of Clay on the tariff was not proven to be essentially different from that of Polk. In addition, the cooperation of the Whigs and Native Americans tended to repel whatever Catholic support the Whigs had previously had. Furthermore, Frelinghuysen, the Whig candidate for the vice-presidency, was especially distasteful to the Catholic voter. Due to this

[1] *Pennsylvania Telegraph*, December 18, 1844.

combination of circumstances, the Democrats, by a small majority, secured the electoral vote of the state.[1]

When the state legislature met in January, 1845, the senate contained twenty-one Democrats, eleven Whigs, and one Native, and the house consisted of fifty-two Democrats, forty Whigs, and eight Natives. On joint ballot the Democrats had seventy-three of the one hundred and thirty-three votes.[2] On January 14 the legislature reelected Daniel Sturgeon to the United States Senate. Each of the three parties strictly supported its caucus nominee, but some indication of Democratic disaffection was manifested, for of the seventy-one votes cast in the caucus Sturgeon received only forty-two.[3]

When the electoral college met in December to cast the vote of the state for Polk, all save one of its members united in an address to the President-elect recommending James Buchanan for Secretary of State.[4] To give added weight to their proceeding, no further solicitations for office were allowed, in the hope that if their recommendation were adopted, other offices would be more easily secured.[5] In due course of time, the secretaryship was offered to and accepted by Buchanan.[6] Buchanan, however, served during the balance

---

[1] B. W. Richards, November 18, 1844, to John McLean, Richard Peters, December 6, 1844, to McLean, McLean Papers, Lib. of Cong.; Wm. D. Lewis, November 30, 1844, to Henry Clay, Colton, *Private Correspondence of Henry Clay*, p. 511.

[2] *North American*, January 3, 1845.

[3] *Public Ledger*, January 13, 14, 15, 1845.

[4] Letter of the electors to Polk, December 5, 1844; Polk Pápers, Lib. of Cong.

[5] Letters of J. W. Forney, E. W. Hutter, Henry Walsh, December 4, J. M. G. Lescure, December 5, 1844, to Buchanan, Buchanan Mss. These men though not members of the electoral college engineered the affair, cooperating with Dr. Geo. F Lehman who was a member.

[6] Moore, *The Works of James Buchanan*, vol. vi, pp. 110, *et seq.*

of the Twenty-eighth Congress as United States Senator.
On March, 5, 1845, he tendered his resignation to the governor, who on the eighth forwarded it to the legislature.[1] To
fill the vacancy the senate made thirty nominations and the
house fifty. The correspondent of the *Public Ledger*
thought that the contest lay between C. J. Ingersoll and
Simon Cameron.[2] It was evident that the election would
be based on the tariff. On March 12, the Democrats held
a caucus which only forty-eight of the seventy-three members
attended. On the sixth ballot G. W. Woodward received
twenty-five votes and was declared to be the nominee of the
caucus. No votes at the caucus were cast for Cameron.[3]

In the meantime, the Whigs were pursuing a policy which
had been urged upon them for filling the full-term senator-
ship. They were planning to throw their votes to a Democrat, who would pledge himself to support the Tariff Act of
1842 and who had enough Democratic votes to enable him
to secure the election with Whig and Native American assistance. On March 12 eleven Whigs addressed a letter
to Cameron, in which they pointed out the fact that although
they were of the minority party yet they might be able, by
proper combination with some Democrats, to elect the
Senator. They, therefore, asked him the following questions:

Are you in favor of the tariff of 1842; and if elected to the
United States senate, will you sustain it without change?
Are you in favor of the distribution of the proceeds of
the sales of the public lands; and if elected will you support
this measure?

To both of these questions Cameron on the same day re-

[1] *Public Ledger*, March 10, 1845.
[2] *Ibid.*, March 12, 13, 1845.
[3] *Ibid.*, March 14, 1845.

plied in the affirmative.[1]   This occurred before the Democrats held their caucus and accounts for the absence of the
Cameron supporters.

The following day Cameron was elected on the sixth
ballot.   The Whigs and Native Americans did not vote for
Cameron on the first five ballots, insisting that his strength
be revealed.   On the final ballot the vote was for Cameron
sixty-seven, Woodward fifty-five, and scattering six.   The
vote for Cameron came from forty-four Whigs, sixteen Democrats, seven from the senate and nine from the house,
and from seven Natives.   On the decisive ballot three
Whigs and one Native did not vote.[2]   The Whigs claimed
that the pledges which had been secured from Cameron
made the election their triumph.   The policy of Woodward
was declared to be favorable to " Free Trade, anti-Distribu-
tion, and opposed to any change of the laws which now
virtually surrender our government to the mercy of foreign
pauper immigrants, although at one time he had previously
denounced the present system." [3]   A leading Democratic
paper declared that the defeat of Woodward was due to
his hostility to a protective tariff.[4]

On March 14 the Woodward supporters in the legislature appointed a committee to prepare an address, which

[1] *Niles' Register,* vol. lxviii, pp. 262, *et seq.,* for the letters.

[2] *House Journal,* 1845, vol. ii, pp. 529, *et seq.*   For a fantastic account
of how religious prejudices were appealed to in order to secure votes
for Cameron, *cf.* McClure, *Old Time Notes,* vol. i, p. 98.   Cameron had
evidently been laying his plans long ahead, for in a postscript to a
letter of February 8, 1845, to Buchanan, he said, " I will tell you one
of these days *in confidence* who will succeed you in the Senate."
Buchanan Mss.   Savidge, *Life of Benjamin Harris Brewster,* p. 71,
gives an account of the disgust of Buchanan when he was told by
Cameron that he intended to succeed him.

[3] *North American,* March 17, 1845.

[4] *Spirit of the Times,* July 16, 1846.

stated how Cameron violated party custom in securing his
election. Furthermore, the suspicion of bribery was not
absent; for, the activity of Cameron inevitably suggested
corruption, just as the mention of corruption inevitably
suggested Cameron. At an adjourned meeting on April
12, letters from Dallas and from Buchanan on the election
of Cameron were read. After protracted debate on the
address the meeting adjourned without taking any definite
action. Due to the impending close of the legislature, no
further meetings were held. Nevertheless, the officers of
these meetings presented an address to the public, in which
they condemned Cameron and his supporters, declaring that
his election was a Whig victory. The letters of Dallas and
Buchanan were also published. Dallas censured those who
refused to support the caucus nominee, but he did not pass
judgment on Cameron because he was elected a member of
the body over which Dallas was to preside. Buchanan,
between whom and Woodward an estrangement had been
developing, hoped that a remedy might be found to prevent
the occurrence of a similar election in the future. He, however, declined to join in the criticism of Cameron, whose
election was an act of the state government, while he was
now associated with the federal government.[1]

During the last session of the Twenty-eighth Congress
attention was again directed to the question of the annexation of Texas. The plan to secure this by joint resolution
was declared to be the abnegation of all the forms of the
Constitution. The contemplated creation of five or six
slave states from this region was regarded " as the perpetuity of the slave power of the South over the free institutions of the North." The Native Americans, in particular, it was urged, should oppose the making of thousands

---

[1] Procedure, address and letters in *Niles' Register*, vol. lxviii, p. 136.

of foreigners citizens by the stroke of the pen.[1]   One Whig
editor declared, " If the free States permit this stupendous
fraud, they will discover, when too late, that they have
forged fetters for themselves, and sacrificed the interests
of northern industry to the *ignis fatuus* of free trade." [2]
After the passage of the resolution, the *North American*
declared that the bond of silence on slavery was now broken.
" Put down by force, we shall not be expected to keep
quiet from courtesy." [3]   After stressing the illegality of
the method pursued in securing annexation, the *Miners'
Journal* continued,

There is no disguising it, the scheme of annexation originated in avarice and lust of dominion of power, and has been
accomplished in direct contempt and violation of the Constitution, in disregard of the just claims of Mexico, and in
utter disrespect of the wills and wishes of two-thirds of the
people in half of the States.   We have not only done a wrong
to Mexico, by playing the part of a highway robber, towards
her, but have encroached upon the common rights of the great
Commonwealth of Nations.[4]

The Whigs of the state viewed the annexation with mis-
giving as they feared that the tariff might suffer as a result.

The Natives, who in 1844 had succeeded in organizing
only for elections in a few counties, prepared for a wider
extension of their movement.   On February 22, 1845, a

[1] *North American,* January 28, 1845.

[2] *United States Gazette,* February 3, 1845.

[3] *North American,* March 3, 1845; analysis of the vote, *ibid.,* March
6, 1845.

[4] March 8, 1845.   The *Public Ledger* (Ind.) viewed the whole affair
with pleasure.   Its circulation was by far the greatest of any paper
in the state, and the workingmen were its chief readers.   On October
1, 1845, its leading editorial was headed, " The Continent, the Whole
Continent, and Nothing but the Continent."

state convention of Native Americans assembled at Harrisburg. Seventy-four delegates, who came from Philadelphia and twelve other counties, were in attendance, but nine of the counties were represented by only one or two delegates. The convention passed resolutions demanding a probationary period of twenty-one years for all foreigners before admitting them to citizenship, and condemned religious creeds which favored a union of church and state.[1] On August 7 a nominating convention assembled at Harrisburg and placed Robert H. Morton before the public as the candidate for canal commissioner.[2]

The Democrats nominated their candidate for canal commissioner in a regular convention. The Whigs, however, were in a great state of disorder, with strong indications that the organization might be discontinued, particularly in Philadelphia where the Native Americans had made such inroads on their party. They held no nominating convention this year, and it was not until the middle of September that the Whig state central committee of the year before selected Captain Samuel D. Karns as the candidate.[3] This action met with the approval of the Whigs. A fourth candidate for this office was furnished by the Liberty party.

There was no issue raised for the campaign, although the *Spirit of the Times,* a Democratic paper, declared that the election was based on the question of the disorders of the year before.[4] As a result of the election the Natives did not return a member to the legislature, thereby losing their

---

[1] *Public Ledger,* February 24, 26, 28, 1845.

[2] *North American,* August 9, 1845.

[3] *United States Gazette,* March 5, 19, April 23; *ibid.,* September 19, 1845, for the address of the committee on September 15.

[4] October 14, 1845.

eight men in the house. The next legislature would contain in the senate eighteen Democrats, fourteen Whigs, and one Native, and in the house sixty-seven Democrats and thirty-three Whigs.[1] The Natives charged that the Whigs had supported the successful Democratic ticket in Philadelphia city and county in return for the clerkships.[2] The Democratic candidate for canal commissioner received 4,500 more votes than his opponents.[3] This election in an off year clearly indicates the strength of the Democratic control of the state.

With the approach of the opening of Congress, the Democracy of the state feared that the national party might attempt to alter the tariff rates. Immediately, it took steps to prevent this alteration. The *Morning Ariel,* a Democratic paper of Philadelphia, said, " If such an attempt is made, we shall oppose it." [4] The movement to indicate in unmistakable terms the attitude of the state culminated in a call, by the Democratic leaders, for a state tariff convention.[5] The Whigs in general favored the convention, but some urged the Whigs not to attend the convention since " A locofoco convention will exert tenfold more influence on our locofoco president and his cabinet than a mixed convention." [6] On November 12 the convention assembled at Hollidaysburg with ex-Governor Porter in the chair.

[1] *North American,* October 28, 1845.

[2] *Daily Sun,* October 16, 1845.

[3] *North American,* October 31, 1845, gives the official returns as follows: Burns (Dem.) 119,510; Karns (Whig) 89,118; Morton (Nat. Am.) 22,434; Latimer (Liberty) 2,851.

[4] September 6, 1845.

[5] *Daily Commercial Journal,* October 21, 1845, for the preliminary meeting.

[6] *Pittsburgh Gazette,* October 23, 1845, quoted in *Niles' Register,* vol. lxix, p. 142.

The resolutions favored the tariff of 1842 because it was a revenue tariff.[1] The Whigs, however, were not satisfied with the resolutions. R. M. Riddle, one of the secretaries of the convention, wrote that the Democrats attempted to reconcile their wishes with the policy of the administration. Furthermore, "the Democrats were so strongly in the majority, that even moves to amend grammatical blunders were swept down—and the party lines inflexibly drawn, even against the crossing of a *t* or the dotting of an *i*." [2]

At the national capital the President was preparing his first message to Congress. As early as September 29, 1845, Buchanan had informed Polk that he could not control the Pennsylvania Democrats if Polk intended to ask for alterations in the tariff of 1842.[3] When on November 11 Secretary of the Treasury Walker read to the cabinet his report to Congress, Buchanan opposed his recommendation for the elimination of specific duties and for the substitution of *ad valorem* duties.[4] Nevertheless, the President embodied this recommendation of Walker in his message.[5] One of the Whig editors characterized the message as " a middling affair, ... excellent in nothing but its piety, and interesting only for the position of its author." [6] The *North American* in reiterating the Whig position said,

A tariff of revenue, a tariff of protection, a tariff with incidental protection, and a dozen other titles, have been mouthed so often by political orators, that most men shrink from the task of splitting the hairs which divide them. The real ques-

[1] Resolutions quoted in *Niles' Register*, vol. lxix, p. 181.
[2] *Daily Commercial Journal*, November 16, 1845.
[3] *Polk's Diary*, vol. i, p. 46.
[4] *Ibid.*, vol. i, p. 94. .
[5] Richardson, *Messages and Papers of the Presidents*, vol. iv, p. 406.
[6] *Daily Commercial Journal*, December 8, 1845.

tion is—shall our domestic manufactures be protected by our revenue laws, or not? It is of little importance by what title the protection is given.[1]

The efforts made to impress Congress with the attitude of the state on the tariff question were continued. The legislature adopted resolutions instructing the Senators and requesting the Representatives to oppose all " attempts to alter or modify " the existing tariff act.[2]   On the passage of these resolutions the Whigs refused to vote because there had been added clauses against a national bank, against the distribution of the proceeds from the sale of the public lands, and for the separation of the government from all banking institutions.[3]   The fact that the legislature had adopted these resolutions with practically no opposition led one of the leading Democratic papers to exclaim that " in Pennsylvania the tariff has never been a party question." [4] Efforts to make the hostility of the state to tariff alteration impressive continued.   The Pennsylvania Representatives at Washington, under the leadership of the Whigs, organized an exhibition of American manufactures " to be compared with the *British* manufactures sent from *Manchester,* and now being exhibited in the room of the ' committee on post office and postroads,' to influence the action of Congress in relation to the proposed modification of the tariff." [5]

[1] December 8, 1845.

[2] *Session Laws,* 1846, p. 511.

[3] *House Journal,* 1846, vol i, pp. 183, 227, 274, 520, 671; *Senate Journal,* 1846, vol. i, pp. 58, 186, 780. The questions involved in the second part of the resolutions did not come before Congress; consequently, there was no clash between Cameron's election pledge and the instructions of the legislature.

[4] *Democratic Union,* quoted in *Niles' Register,* vol. lxix, p. 336. The senate had just unanimously passed the tariff portion of the resolutions.

[5] Address of March 24, 1846, in *Niles' Register,* vol. lxx, p. 51.

The efforts of Pennsylvania to stay the passage of the tariff bill were of no avail, for on July 3, 1846, it was adopted by the House. The *North American* gave an analysis of the vote and said,

Sir Robert Walker's Free Trade Bill for reducing the revenue and destroying the industrial pursuits of our country passed the House of Representatives, by the aid of 113 Democratic and 1 Whig vote. It was resisted by 71 Whigs, 18 Democrats, and 6 Native Americans, in all 95. Either New York or Ohio could have saved the bill, but Party triumphed over Country. But 4 Democratic votes from New York were obtained, and none from Ohio, after all its blustering against the bill.[1]

That the bill was a Democratic measure was clearly shown by the vote. The Whigs maintained that the Democratic Representatives from Pennsylvania had been forced to follow their lead in opposing the bill.[2]

[1] July 7, 1846.

[2] *Daily Commercial Journal,* July 10, 1846. Of the twelve Democratic Representatives from Pennsylvania, David Wilmot alone voted for the bill. On December 2, 1845, Wilmot had endorsed the views of Polk, which were to be embodied in the message; *Polk's Diary,* vol. i, p. 110. Wilmot had been elected as a free-trade candidate from a district in the northern tier of counties. In defending his course, the leading Democratic paper of the district proposed " the Divorce of Pennsylvania from Massachusetts;" *Bradford Reporter,* August 26, 1846. It also claimed that " the ' cotton lords ' have waxed rich upon the industry of the land; capital has accumulated capital, and bloated wealth has added to its riches. But we ask the Farmers of Bradford, has it added to your purse or your provisions?" *ibid.,* July 15, 1846. When Wilmot discovered the hostility of the other Democrats from Pennsylvania to alterations in the tariff schedules, he wrote John Laporte on December 15, 1845, " I learn by letter that Miller speaks unfavourably of the President's views upon the subject of the Tariff. This if so is disgraceful. I have no charity for those who knowing the right will not or dare not pursue it. If I am to stand entirely alone on that question, receiving no countenance or support or encouragement from any quarter, I shall look out sharply for myself." Ms. letter in the Society Collection, Hist. Soc. of Penna.

The fact that the bill had passed the House did not deter the Democrats of the state from declaring that it would be defeated in the Senate. They urged the people of the state to continue voicing their opposition to altering the law.[1] When it became evident that there might be a tie-vote in the Senate, necessitating a decision by the Vice-President, they assured the citizens of the state that the bill would be defeated. Defeat of the bill depended then on the capacity in which the Vice-President voted. It was argued that according to the Constitution he would vote as a Senator; consequently he would be bound to vote with Pennsylvania, from which state he came. If the Senate were equally divided, they argued, he could not urge that a majority was against Pennsylvania, which had spoken unanimously in adopting resolutions against the proposed bill. If the Vice-President voted for the bill, he would nullify one of the votes of Pennsylvania in the Senate and give her "a bill that will do her more harm than a short war with Great Britain. For the bill of Mr. McKay makes a long and blasting war upon the *workingmen* of our country." If the Vice-President did not vote as a Senator, he would vote as the "Representative of the People." The bill would then become law "*without* the vote of the Senate, but merely upon the *Representative* vote of Mr. Dallas, if he does not *vote as a Senator.*"[2] Other Democratic papers were not so certain that the interests of the state were secure merely because one of the citizens of the state chanced to be Vice-President.[3]

[1] *American Sentinel,* July 13, 1846; for summaries of the action taken by mass meetings in the state, *cf. Niles' Register,* vol. lxx, p. 309.

[2] *American Sentinel,* July 15, 1846.

[3] *Spirit of the Times,* July 22, 1846. In its issue of July 21 it warned the South of a rebellion at the ballot box if the bill passed. "There

The Whig Senators, much to his embarrassment, forced
the Vice-President to cast a ballot for the engrossing of the
bill, whereby he saved the measure from defeat.[1] The
attack on Dallas by the majority of the Democratic papers
of the state for his vote was terrific. One of his former
supporters said,

Should Mr. Dallas live to the age of Mathuzalah, he will
never be able to make ample atonement for his severe on-
slaught upon the home industry of Pennsylvania. Farewell
to all vice-presidents for the future from Pennsylvania.—
We have had enough of one to last us, while all who live
now shall continue to breathe the breath of existence in our
land.[2]

Another Democratic journal cried aloud, " The Old Keystone has been blasted by the ingrate hand of a treacherous
son!" It shouted " REPEAL is the word! Take it up Democrats! echo it iron men! echo it miners and laborers;
shout it mechanics! There shall be no rest, no reposing
until the British Tariff Bill is repealed! " [3] Buchanan in two

are times when wrongs make rebellions sacred; there are occasions
when submission is dishonorable. Think not because we have borne
long and patiently we will bear the ass' load forever."

[1] For the method in which this was accomplished, although their
other plans failed, cf. The Writings and Speeches of Daniel Webster,
vol. xvi, p. 459. For Dallas' defense see his letter in the Pennsylvanian, August 5, 1846.

[2] American Sentinel, July 29, 1846. Hostility to Dallas was intense.
He was burned in effigy in Philadelphia and elsewhere; Pennsylvanian,
July 31; United States Gazette, August 7, 1846.

[3] Spirit of the Times, July 29, 30, 1846. Dallas of course had his
supporters. A list of voters, in the Pennsylvanian, August 5, 1846,
who congratulated him upon his vote, contains the name of Wm. D.
Kelley, later because of his extreme views in favor of protection known
as " Pig Iron" Kelley. At this time Kelley was a free-trader; Kelley,
Speeches, Addresses and Letters on Industrial and Financial Questions, p. vi.

letters to John W. Forney, who had recently acquired the
Pennsylvanian, indicating a plan to offset the disastrous
effect of the passage of the act on the Democracy of the
state, declared, "Repeal is not the word, but modification.
A protective Tariff is not the word; but a revenue Tariff
with sufficient discriminations to maintain our home industry."[1] The cry of "repeal" was, however, eagerly
caught up and was written into the resolutions of Democratic mass meetings in all parts of the state.[2]

The Whigs did not, as did the Democrats, attribute the
odium for the passage of the bill to the Vice-President.
They criticized their political opponents, particularly those
from the South, for the passage of the act. One editor
complained,

The South enters into a political contest with the feelings
engendered at the race course, and having wagered upon a
chance, urges it to the uttermost, careless of consequences.
The repeal of the Tariff may ruin the country, but what
matter, if the gamesters of the South, who now stake negroes,
and anon wager the rights of a people, win the game? The
South itself will suffer from the derangement of our policy
—but it will win the race. That the triumph is appreciated
is manifest from the epileptic glee of the *Union*.[3]

The fact that many Democratic banners in the state had
proclaimed for the tariff of 1842 was bitterly recalled.[4]
The Whigs declared that all attempts to secure a com-

---

[1] Moore, *The Works of James Buchanan*, vol. vii, pp. 43, 46. This
suggestion was followed by Forney, and adopted gradually by other
Democratic editors; *Pennsylvanian*, August 4, 5, 8, 10, 1846.

[2] Some of the resolutions in the *North American*, August 21; *United
States Gazette*, September 2, 1846; *Niles' Register*, vol. lxx, p. 405.

[3] *North American*, July 11, 1846.

[4] *Ibid.*, July 14, 15; *United States Gazette*, July 9, 30, 1846.

promise tariff should be rejected, as this plan involved a surrender of principle.[1] It was declared that the new tariff would bear most heavily on the small capitalist, who would soon be forced to abandon his business.[2] The act was characterized as being thoroughly British and as being of especial benefit to the Duke of York in the operation of his large coal mines in Nova Scotia, since the products of these mines could now be sold in New England to the exclusion of anthracite coal from the Pennsylvania mines unless the wages paid the miners were reduced.[3] In fact, it was noted that miners were leaving Pennsylvania, bound for the coal fields of Nova Scotia.[4]

In the act the Whigs saw the triumph of the South, and in the triumph of the South they saw the victory of slave over free labor. The *Daily Commercial Journal* asserted,

The perpetuity of the slave institution depends upon its success in overthrowing and destroying free labor. With this view was the Tariff of 1846 framed, and no act was ever better fitted to accomplish its aim. From one end to the other, it is a bill, not alone to protect slave capital, but to war upon free labor.

If the act of 1842 was unconstitutional, as the people of the South claimed, because of its protective features, so was the act of 1846; " both acts are protective—but that of '42 encouraged free labor—this of '46 protects slave labor." [5] The *North American* in a series of editorials

---

[1] *North American,* July 25, 1846.

[2] *Daily Commercial Journal,* July 20, 1846.

[3] *North American,* August 3; *United States Gazette,* July 10, August 19, September 24, 26, 29, 1846.

[4] *United States Gazette,* September 30, 1846.

[5] August 6, 1846.

maintained that slave and free labor were antithetical in the same country.[1] In one of them it said,

Our duty is now a plain one—the North must take care of herself. She must become the unflinching advocate of freedom and—since Northern industry stinks in Southern nostrils —the hearty hater of *slave labor*. Pennsylvania has stood too long the champion of the South. She must now become the unceasing, sleepless sentinel of freedom. She is now spit upon and scorned, and in her hour of distress and dismay, let her learn that the hand that has wronged her can be extended in friendship no more.[2]

This triumph of the South over the North had come as the result of the annexation of Texas, it was felt, for " by the aid of Texas Senators," the South has " cursed us with Free Trade." [3] The fact that the act would have been defeated in the Senate without the votes of the two Senators from Texas, always remained to the protectionist

[1] August 1, 5, 6, 10, 1846.

[2] August 5, 1846.

[3] *Daily Commercial Journal*, August 6, 1846. A correspondent, " X ", in the *United States Gazette*, July 31, ironically stated that Texas would be of great value since it had cost so much. " The coal and iron interests of Pennsylvania too may be prostrated by the repeal of that Tariff—and the *diminished* revenue arising from such repeal *may* and most certainly *will* render it necessary to lay a United States tax to meet the increased expenditures of the government.—But what of all this? 'Issachar is a strong ass crushing down between two burdens,' and we Pennsylvanians have always, as in duty bound, most *patiently* followed the *illustrious* example. 'Huzza for Polk, Dallas and the Tariff of '42.'" The *Pennsylvania Telegraph*, July 29, 1846, complained, " Pennsylvania gave her vote in favor of the annexation of Texas, which added two Free Trade Senators to the United States Senate, by whose votes the Tariff of 1842 has been repealed, and this free trade system introduced, prostrating her energy, destroying her manufactures, and her iron and coal interests. She built the gallows to hang herself, and her neck is now in the noose."

Whigs a reminder of the injustice caused by the admission of that state into the Union.[1]

The course of the administration in the peaceful settlement of the Oregon question met, in general, with the approval of the Whigs.[2] Some of them felt that the former enthusiasm for Oregon had been feigned. One of them said, " The Administration but *pretended* its zeal for the ' whole of Oregon,' to secure the assistance of its Northern friends in the cause of annexation and the crusade against the Tariff." [3] The veto of the River and Harbor Bill was declared to be another blow at the North, although it also seriously affected the West and the Southwest.[4]

The Whig nominee for canal commissioner in 1845 had been nominated by the Whig state central committee, which had kept itself in existence from the year before. After the election of 1845 this committee considered its labors as more than completed and made no arrangements for its successor. Therefore, on January 13, 1846, the Whig members of the state legislature met and appointed a committee of three to prepare a call for a convention to meet on March 11 for the purpose of nominating a candidate for canal commissioner.[5] According to call the convention assembled and on the third ballot nominated James M. Power of Mercer county.[6] On March 4 the Democratic convention renominated William B. Foster.[7] The Native

[1] *Cf.* the message of Governor Johnston in 1850 in reply to the resolutions of Georgia and Virginia on the compromises of 1850; *House Journal,* 1850, vol. ii, pp. 419, *et seq.*

[2] *North American,* June 12, 13, 1846.

[3] *Daily Commercial Journal,* June 18, 1846.

[4] *Ibid.,* August 6, 1846.

[5] *Ibid.,* January 20, 1846.

[6] *Public Ledger,* March 13, 1846.

[7] *Ibid.,* March 6, 1846.

American convention of February 24 placed Robert H. Morton before the people as its candidate.[1] William L. Elder received the nomination of the Liberty party.

The Whigs fought the campaign of 1846 on the question of the tariff and on that question alone. It was not necessary to argue the advisability of a protective tariff. It was necessary merely to state that the Tariff Act of 1842 had been repealed, and that too by the Democrats, who in 1844 had made loud protestations that their party would be the only one to preserve the act of 1842. A corollary to the statement that the act had been repealed was that the country was being ruined thereby. Although the Tariff Act of 1846 was not to go into effect until December, its effects, it was claimed, were already in evidence. Shortly after the passage of the act, pig iron had dropped four to five dollars a ton, and wool two cents a pound.[2] Factories began to curtail their production.[3] It was noted that furnaces in the Schuylkill district were closing and that the shipment of coal was decreasing.[4] The closing of a bale-rope factory in Philadelphia was referred to as "The Dallas Night Cap" and the decrease in the shipment of coal as "The Free Trade Blight."[5] The attempt of the Democrats to prove that the Whigs were endeavoring to create a panic met with little success.[6] The argument of the Democrats that the Tariff Act of 1846 protected the agriculturalist, while the act which had been repealed had

[1] *Public Ledger*, February 26, 1846.

[2] *Butler Whig*, August 5, 1846. The decline in prices was constantly stressed by the *United States Gazette*, August 3, 5, 22, 1846.

[3] *United States Gazette*, July 31, 1846.

[4] *Miners' Journal*, August 1; *North American*, September 18; *United States Gazette*, August 28, 1846.

[5] *North American*, September 28, 1846.

[6] *Pennsylvanian*, July 30, 31, August 1, 4, 7; *United States Gazette*, August 4, 5, 1846.

not done so, attracted slight attention.[1] Their effort to
prove this because of the slight rise in the price of foodstuffs
was, inconsistently, declared by the Whigs to be illogical in-
asmuch as the act had not yet gone into effect.[2] It was con-
tended that on election day the American workingmen in
Pennsylvania would demand " An American Protective
System; the Repeal of Walker's British Bill; No Special
Legislation for Cotton Growers; Protection of Free White
Labor above that of Southern Slave Labor; No Sub-
Treasury Rags; and a Currency the same for the Rich and
Poor." [3]

In the early part of 1846 it seemed possible that the state
might be divided politically into two sections because of the
railroad question. The people of Pittsburgh wanted a
charter granted to the Baltimore and Ohio Railroad for
the construction of a branch line to Pittsburgh. The citizens
of Philadelphia, fearing that some of the western trade
might be diverted, opposed the grant. They favored the
construction of a railroad from Harrisburg to Pittsburgh,
which would then have an all-rail connection with Philadelphia. The citizens of western Pennsylvania were paci-
fied by a charter to the Baltimore and Ohio Railroad Company, contingent, however, upon the failure of the new
railroad, the Pennsylvania, to secure the required capital
by a specified day. In the meantime, they secured a modification of an existing charter and under its provisions proceeded to construct the desired outlet for Pittsburgh.[4] One

---

[1] *Pennsylvanian*, July 30, August 1, 1846.

[2] *Daily Commercial Journal*, September 28, 1846.

[3] *North American*, October 10, 1846. On August 6 it called the act of
1846 " the late proclamation of war against the laborers of the North."
On August 10 it claimed that the administration journals were raising "the banner of Slavery against Freedom—the South against the
North—the whip and shackle against the loom and shuttle."

[4] *Public Ledger*, January 14, February 18, 25, 27, March 5, 6, April 13,
May 6, July 8, 14; *Daily Commercial Journal*, March 1, 19, 20, 23, 25,
27, April 9, 24, 28, October 22, 1846.

of the Democratic journals of Philadelphia attempted to
make this an issue in raising the cry, " Power and Pittsburgh! Foster and Philadelphia!" [1] In the election for
municipal officers of Philadelphia city, the question arose
whether the city as a corporation could subscribe to the
stock of the Pennsylvania Railroad.[2] A " Railroad " and
an " Anti-Railroad " ticket were formed from men of
the three parties. The candidates were pledged for or
against the subscription. Although only Whigs were
elected to the select council, yet those whose names were on
the " Railroad " ticket received a thousand more votes than
the other Whig candidates.[3]

The Whigs made nominations in all the congressional districts, save in that represented by Wilmot, where they endorsed a tariff Democrat. The Natives ran candidates in
eight of the eleven districts in the southeastern portion of
the state and also a candidate in the Allegheny district.
In five of the congressional districts of western Pennsylvania and in the four Philadelphia districts, the Liberty
party had candidates.[4] The four Philadelphia Congressmen were all elected by minorities; the Natives and the
Whigs secured one each and the Democrats the other two.
Of the remaining twenty Congressmen of the state the Democrats secured only five. In the Twenty-ninth Congress
the Democrats had controlled twelve of the twenty-four
members from the state, in the coming Congress they would
have only seven.[5] David Wilmot, who alone of the Penn-

[1] *Daily Keystone and People's Journal*, October 13, 1846.

[2] *United States Gazette*, June 18, October 9, 1846; Binney, *Life of
Horace Binney*, pp. 246, *et seq.*

[3] *Public Ledger*, October 10, 15, 1846.

[4] *Ibid.*, October 8, 13, 1846.

[5] Election returns from the *Pennsylvania* quoted in *Niles' Register*,
vol. lxxi, p. 150.

Whig

Erie / Crawford / Warren / McKean / Potter / Tioga / Bradford / Susquehanna / Wayne / Pike / Monroe / Carbon / Northampton / Bucks / Phila / Montgomery / Delaware / Chester / Wyoming / Luzerne / Lehigh / Berks / Lycoming / Columbia / Northumberland / Schuylkill / Lancaster / Mercer / Venango / Clarion / Jefferson / Elk / Clinton / Centre / Union / Juniata / Dauphin / Lebanon / York / Beaver / Butler / Armstrong / Indiana / Clearfield / Mifflin / Perry / Cumberland / Adams / Allegheny / Westmoreland / Cambria / Blair / Huntingdon / Franklin / Washington / Fayette / Somerset / Bedford / Greene

ELECTION FOR CANAL COMMISSIONER IN 1847

sylvania delegation in Congress had voted for the Tariff
Bill of 1846, was returned.[1]   The election to the legislature resulted favorably for the Whigs, for they would control eighteen of the thirty-three senators and fifty-six of the
one hundred representatives.[2]   The Whig candidate for
the office of canal commissioner was elected by a plurality
of more than 7,500.[3]   He was the only canal commissioner
the Whigs elected.

The vote cast at this election was small, which may in
some degree be accounted for by the inclement weather.[4]
The small vote was, however, chiefly due to the disgust of
the electorate.   The total vote was approximately 20,000
less than in 1845 when there had been no congressional
elections.   The Whig vote was about 7,500 more than in
1845, the Native American about 7,000 less, and the Democrats registered a loss of more than 20,000.   Many of the
strongest Democratic counties were in this election carried
by the Whigs, clearly indicating disgust with the course
pursued by the Democracy on the tariff.   The election also
showed that the Native American party could not hope to
assume any dignity even in state politics.   Over 14,000 of
their 15,000 votes came from Philadelphia city and county;
the balance came from a few strong Whig counties.[5]

[1] Ex-Governor Porter was alleged to have said that Wilmot's district
went for free trade because "in that region of country the only
thing the people manufactured were shingles, and they stole the
lumber to make them, and the only *protection* they wanted was protection from the officers of justice!" *North American*, November 18,
1846.

[2] *Public Ledger*, January 6, 1847.

[3] Official returns: Power (Whig) 97,963; Foster (Dem.) 89,064;
Morton (Nat. Am.) 15,424; Elder (Liberty) 2,028; *ibid.*, October 27,
1846.

[4] *Pennsylvanian*, October 16, 1846.

[5] The Natives reelected Levin to Congress, but elected no member of
the legislature.

When the legislature met in January, 1847, it was fully under the control of the Whigs. They were urged to expedite business, to make the session short, and to grant no charters, which would, at any rate, be vetoed by the Democratic governor.[1] On March 3, 1847, the governor signed a bill affecting the status of slaves within the state. The act made kidnaping a high misdemeanor and provided heavy penalties therefor. Judges were authorized to issue writs of *habeas corpus* and to inquire into the cause of imprisonment of any human being within the commonwealth. It denied the use of the state jails for the detention of captured fugitive slaves. It repealed the portions of the sojourning act of March 1, 1780, which had allowed slaves to be brought into and retained within the commonwealth for a period of six months. The act also permitted slaves to be witnesses in judicial proceedings.[2] The bill passed both the senate and the house without a roll-call and received the signature of the Democratic governor.[3] It was claimed that the act was made necessary by the decision of the Supreme Court of the United States in the case of Prigg *v.* Pennsylvania, which had been handed down in 1842. The decision held that the state act of March 25, 1826,[4] which provided for state assistance in the rendition of fugitive slaves, was unconstitutional on the ground that the rendition of fugitive slaves was a subject for exclusive

[1] *North American*, October 27, 1846.

[2] *Session Laws*, 1847, p. 206; the act was entitled "An act to prevent kidnapping, preserve the public peace, prohibit the exercise of certain powers heretofore exercised by judges, justices of the peace, aldermen and jailors in this commonwealth, and to repeal certain slave laws." *Cf.* Turner, *The Negro in Pennsylvania*, pp. 227-249, for the history of the rendition of fugitive slaves from the state.

[3] *House Journal*, 1847, vol. i, pp. 76, 207, 355, 394; *Senate Journal*, 1847, vol. i, pp. 217, 312, 343.

[4] *Session Laws*, 1825-26, p. 150.

federal legislation.[1]   It must be borne in mind that the act of March 3, 1847, was passed five years after the decision of the Supreme Court, and that it followed hard on the passage of the Tariff Act of 1846.   The act must, therefore, be considered as the reply of the state to the repeal of the Tariff Act of 1842.   The support of the Tariff Act of 1842 had been non-partisan, so the adoption of the act of March 3, 1847, was not a party measure.   The passage of the act together with the fact that the Democrats in this legislature joined in endorsing the Wilmot Proviso indicates how complete the disorganization of the Democracy within the state was as a result of the passage of the Tariff Act of 1846.   From this disorganization they were to recover, however, before the end of the year.   The repeal of the Tariff Act of 1842 had given the Whig party of the state a moment of triumph, but it made the party anti-slavery.

[1] 16 *Peters* 539.

CHAPTER IV

A POLITICAL INTERLUDE

1847-1848.

THE war with Mexico called attention to the question of slavery in the territory, which it was assumed would be acquired. Although the war was in progress during the political campaign of 1846, yet none of its issues entered directly into the struggle, which was fought on the repeal of the Tariff Act of 1842. Although the Whigs of the state questioned the justice of the course of the President in asserting that the Rio Grande was the boundary of the United States, yet, when the assertion of this claim led to war, they urged all to join in the defense of their country. One of their leading journals in Philadelphia said,

The war was uncalled for, but being declared, there is but one duty for every man who claims the name of American (and is not conscientiously scrupulous on the subject of arms), he must aid to carry on that war with vigor, that its termination may be the more speedily secured. Our country, our whole country, and nothing but our country, when she is endangered by a war, no matter how that war happened. But let us not, in our enthusiasm, forget the high duties of patriots and men. Let us not fall into the miserable error of supposing that *success* in a campaign, is a justification of war.[1]

[1] *United States Gazette,* May 27, 1846; *ibid.,* May 8, 11, 12, 13, 16, 19, 20, June 3, July 1, November 24, December 10; *Daily Commercial Journal,* May 13; *North American,* November 25, December 17, 18; *Pennsylvania Telegraph,* June 3, 17, 1846.

Opposition to the annexation of any territory, even that of California, was freely voiced. The people inhabiting this area were declared to be unfit to become citizens of the United States.[1] A Pittsburgh journal condemned the war and urged the hastening of peace.

The spoliation of Mexico has assumed the attitude of a wrong; and whether in nations or individuals, wrong if persisted in cannot prosper. Let peace be concluded with Mexico—on no grinding terms either, but such as it would become the generosity of a great nation to grant to a prostrate though gallant foe.[2]

The insistence of the Whigs upon inquiring into the causes of the war led to their being charged by the Democrats with a lack of patriotism and to their being branded Federalists; both of which charges they, of course, vigorously denied.[3]

On August 8, 1846, a two-million-dollar appropriation bill for the purpose of conducting preliminary peace negotiations with Mexico passed the House of Representatives, although the Wilmot Proviso had been attached to it. Not a dissenting vote from Pennsylvania was cast against the measure.[4] The bill was before the Senate when Congress adjourned. The comments on the bill, made

[1] *North American,* June 6, 12, 1846.

[2] *Daily Commercial Journal,* July 25, 1846.

[3] *Ibid.,* June 8; *North American,* November 11, 13, 25, 28, December 18, 22, 1846, January 22, February 1, 1847. In its issue of November 11, 1846, the *North American* printed a fictitious address signed by twenty-eight leading Democrats. The address stated that the signers, old Federalists, have secured control of the Democratic party and they now ask for the support of all former Federalists. The alleged signers from Pennsylvania are James Buchanan, William Wilkins, Richard Rush, John M. Read, Henry D. Gilpin, John K. Kane, and Ellis Lewis.

[4] *House Journal,* 29th Congress, 1st session, p. 1284.

by the Whig press, were criticisms on the purpose of the appropriation and not on the proviso.[1] When it became evident that the acquisition of territory would be one of the results of the war, the adoption of the proviso, not as a Whig but as a Northern measure, was advocated.[2] A resolution, adopted by the state legislature on January 22, 1847, instructed the Senators and requested the Representatives " to vote against any measure whatever, by which territory will accrue to the Union, unless, as a part of the fundamental law upon which any compact or treaty for this purpose is based, slavery or involuntary servitude, except for crime, shall be forever prohibited." [3] The adoption of this resolution was not a partisan measure, for it passed the house by a vote of 96 to 0, and the senate by a vote of 24 to 3.[4]

During the second session of the Twenty-ninth Congress another appropriation bill, but for three million dollars, to conduct preliminary peace negotiations was introduced. When the Wilmot Proviso was attached in the House to this bill, the *North American* was led to exclaim, " The Freedom Proviso has again been attached to the Bribery Bill." [5] Five of the Pennsylvania Democrats in the House voted against the adoption of the proviso.[6] When the bill was returned to the House with the proviso rejected by the Senate, the House failed to sustain its former vote. Amongst those who changed their votes were three Demo-

---

[1] *North American*, August 17; *Daily Commercial Journal*, August 11, 1846. The latter paper said Polk had started to conquer a peace but now he proposed to buy one.

[2] *North American*, January 18, 1847.

[3] *Session Laws*, 1847, p. 489.

[4] This resolution was introduced by a Democrat. *House Journal*, 1847, vol. i, p. 143; *Senate Journal*, 1847, vol. i, p. 129.

[5] February 10, 1847.

[6] Analysis of vote in *North American*, February 19, 1847.

crats from Pennsylvania.[1] The defeat of the proviso was attributed to the failure of the Democrats to stand by their previously expressed opinion.[2] The Twenty-ninth Congress, it was stated, had been particularly under the control of the South. "Every measure of the North and West was strangled either by the votes of Congress or the Executive Veto."[3]

The shifting of the Democracy in Pennsylvania from support of to opposition to the Wilmot Proviso has been indicated by the voting in Congress. Definite argument against the measure was furnished in a letter from Buchanan to the Democrats of Berks county, who on August 28, 1847, were holding a Harvest Home Festival at Reading. Buchanan urged the extension of the Missouri Compromise line through the territory which might be acquired from Mexico. He had previously advocated the plan at cabinet meetings, winning the President to its support. He claimed that the nature of the region and the type of immigrants who would be attracted to the area would be a bar to slavery; consequently it was unwise to agitate for the proviso.[4] Dallas in a speech at Pittsburgh took position with Lewis Cass and others and advocated " leaving to the people of the territory to be acquired the business of settling the matter for themselves."[5] The anti-slavery Whigs considered the proviso the means of deciding the conflict between free and slave labor. At this time there occurred at the Tredegar Iron Works, Richmond, Virginia, a strike

[1] Analysis of vote in *Niles' Register*, vol. lxxii, p. 18.

[2] *North American*, March 15, 17; *Lancaster Union and Tribune*, March 23, 1847.

[3] *Daily Commercial Journal*, March 6, 1847.

[4] Moore, *Works of James Buchanan*, vol. vii, p. 385; *Polk's Diary*, vol. ii, pp. 308-9, 334-5.

[5] *Public Ledger*, September 29, 1847.

because of the introduction of slave labor into several departments of the plant. This strike in the home of slave labor was held clearly to illustrate the inherent conflict between free and slave labor.[1]

On the question of the tariff the Democrats were taking new ground. In the election of 1846 they had been completely disorganized and had had no defense against the attacks of the Whigs. Now they were beginning to argue that the Tariff Act of 1846 was an excellent one.[2] The basis for this claim was the high prices obtained for foodstuffs, as a result of the failure of the crops in Europe. The extension of the railroads and the substitution of solid for plate rails were beneficial to the iron industry.[3] To the charge

[1] *Daily Commercial Journal,* June 8, 1847; the proceedings and communications of the strikers are in the *Richmond Enquirer,* May 29, 1847. The Whigs declared the proviso was nothing new as it contained Jefferson's anti-slavery resolutions of 1784; *North American,* August 13, 1847.

[2] Even the *Spirit of the Times,* which the year before had shouted, "Repeal is the word," took this position; September 6, 11; *York Gazette,* October 5, 1847. The Whigs in the legislature had not been able to have resolutions, favoring the restoration of the tariff of 1842, adopted. The Whig majority of the special committee in the senate, to which was referred so much of the governor's message as related to the tariff, reported as follows to the senate: "' Polk, Dallas, Shunk, and the Tariff of 1842!' was their battle cry in our State, and (admitting that no frauds were committed at the polls) the people of Pennsylvania decided in favor of the Democratic candidates. But their vote was for Polk, Dallas, Shunk, and *the tariff of* 1842. The tariff was as much a part of the ticket voted, as if it had been printed on it, and but for it the then candidates, whose names were thus connected with it, would now be in the obscurity of private life." *Senate Journal,* 1847, vol. i, p. 252. The Democratic minority reported, "If ' Polk, Dallas, Shunk, and the tariff of 1842', were in any instance adopted as the 'battle cry' of the democracy, it was rather as idle bravado than the deliberate manifestation of political sentiment." *Ibid.,* p. 427.

[3] Jesse Miller, November 9, 1846, to Buchanan, Buchanan Mss; R. I. Arundel, October 15, 1847, to John McLean, McLean Papers, Lib. of Cong.; *Daily Commercial Journal,* October 28, November 22; *Spirit of the Times,* September 11, 1847.

that their dire predictions of 1846 had not materialized, the Whigs replied that the Democrats had made the same prophecies.[1] The fact that prices were high could not be denied and warnings of a dismal future received little attention.

Although the four parties made nominations for governor and canal commissioner, yet the contest lay between the Democrats and the Whigs. For governor the Whigs nominated James Irvin and for canal commissioner Joseph H. Patton. Irvin was extensively engaged in the iron industry in Centre county, was a strong advocate of a protective tariff and consequently would appeal to the like-minded individuals of the state. Originally a Democrat, he had left that party as the result of Jackson's attack on the bank. He had been elected to the Twenty-seventh and the Twenty-eighth Congresses and had supported the Tariff Act of 1842. The Democrats renominated Governor Shunk and for canal commissioner they nominated Morris Longstreth. The contest was more bitterly personal than any which had recently preceded.[2] Behind these recrimina-

[1] *Daily Commercial Journal,* June 4, 1847.

[2] The Democrats made the following charges against Irvin: he is, " 1. An Aristocratic Iron Master! 2. The Father of the Bankrupt Law! 3. The Advocate of Taxing Tea and Coffee! 4. The Reviler of General Jackson! 5. The Friend of Thaddeus Stevens! 6. The Supporter of the Buckshot War! 7. The Advocate of the Gettysburg Railroad! 8. The Worshipper of a United States Bank! 9. The Trumpeter of his own Acts of Charity! 10. An Old-school, Anti-war Federalist!" quoted from the *Bedford Gazette* in the *North American,* August 19, 1847; other Democratic attacks *American Volunteer,* September 16; *York Gazette,* October 5; *Spirit of the Times,* October 12; *Lancaster Intelligencer,* August 24, September 21, 1847. For Whig attacks *cf. North American,* April 7, 8, May 18, 25, June 19, 22, July 2, 3, September 11, 16, 17, 23, 25, 27, October 2, 6; *Miners' Journal,* March 20; *Butler Whig,* May 26; *Daily Commercial Journal,* September 27, 28, 29, 30, 1847.

tions was the effort of the Whigs to make the tariff and
the Wilmot Proviso the issues of the campaign.[1] In this
they failed, and Shunk was reelected by a plurality of more
than 18,000 votes.[2] The total vote was 42,000 less than in
1844, but 80,000 more than in 1846. The decline in the
vote of the Native American party continued. The legislature did not pass into the hands of the Democrats; they
secured control of the house, but the senate, due to hold-
overs, remained Whig.[3]

In the main, the Whigs contended that the victory of
their opponents was temporary and indecisive. " It has
been induced by the false confidence in the high prices for
produce consequent upon the famine in Europe," said one.[4]
A leading Democratic journal in the eastern portion of the
state declared, " The sovereign people have recorded their
verdict upon the War with Mexico, the Tariff of '46, the
Sub-Treasury, as well as Federal treason to our native
land ! "[5] Despondently a Whig paper in the western part
of the state replied, " It is even so. Pennsylvania adheres
to Polk, Dallas, and Buchanan—repudiates the Wilmot
Proviso, though introduced by one of her own representatives—adheres to this wicked war of conquest and land

[1] *Daily Commercial Journal*, September 20, October 12; *North American*, June 12, July 3, 17; *York Gazette*, October 5, 1847.

[2] *Smull's Legislative Hand-Book*, 1919, p. 720; the official returns for
governor were: Francis R. Shunk (Dem.) 146,081; James Irvin
(Whig) 128,148; E. C. Reigart (Nat. Am.) 11,247; F. J. Lamoyne
(Liberty) 1,861; scattering 6. A number of former Anti-Masons supported Reigart in preference to Irvin.

[3] *North American*, January 4, 1848. In the senate were 19 Whigs,
and 14 Democrats; in the house 36 Whigs, and 64 Democrats. Wm.
F. Johnston, a former Democrat, was sent, by a small majority, to the
senate from a normally Democratic district.

[4] *Ibid.*, October 16, 1847.

[5] *Spirit of the Times*, October 15, 1847.

robbery—and covers with its large popular sanction even the enormous maladministration of this war, which it approves."[1]   The Whigs had failed in raising these issues, for they had determined to conduct a quiet campaign, with the result that the Democrats polled a larger percentage of their full strength.[2]

Attention for some time had been directed to the presidential election of 1848. The news had scarcely reached the country that General Taylor had won several battles from the Mexicans before he was placed in nomination for the presidency by a mass meeting at Trenton, New Jersey.[3]   As his military success continued, he became a stronger and stronger presidential possibility; but it was not known to what party he professed to belong.   There was no doubt but that Buchanan would again endeavor to secure the endorsement of the state for the presidential nomination at the next Democratic national convention.   There was, however, a strong faction in the state, led by Simon Cameron, ex-Governor Porter, ex-Secretary of War J. M. Porter, Reah Frazer, and Henry A. Muhlenberg, which opposed Buchanan's control of the Democracy in the state. They decided, inasmuch as the nature of Taylor's politics was not known, to avail themselves of his growing popularity to overthrow Buchanan.   Taylor's military achievements would make him all the more attractive, as General Scott was frequently mentioned for the Whig nomination. On April 25, 1847, Cameron wrote a letter to the editor of the *Norristown Register,* in which he stated his belief that Taylor was a Democrat.[4]   To give definiteness to the move-

---

[1] *Daily Commercial Journal,* October 21, 1847.

[2] *Pennsylvania Inquirer,* October 20, 1847; McClure, *Old Time Notes,* vol. i, p. 171.

[3] *Niles' Register,* vol. lxx, p. 256.

[4] Republished in the *Daily Commercial Journal,* June 4, 1847.

ment, a convention assembled early in July at Harrisburg; a " Democratic Taylor Central Committee " was appointed to organize the movement.[1] It decided to hold a Democratic Taylor mass meeting at Harrisburg on September 24, 1847. The mass meeting enthusiastically endorsed Taylor for the presidency.[2]

In the meantime, the Native Americans had assembled at Pittsburgh on May 11, 1847, in what they grandiloquently called a national convention.[3] Letters had previously been written to leading politicians asking them whether they would accept the nomination of the party for the presidency, if it were unanimously given them. The recipients of this offer either rejected it or neglected to answer the letter making it.[4] At this convention no nomination was made, and an adjournment was made to Philadelphia, where the convention was to reassemble on September 10. In the interval between the two conventions, the president of the

---

[1] *Pennsylvania Inquirer*, July 31, August 6, 1847. On the committee were the following prominent Democrats: Seth Salisbury, John M. Read, Richard Vaux, Simon Cameron, Ellis Lewis, George Kremer, H. B. Wright, and Henry A. Muhlenberg.

[2] *Evening Bulletin*, October 6, 1847.

[3] *Daily Commercial Journal*, May 12, 1847. Delegates from Pennsylvania, New York, Kentucky, Illinois, Indiana, and Massachusetts were said to be present.

[4] Peter Sken Smith acted as chief interrogator. On March 16, 1847, he wrote John McLean, who replied that he considered such an early nomination of doubtful value; McLean Papers, Lib. of Cong. On March 19 a letter was sent to Henry Clay, who on April 2 refused to consider the offer. On March 26 Commodore Charles Stewart declined the offer in Smith's letter of March 18. On May 1 Smith received a reply from Ogden Edwards stating that he considered the time inauspicious for a nomination. Letters published in the *Daily Commercial Journal*, September 15, 1847. On April 24, John C. Calhoun was sent one of these letters, which he apparently never answered; *Report of the American Historical Society*, 1899, vol. ii, p. 1116.

convention inquired of General Taylor whether he would accept the nomination if it were tendered him. On July 13 Taylor replied, in his usual form, that he would yield to the wishes of the people.[1] Upon the reassembling of the convention at Philadelphia, General Taylor was "proposed" as the "People's Candidate" for the presidency and General H. A. S. Dearborn was nominated by the Native Americans for the vice-presidency.[2] The Native Americans were now in a position to cooperate with the Taylor Democrats or any other group favoring Taylor for the presidency.

On February 22, 1848, there assembled at Harrisburg a "Peoples' Convention," over which James M. Porter presided. The members of the convention were chiefly Native Americans and anti-Buchanan Democrats. An electoral ticket pledged to Taylor was reported and a central committee was formed.[3] But the hopes of the Taylor Democrats were soon blighted; on the same day, at a Whig celebration at Philadelphia, Taylor's letter of August 3, 1847, to Joseph R. Ingersoll was read. In this letter Taylor endorsed Ingersoll's statement on the floor of Congress that Taylor was "a Whig—not indeed an ultra-partisan Whig— but a Whig in principle."[4] The Democrats in the Taylor movement individually began immediately to reject him on the ground that he had declared that he was not a Democrat.[5] After the nomination of Taylor by the Whigs, this prior endorsement of Taylor by these Democrats was given due publicity by the Whigs.[6]

[1] *Daily Commercial Journal*, September 15, 1847.

[2] *American Press and Republican*, September 18, 1847.

[3] *Public Ledger*, February 23, 25, 1848.

[4] *Niles' Register*, vol. lxxiii, p. 407.

[5] Letter of Henry A, Muhlenberg, dated March 2, 1848, in the *Daily Commercial Journal*, March 15, 1848.

[6] *Ibid.*, November 6, 1848.

The Whigs of the eastern portion of the state were likewise considering Taylor as a favorite candidate for the presidency.   On April 10, 1847, he was endorsed for that office
by a convention of the " Democratic Whigs of the City and
County of Philadelphia." [1]   No further action was taken
this year.   At the Buena Vista Festival of February 22,
1848, at Philadelphia, at which Taylor's letter declaring
that he was a Whig was read, one of the speakers after
condemning Clay for his Lexington speech said he had three
reasons for urging his audience to support Taylor; they
were, " 1. Because he is honest and capable; 2. because he
is a Whig; 3. because he can be elected." [2]

In the western part of the state, Scott and Clay appealed
more to the Whigs than did Taylor; and huge mass meetings
endorsing the one or the other of them were held. [3]   On
March 1, 1848, the Allegheny county convention instructed
its delegate to the national convention to support Clay. [4]   It
was not, however, until April 10 that Clay announced that
he would allow his name to be presented to the Whig
national convention. [5]   Previously, however, Clay had alienated many of his admirers by delivering on November 13,
1847, what was popularly known as his Lexington speech.
In it he condemned the President for pursuing a policy
which had caused the war and for conducting it without
properly consulting Congress.   The war was declared to
be one not of defense but one of aggression.   If Mexico
were conquered, what then?   To the forcible annexation
of territory, even in the shape of an indemnity, he was op-

[1] *North American,* April 12, 1847.

[2] *Public Ledger,* February 24, 1848.

[3] *Ibid.,* February 29; *Daily Commercial Journal,* February 3, 24, 1848.

[4] *Daily Commercial Journal,* March 2, 1848.

[5] *North American,* April 13, 1848, for Clay's letter to the public.

posed. If the people of the United States desired it, California, including the Bay of San Francisco, should be purchased. The purposes of the war should be proclaimed by Congress and the war should be continued only until these aims had been accomplished. Throughout the speech there was an insistence on the Whig principle that the Executive be controlled by Congress.[1] Whig opinion on the speech was divided. On December 6, 1847, a large mass meeting in Philadelphia adopted the resolutions which Clay had proposed in his speech,[2] but the mass meeting of February 22, 1848, declared that the speech had made him a presidential impossibility. One of his ardent admirers in the western part of the state affirmed that the movement in his favor had been ended, for " our conviction is that this speech settles the point—that Mr. Clay cannot be nominated as the Whig candidate—or, if nominated, that he could not be elected." [3]

On March 15, 1848, the Whig state convention assembled at Harrisburg. Its duties were to nominate a candidate for canal commissioner, to select senatorial delegates to the national convention, and to form an electoral ticket. On the second ballot Ner Middleswarth, a former leader of the Anti-Masons, was chosen as the standard bearer. The convention refused to take even a vote on its preference of a presidential candidate, consequently it refused to instruct the senatorial delegates. It resolved, " That the Whig candidate for the Presidency, to be worthy of the support of the Whig party, must be known to be devoted to its principles, willing to become their exponent and champion, and

[1] The speech is reported in full in *Pennsylvania Telegraph*, November 30, 1847; extracts and the resolutions are in Sargent, *Life and Public Services of Henry Clay*, pp. 105, *et seq.*

[2] *Evening Bulletin*, December 7, 1847.

[3] *Daily Commercial Journal*, December 2, 1847.

prepared to carry them faithfully out in the execution of his official duties." In another resolution they expressed their belief that such a candidate would be nominated and to him they pledged the support of Pennsylvania.[1] Many doubts still existed as to the Whig orthodoxy of Taylor and these resolutions were an attempt to meet the situation. These doubts were somewhat quieted by the publication of his letter of April 22, 1848, to J. S. Allison in which he stated that he was a Whig but not an ultra Whig.[2]

The Whig national convention had been called, by caucuses of the Whig members of Congress on January 27 and February 3, 1848, to meet at Philadelphia on June 7.[3] The convention nominated Taylor and Fillmore, but adopted no resolutions.[4] On no ballot did Taylor receive a majority of the votes from the Pennsylvania delegates, but they naturally pledged their united support to him.[5]

Inasmuch as the Whigs had nominated Taylor, the way was open for them to secure the votes of the Native Americans for their candidate. Prior to the national convention the " Whig Rough and Ready Club of the City and County of Philadelphia " had been formed.[6] After the nomination of Taylor, the name was changed to the " National Rough and Ready Club." It was resolved,

[1] Proceedings in the *Public Ledger,* March 16, 17, 1848.

[2] *Daily Commercial Journal,* May 6, 1848.

[3] *North American,* February 7, 1848.

[4] Proceedings in *Public Ledger,* June 9, 10, 1848. The nominations split the Whig party in Massachusetts and for a time threatened to do the same thing in New York. No opposition to the nominations developed in Pennsylvania.

[5] Pennsylvania's vote on the various ballots was 1. Taylor 8; Clay 12; Scott 6. 2. Taylor 9; Clay 7; Scott 10. 3. Taylor 12; Clay 4; Scott 10. 4. Taylor 12; Clay 4; Scott 10.

[6] *North American,* March 27, 1848.

" That the friends of Taylor and Fillmore be invited to join the Club at its meetings, and become members, to aid in promoting the election of Zachary Taylor, of Louisiana, and Millard Fillmore, of New York." [1] In counties other than Philadelphia, where the Native Americans had effected an organization, the same policy of conciliation was pursued by the Whigs. As a result the Native Americans did not form a ticket for either local or state offices. [2]

Before the fall elections it was necessary to make nominations for governor. Governor Shunk was slowly dying. On Sunday, July 9, the last day on which he could do so in order to make an election possible that year, the governor resigned. [3] The Whigs immediately charged their opponents with thrusting themselves on the dying man in order to secure the resignation. [4] Some of the Whigs also raised the question of whether it would be possible to have a legal election this year because of certain technicalities and ambiguities in the law. William F. Johnston, speaker of the senate, who had become acting governor, did not lend himself to the schemes of postponing the election to the follow-

[1] *Pennsylvania Inquirer,* June 21, 1848.

[2] In printing the list of candidates, which it supported, the *American Press and Republican* (Native American), September 9, 1848, *et seq.,* made the following distinctions: 1. " The People's Candidate for President, Endorsed by the Whig National Convention "—General Taylor. 2. " Whig Nominations "—for Vice-President, Millard Fillmore; for canal commissioner, Ner Middleswarth. 3. " Independent Rough and Ready Electoral Ticket." 4. " Rough and Ready Nominations "— for Governor, Wm. F. Johnston; for Congress, Thaddeus Stevens; for the legislature.

[3] *Pennsylvania Archives,* series iv, vol. vii, pp. 275-6.

[4] *North American,* July 11, 13; *Miners' Journal,* July 15; *Pennsylvania Inquirer,* July 11, 1848. For an account, by a witness, of the securing of the resignation, *cf.* DeWitt, *A Discourse on the Life and Character of Francis R. Shunk,* p. 10.

ing year, so on August 12 he issued his proclamation calling for an election in the Fall.[1]   He had earlier indicated that this would be the course which he would pursue.   Therefore, on July 20, the Whig state central committee called on the " friends of General Zachary Taylor and Millard Fillmore in the State of Pennsylvania " to elect delegates to a convention to meet at Harrisburg on August 31 to name a gubernatorial candidate.[2]   The convention unanimously nominated Johnston on the first ballot.   The resolutions favored a protective tariff, opposed the extension of slavery, and denounced executive usurpation.[3]   As the opponent of Johnston, the Democrats after a warm controversy nominated Morris Longstreth.[4]

The nomination of Johnston was a happy one, for which the way had been previously paved.   He had been a protectionist Democrat of considerable influence in the western portion of the state, serving a number of terms in the lower house.   He had not consistently acted with his party, and in 1841 had introduced the measure providing for the payment of the interest on the state debt by means of the relief notes.   The passage of the Tariff Act of 1846 he viewed as a violation of the Democratic pledges made during the presidential campaign of 1844.   Thereupon, he abandoned his old party and was elected by the Whigs in 1847 to the senate.   His accession to the Whig ranks was hailed with delight, for he was a man of marked ability and of honest convictions.   At the close of his first year in the senate, it was evident that the speaker of that body, according to the terms of the constitution, would be governor *pro tempore* upon the death of Governor Shunk, which was imminent.

[1] *Pennsylvania Archives,* series iv, vol. vii, p. 283.

[2] *Pennsylvania Telegraph,* July 25, 1848.

[3] *Daily Commercial Journal,* September 6, 1848.

[4] *Public Ledger,* August 31, September 1, 1848.

The Whigs, who controlled the senate, secured the resignation of the speaker, whose term would expire with this session. They then honored Johnston by electing him speaker, thereby assuring themselves of the support of many protectionist Democrats.

The nomination of Cass by the Democrats led to the disaffection of Van Buren, who with Charles Francis Adams was nominated as the standard bearer at a convention of Free Soil men at Buffalo on August 9.[1] The movement in Pennsylvania was led by David Wilmot. On June 29 he wrote a letter in which he said, " I shall support Van Buren with the whole strength of my patriotism, and do all in my power to get up an electoral ticket for him in Pennsylvania." [2] The Buffalo nominations were endorsed at county mass meetings in various parts of the state.[3] These mass meetings chose delegates to a state convention, which had been called for Reading by the Pennsylvania delegates to the Buffalo convention.[4] The state convention upon assembling on September 13 formed an electoral ticket, but, despite the desires of the delegates from western Pennsylvania, refused to form a state ticket.[5] It was hoped that this movement would attract the free-soil Whigs, who, however, being in control of their party, asserted that the Whig party " has been and is the bulwark of freedom." [6]

One characteristic of this election was the writing of numerous letters by Taylor. As no platform had been adopted by the national convention, the Whig journals began

---

[1] *Public Ledger,* August 10, 11, 12, 1848.

[2] *Ibid.,* July 19, 1848.

[3] *Ibid.,* August 28, September 1, 7, 1848.

[4] *Ibid.,* August 16, 1848.

[5] *Ibid.,* September 14, 15, 1848.

[6] *Daily Commercial Journal,* September 2, 1848.

publishing as the party's policy the letter of Taylor to J. S. Allison, dated April 22, 1848, and his letter of acceptance, dated July 15, 1848, to J. M. Morehead.[1] Taylor, in the mean time, naively continued to insist that he was not a party candidate.[2] He even accepted from the " Democratic citizens of Charleston," South Carolina, a nomination for the presidency on the same ticket with W. O. Butler, the regularly nominated Democratic candidate for the vice-presidency.[3] These numerous letters of Taylor were causing so much trouble that he was forced finally to yield to the insistence of his political advisers that he write no more letters for publication.[4]

A new method was introduced into the mechanics of campaigning in Pennsylvania when Johnston toured the state. The *Public Ledger,* an independent journal, approved of this plan, as it gave the voters the opportunity of seeing and of hearing the candidate. Because of the large number of newspapers in the East, this method had not been considered as essential as it had been in the South and in the West.[5] In his tour Johnston stated that the issues involved were the tariff and the extension of human slavery. He contended that in contrasting the effects of the tariff of 1842 and the tariff of 1846 it would be found that " the former had covered the country with blessings, while the latter in giving (according to the Baltimore Convention) ' a renewed impulse to the cause of Free Trade,' had brought or was bringing ruin, stagnation, and business revulsion."

[1] *Daily Commercial Journal,* August 11, 1848, *et seq.*

[2] Letters in the *Public Ledger,* August 15, 22, 1848.

[3] *Ibid.,* August 28, 1848.

[4] Taylor to J. J. Crittenden, September 23, 1848; Miscellaneous Manuscript Collection of the New York Historical Society.

[5] September 7, 1848.

In regard to slavery, he declared that the policy of the state had been always to oppose its extension.[1]

On the question of the tariff the Whigs in the state were everywhere united, but they did not all join in the support of the Wilmot Proviso. The *Pennsylvania Inquirer,* for example, limited itself during the entire campaign to a discussion of the military renown of General Taylor and to the need of adequate protection to home industry. It specifically stated the issue to be " Taylor and the Tariff of '42." It did not discuss the Wilmot Proviso.[2] That the issue of the tariff was not without force was shown by an address of tariff Democrats in Clarion county. They rejected the Baltimore platform and the Democratic candidates, declaring that " what was democratic doctrine in '44 should be the same in '48." [3] As the campaign progressed, it became evident that Pennsylvania was " the real battle ground " and that this was due to the tariff.[4]

The free-soil Whigs, however, had control of the state party and pushed the issue of the Wilmot Proviso as well as the issue of the tariff. The fate of this measure, it was pointed out, rested not only on the Congressmen but also on the President. Cass was pledged to veto the measure should it be presented to him. Since Van Buren could not be elected, those, who were interested in the proviso, were urged to vote for Taylor.[5] Wide publicity was given to a Democratic pamphlet, distributed in the South, which the

[1] *Public Ledger,* September 2, 1848.

[2] October 10, 19, November 3, 1848.

[3] *Pennsylvania Inquirer,* September 27, 1848.

[4] *The Writings and Speeches of Daniel Webster,* vol. xvi, p. 500.

[5] *North American,* August 2, 16, September 5; *Daily Commercial Journal,* May 30, June 21, July 7, 1848. Cass' letter of February 19, 1847, giving his views on the Wilmot Proviso in the *Public Ledger,* September 1, 1848.

Whigs republished for distribution in Pennsylvania. The pamphlet was entitled, " A Statement proving Millard Fillmore, the Candidate of the Whig Party for the Office of Vice President, to be an Abolitionist, by a Review of his Course in the 25th, 26th, and 27th Congress. Also, showing General Taylor to be in favor of extending the Ordinance of 1787 over the Continent, beyond the Rio Grande; in other words to be in favor of the Wilmot Proviso." [1]

The strong Whig counties of Allegheny and Lancaster were completely under the control of the free-soil element. In Allegheny county, Moses Hampton secured the Whig renomination to Congress only by pledging himself definitely to support the Wilmot Proviso.[2] In Lancaster county Thaddeus Stevens through the adroit manipulation of the Native American delegates to the " Rough and Ready County Convention " secured his nomination as the congressional candidate.[3] This nomination was tantamount to an election. His anti-slavery views were well known and pronounced. The abolition leaders in the county, however, addressed a letter to both Stevens and Emanuel Schaeffer, the Democratic candidate, and asked the following questions :

1. If elected to a seat in the Congress of the United States will you vote for and support at all times the principles of the Jeffersonian Ordinance of 1787 in their application to the whole of our newly acquired territories, so far as the same may be necessary to exclude slavery and involuntary servitude from them forever?

2. If elected will you support a bill for the extinction of this

---

[1] Reprinted entire in the *Daily Commercial Journal,* September 12, 1848.

[2] *Ibid.,* May 10, 18, 19; June 9, 26, July 28, 1848.

[3] *Public Ledger,* August 17, 21, 24; *American Press and Republican,* August 26; *Lancaster Intelligencer,* August 29, 1848.

institution (Slavery) wherever Congress possesses Constitutional jurisdiction over it?

The Democratic candidate replied that the people of each state and territory had the right of controlling and of checking the advance of this institution. Stevens answered both questions in the affirmative and requested the committee to consider his answers " as expressing merely opinions and feelings long entertained, and not as pledges, given for the occasion. . . . . I will further add, what, perhaps, your letter does not require; that I will vote for no man for any office, who I believe would interpose any official obstacles to the accomplishment of these objects." [1]

In all of the congressional districts the Whigs nominated candidates, and did not endorse any tariff Democrats, as they had done in 1844.   In two of the Philadelphia districts, however, they endorsed two of the nominees of the Native Americans in return for their acceptance of the balance of the Whig ticket.[2]   The Democrats used the Ten Hour Law in an appeal to the factory workers. This law of March 28, 1848, declared that a legal day's work in the textile mills in the state consisted of ten hours of labor. Trouble had developed in some mills over the enforcement of the law. Although there was no large gain as a result of this appeal, yet, inasmuch as the election was close, the defeat of Middleswarth, Whig candidate for canal commissioner, was partly due to his opposition in the senate to this bill.[3]

---

[1] Correspondence in the *Lancaster Intelligencer,* September 26, 1848.

[2] *Public Ledger,* September 28, 1848. The Whigs endorsed Congressman L. C. Levin for reelection and John S. Littell, a former Whig. A few Whigs, who were opposed to Levin, nominated their own candidate.

[3] Parke, *Historical Gleanings,* p. 78; *Public Ledger,* July 7, 15, 25, September 19, 1848. McClure, *Old Time Notes,* vol. i, p. 177, attributes Middleswarth's defeat to his opposition to the law. For the act, see *Session Laws,* 1848, p. 278.

It is difficult, on the basis of the returns, to state definitely who carried the October elections. The Whigs secured the greater portion of the offices, but the Democratic majority seems to have been about 3,000. Of the twenty-four Congressmen, fourteen Whigs, one Native American-Whig, eight Democrats, and one Free Soil Democrat, David Wilmot, were elected.[1] In the eleventh district, a mining region, the Democrats had nominated two candidates, with the result that the Whig had been elected by a very small plurality.[2] Wilmot had been elected by a huge majority.[3] On joint ballot the Whigs would control the legislature, assuring the election of a Whig Senator. In the senate the Whigs had twenty-one of the thirty-three members; the house contained fifty Democrats, forty-five Whigs, and five Native Americans, who had been elected in Philadelphia county with the assistance of the Whigs.[4]

The early returns for governor and canal commissioner indicated that the Whigs had elected both of them. It soon was evident, however, that Middleswarth had been defeated. For a period of ten days, it was doubtful whether Johnston or Longstreth had been elected governor, but then it became clear that Johnston had been chosen by a majority of over two hundred votes.[5] The Democratic candidate for canal

[1] *Public Ledger,* October 20, 1848.

[2] H. B. Wright, in a letter of October 16, 1848, to Buchanan, attributed his defeat in this district to the "amalgamation of Abolitionists—free-soil men—the Beaumont and Collings men on Butler the federal candidate." Buchanan Mss. The split in the party was due to the "rotten" delegate system to the county convention. "Free Trade has got its quietus — and hereafter men must learn wisdom," said the leading county paper, the *Luzerne Democrat,* October 11, 1848.

[3] *Public Ledger,* October 23, 1848.

[4] *Ibid.,* October 21, 1848.

[5] *Smull's Legislative Hand-Book,* 1919, p. 720; the official returns were William F. Johnston (Whig) 168,522; Morris Longstreth (Dem.) 168,225; scattering 72.

commissioner secured a majority of over three thousand. The vote for commissioner as compared with that for governor showed a decline in the Whig vote of 4,400 and in the Democratic vote of 1,100. The larger falling off in the Whig total than in the Democratic represented the refusal of the factory workers and of the free-soil Democrats to support Middleswarth. The former had been antagonized by his opposition to the Ten Hour Bill. In Allegheny county alone, he lost over 600 of the factory workers' votes. In Wilmot's district, he lost over 425 of the free-soil votes which had been cast for Johnston. This defection is not so noticeable in the southeastern part of the state.[1] Painter, the successful candidate, received the votes of the Taylor Democrats, since he had been one of those who had worked for Taylor, being a signer of the resolutions of June 26, 1847.[2]

The election of Johnston by so small a majority indicated that there had not been a political upheaval in the state. Johnston had been a Democrat, but had abandoned that party after its tariff pledges of 1844 had been violated. Support came to him from similarly minded Democrats. The manner in which the death chamber of Governor Shunk had been entered by the politicians disgusted a number of the voters. In his tour of the state Johnston had made many friends. He argued the tariff question closely and consequently secured the normal Democratic counties of Schuyl-kill, an iron- and coal-producing area, and of Washington, a wool-growing region. The fact that the Native Americans did not have an independent state ticket assured him of their support. The Free Soil Democrats did not have a state ticket and his views on the Wilmot Proviso

---

[1] *Senate Journal,* 1849, vol. ii, p. 347.
[2] *Pennsylvania Telegraph,* July 11, October 31, 1848.

were acceptable to them. In Wilmot's district, although he received a minority of the votes cast, yet he secured 1,250 more votes than did the Whig candidate for Congress. Since the majority of Johnston was so small, any and all of these elements were decisive factors.

The election of Johnston, their first governor, highly elated the Whigs, for it also presaged the election of Taylor in November.[1] For the first time, the election for President was to occur on the same day in all parts of the Union. It had become quite clear that New York and Pennsylvania would determine the election. The Whigs were certain that they would carry the former because of the wide breach in the Democracy of the state. Their efforts were consequently concentrated on Pennsylvania, where both parties more systematically used the customary campaign methods.[2] The result of the efforts to obtain a full vote was the polling of the largest vote hitherto cast. Taylor secured a plurality of 13,500 over Cass, and a majority over Cass and Van Buren of 2,250 in a total vote of over 368,000.[3]

The reason for their defeat, said the chairman of the Democratic state central committee, was due to "Taylorism, and 'nothing else.' This is Jacksonism and Harrisonism over again."[4] The recession from high prices for agricultural products, which had prevailed during the past two years because of the failure of crops in Europe and

[1] Nathan Sargent, October 12, 1848, to J. R. Chandler, "Only think of a *WHIG* governor of Pa.! Hurrah! Hurrah!! Hurrah!!!" Society Collection, Hist. Soc. of Penna.

[2] E. W. Hutter, chairman of the Democratic state central committee, on October 31, 1848, wrote Buchanan that the Whigs had an "ocean of money." Their committees of visitation were actively engaged in house to house canvasses; Buchanan Mss.

[3] *Smull's Legislative Hand-Book*, 1919, p. 715, gives the official returns as Taylor 185,513; Cass 171,976; Van Buren 11,263.

[4] E. W. Hutter, November 8, 1848, to Buchanan; Buchanan Mss.

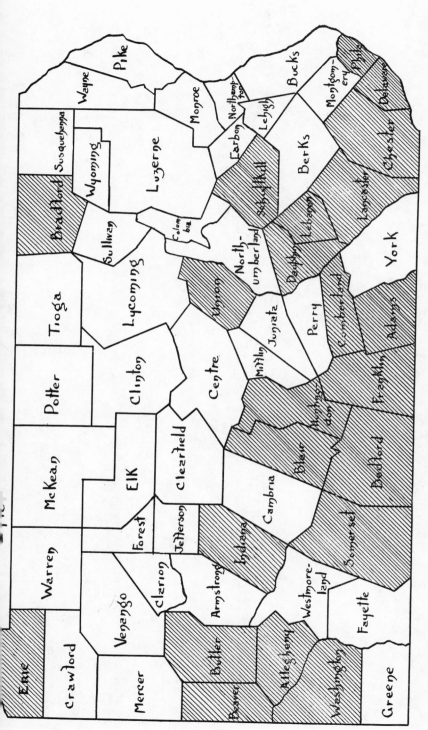

PRESIDENTIAL ELECTION OF 1848

because of the repeal of the British Corn Laws, helped the Whigs in their argument on the tariff. One of the Democratic leaders in the mining region attributed the result of the election " to gunpowder and the Tariff! which of these had the greatest influence—it will be hard to ascertain." According to him, the Democrats in the coal and iron districts could not be controlled. " They said it was bread and they would not stand to principle." [1]

[1] H. B. Wright, November 13, 1848, to Buchanan; also J. W. Forney to Buchanan, November 11, 1848; Buchanan Mss.

CHAPTER V

The Slavery Question in State Politics

1849-1851.

UPON the assembling of the state legislature in 1849, the Whigs without any trouble secured control of the senate. In the house the Democrats had exactly one half of the one hundred members, the Whigs forty-five and the Native Americans five. On the first ballot for speaker none of the Native Americans voted for the Whig candidate, but on the second ballot two did so. Twenty-one ballots were cast without an election. On January 5 one of the Native Americans announced that if three votes would break the deadlock, he with two other Native Americans would change their vote in order to prevent a further waste of time. On the next ballot William F. Packer, a Democrat, was elected with fifty-two votes.[1] By casting their votes as a unit, the Democrats elected the other officers of the house.

On joint ballot, however, the Whigs and Native Americans had a majority, and were able on the third ballot to elect James Cooper to the United States Senate. Cooper had been appointed attorney-general by the governor, but an estrangement had been developing. It was increased by the refusal of the governor to favor any of the candidates for Senator.[2] The Whigs because of the failure of the

---

[1] *Public Ledger,* January 2, 3, 4, 5, 6, 1849.

[2] *House Journal,* 1849, vol. ii, p. 74; *Public Ledger,* January 11, 1849; McClure, *Old Time Notes,* vol. i, p. 180.

Native Americans to cooperate lost a number of the state offices. For state treasurer they nominated a member of the legislature and secured his election by his own vote, an action which they endorsed at a subsequent caucus of their party.[1]

It was assumed that Pennsylvania would be represented in the cabinet of President Taylor, inasmuch as it had been influential in securing his nomination and election. The same problem confronted Taylor that had worried Harrison. The two branches of his supporters in the state made a choice difficult.[2] The Whig Congressmen from Pennsylvania, willing to aid Taylor with unsought advice, at a caucus recommended Andrew Stewart for the Treasury Department.[3] Stewart came from western Pennsylvania and was known to be in favor of sweeping changes in the tariff and in the sub-treasury system. His views on these questions made him acceptable to the northern but unacceptable to the southern supporters of Taylor. As a result, Stewart was rejected and William M. Meredith, a Philadelphia lawyer, was given the portfolio.

The distribution of the federal patronage caused trouble, inasmuch as both Governor Johnston and Senator Cooper were striving to control the Whig party in the state. The governor requested the national leaders to allow no nominations in Pennsylvania to be made which were hostile to him, as this would disrupt the party.[4] In compliance with

[1] *House Journal*, 1849, vol. ii, p. 165; *Public Ledger*, January 16, 17, 1849.

[2] Charles B. Penrose, January 2, 1849, and John M. Kennedy, November 26, 1848, to J. J. Crittenden; Crittenden Papers, Lib. of Cong. Wm. D. Lewis, December 18, 1848, and E. C. Reigart, February 19, 1849, to John M. Clayton; Clayton Papers, Lib. of Cong.

[3] *Public Ledger*, January 22, 24, 25, 26, 1849.

[4] Wm. F. Johnston, January 17, 1849, to J. J. Crittenden; Crittenden Papers, Lib. of Cong.

his request, William D. Lewis was appointed collector of the port of Philadelphia, one of the most remunerative offices within the state. The collector had great power in appointing subordinates. The appointment of Lewis was declared to be unfair to the "Working Whigs."[1] It indicated clearly that the national administration was favoring Johnston rather than Cooper. The former was supported by the free-soil element in the party and, consequently, those who opposed this policy turned to Cooper. Cooper was dissatisfied with the neglect of his wing of the Whig party and with the refusal of Lewis to appoint his followers to subordinate positions in the customs house. Despite the strenuous opposition of Cooper, confirmation of the appointment of Lewis was secured, but not until September 18, 1850.[2]

The governor and the senate of the legislature were Whig, but the house was under the control of the Democrats. It was, therefore, impossible for the Whigs to adopt any distinctively Whig measures. Acting upon the suggestion of the governor, a sinking fund for the state debt was established, but as a non-partisan measure.[3] There was consequently nothing in the acts of the administration which could be used as an issue.

The Democrats were the first to hold their state convention, which assembled on July 4 at Pittsburgh and placed John A. Gamble in nomination for the canal commissionership.[4] The Whigs met at Harrisburg on August 16 and

[1] *Daily News,* June 23, July 3, 1849.

[2] *Senate Executive Journal,* vol. viii, p. 233. The vote on confirmation was 36 to 7. Cooper was the only Whig who voted against it.

[3] Message of January 6, 1849; *Pennsylvania Archives,* series iv, vol. vii, p. 322.

[4] *Daily Commercial Journal,* July 6, 7, 1849.

nominated Henry M. Fuller.[1] The Democrats at their convention rejected the national plank of 1848 on the slavery question and now took a position virtually the same as that of the Whigs. The Native Americans did not hold a state convention, but in some of the counties they endorsed Kimber Cleaver.[2] Unless the Whigs could secure the support of the Native Americans, they could not elect the canal commissioner nor the county officials in Philadelphia. The Native Americans were dissatisfied with the distribution of the patronage, as many of them felt that only the friends of Congressman Levin were favored.[3] Furthermore, as a body they felt that they had been slighted. Their endorsement of Taylor had come first in point of time, and they felt that in the distribution of the federal patronage they in turn should have come first.

The Whigs were ready to continue the alliance with the Native Americans in Philadelphia county but they were opposed to abandoning their own organization and forming the " Taylor Republican Association." [4] The " Rough and Ready City and County Convention," meeting in the latter part of August and in the beginning of September, made nominations for the county offices.[5] In this joint organization of the Whigs and Native Americans, the anti-Levin Native Americans refused to participate and named their own candidates.[6] About half of these candidates were endorsed by the joint organization. When the elections

[1] *Pennsylvania Inquirer,* August 18, 1849.

[2] *Public Ledger,* September 26, 1849.

[3] A. D Chaloner, August 18, 1849, to J. M. Clayton; Clayton Papers, Lib. of Cong.

[4] *Daily News,* July 6, 10, 11, 24, 1849.

[5] *Pennsylvania Inquirer,* August 24, September 6, 11, 12, 15, 1849.

[6] *Public Ledger,* September 5, 1849.

were held, those candidates who had been endorsed by
both bodies were elected. The candidate of the exclusive
Native Americans for county auditor showed unusual
strength and was elected. The returns clearly indicated
that the so-called " Rough and Ready " party had more supporters than the exclusive Native American, which polled an
average of only 2,000 votes but which had nevertheless decided the election. This led the Whigs to determine
that in the future they would have an exclusively Whig
ticket.[1] In Philadelphia city, ordinarily a Whig stronghold, a combination of dissatisfied Whigs, Democrats, and
Native Americans elected Joel Jones mayor on the " Independent People's Ticket." [2]

Throughout the state the election was remarkable for the
apathy displayed and for the lack of partisan zeal.[3] When
the President made a tour of the state, an endeavor was
made to convert it into a Whig procession and to impress
upon him the need of protection to the industries of the
state. The President, however, refused to consider his
tour as anything but non-partisan in nature.[4] During the
campaign the Whigs reiterated the claim that they were the
free-soil party but asserted that need for the Wilmot Proviso was " now a thing of the past : it has ceased to be necessary, and dies with the exigency that created it." [5] They
generally kept this issue in the background and confined their

---

[1] *Daily News*, October 13, 1849. Compare the following returns for
the influence of the Native American vote: for treasurer—Wagner
(Rough and Ready; Native) 21,265; Thomas (Dem.) 19,514; for
register—Vinyard (Rough and Ready) 18,446; Bunton (Dem.) 19,735;
Bonsall (Nat. Am.) 2,828.

[2] *Public Ledger*, September 4, 11, 25, October 1, 6, 12, 1849.

[3] *Ibid.*, October 8, 1849.

[4] *Ibid.*, August 11-27, 1849.

[5] *Daily News*, May 24; *Miners' Journal*, April 28, 1849.

discussions to the tariff. The reference by the *Washington Union* to the " periodical ' pig iron ' clamor raised by the iron masters of Pennsylvania " was resented.[1] The failure of the tariff of 1846 to give protection to industry when prices were low was attributed to its *ad valorem* schedule and was declared to be reason for changing to specific rates.[2] That the method of levying the duties was causing unemployment was shown by the fact that large orders for railroad iron were being placed with British firms.[3] Because of the low prices which were prevailing, it was reported, the Hudson River Railroad had found it profitable to pay Peter Cooper of Trenton, New Jersey, $54,000 for the cancellation of a contract made several years previously.[4] Henry M. Fuller, Whig candidate for canal commissioner, claimed on good authority that in the period 1842 to 1846 seventy-five iron furnaces had been erected west of the mountains in Pennsylvania, but from 1846 to 1849 only three had been erected.[5] In an address to the Whig young men of Pennsylvania, it was asserted that less protection was required now because of the protection which had been previously given, and that if the policy of protection were continued, less and less would be required until the country ultimately could without danger be placed on a tariff revenue basis.[6] The fate of the tariff was said to depend on Pennsylvania.[7]

The Democrats tried, as much as possible, to avoid the

---

[1] *Miners' Journal*, September 29, 1849.

[2] *Daily News*, June 28, 1849.

[3] *Daily Commercial Journal*, April 13, 1849.

[4] *Daily News*, August 28, 1849.

[5] *Pennsylvania Inquirer*, September 4, 1849.

[6] *Ibid.*, August 31, 1849.

[7] *Miners' Journal*, September 22, 1849.

tariff question.[1]   They appealed to the workingman by asserting that the Ten Hour Law of March 28, 1848, which
declared ten hours of labor constituted a legal day's work
in the textile mills of the state, was an exclusively Democratic measure.   They raised this issue particularly in Allegheny county where the year before there had been rioting
over the enforcement of the law.   In this county the Whig
press attacked the law because of its inequitable operation
even within the state, and because of its consequent manifest unfairness to the local capitalist.[2]   The Whig press was
compelled by the Democrats to take strong ground against
the law, and asserted that a man could not possibly do as
much work in ten as he could in twelve hours.   The agri-
culturists were appealed to by the statement that the law
in order to be equitable would have to apply to them too.[3]
In the election the county was retained by the Whigs, but
the Democrats succeeded in electing one of the four as-
semblymen.[4]

The state election resulted in the choice of a Democratic
canal commissioner.[5]   The legislature came fully under the
control of the Democrats, who now had seventeen of the
thirty-three senators, and fifty-nine of the one hundred representatives.[6]   This control was of importance as it was
the duty of this legislature to reapportion the state.   The
free-soil Whigs claimed that they had been defeated " not

[1] *Pittsburgh Gazette*, September 6, 1849, for the proceedings of the
Allegheny county Democratic convention.

[2] *Daily Commercial Journal*, January-February, 1849.

[3] *Pittsburgh Gazette*, July 24, 25, 1849.   Attacks on the law were continued after the election; *ibid.*, November 22, 1849; February 27, 1850.

[4] *Daily Commercial Journal*, October 11, 16, 1849.

[5] Official returns in *Public Ledger*, October 25, 1849.

[6] *Pennsylvania Inquirer*, October 19, 1849.

through weakness, but through a reprehensible indifference." [1]   The supporters of Senator Cooper, on the other hand, asserted that the overthrow was due to appointing " Parlor Politicians " and not " Working Whigs " to office.[2] The election illustrated, just as did the election of 1847, the fact that the Democrats due to their superior organization could wrest the control of the state away from the Whigs in the year following a disastrous defeat. Although the Democrats had a majority in both houses of the legislature, yet they were not to control the organization of the senate. On the seventh ballot for speaker of the senate, the Whigs voted for Valentine Best, a Democrat who had not attended his party caucus. On the following ballot he voted for himself and was elected. The Whigs received their reward in obtaining the chief senate offices.[3]

It was with an endeavor to influence the new Congress that an iron masters' convention was held at Pittsburgh in November, 1849. The *ad valorem* duties of the tariff of 1846, with the sliding scale of low rates for declared high values, were attacked on the ground that they made fraud possible. The convention asked for a " duty of $10 per ton on Pig Iron, and $20 per ton on common bar, and a corresponding increase on all other iron and manufactories of iron, in proportion to cost of make." The largest number of the delegates came from western Pennsylvania, but there were representatives present from other states. The convention was not distinctively Whig, and yet Colonel McCandless, a leading Democrat of western Pennsylvania, refused to address the convention, claiming that his views

[1] *Pittsburgh Gazette*, October 17, 1849.

[2] *Daily News*, October 16, 1849.

[3] *Public Ledger*, January 2, 3, 5, 1850; McClure, *Old Time Notes,* vol. i, p. 185.

on the subject of protection were different from those of the great majority of the delegates in the convention.[1]

The control of the Thirty-first Congress was in doubt.[2] The struggle over the election of the Speaker of the House indicated that the chief issue before Congress would be the question of the extension of the slave area, as involved in the admission of California as a state and in the erection of new territories. After many unsuccessful ballots the House chose Howell Cobb. Many of the Pennsylvania Whigs considered him the least objectionable of the southern Democrats because he had voted to add the anti-slavery provisions of the Northwest Ordinance of 1787 to the Oregon Bill. One free-soil Whig paper declared,

Oregon free, and California once admitted as a free State, the Free Soiler will have nothing left to contend for, and the Wilmot Proviso, having performed its office, ceases to be an issue before the country. . . . We lose nothing as friends of freedom in the new territories by the election of Mr. Cobb to the Speakership.[3]

In his message of January 6, 1849, Governor Johnston urged the legislature to adopt resolutions opposing the further extension of slavery The senate by a vote of 30 to 2 passed such resolutions, on which, however, the house took no action.[4] In February, 1850, the legislatures of

[1] *Public Ledger*, November 26, 27, December 20, 22; *Pittsburgh Gazette*, November 22, 23, 24, 1849.

[2] All the states did not hold their congressional elections in 1848. Only 138 of the 231 Congressmen were chosen in that year. The Whigs, therefore, lost the advantage which would have come to them from having the elections in the same year as the successful presidential election.

[3] *Daily Commercial Journal*, December 24, 1849.

[4] *Senate Journal*, 1849, vol. i, p. 375; *House Journal*, 1849, vol. i, pp. 51, 669.

Georgia and Virginia passed resolutions asserting that the
northern states in not aiding in the rendition of fugitive
slaves were not living up to the compromises of the Constitution.   They denied that Congress had the power to interfere with slavery in the District of Columbia or in the
new territories.   In a strong message to the legislature the
governor vigorously denied that Pennsylvania had not been
living up to the compromises of the Constitution.   That
Pennsylvania had always been opposed to the extension of
slavery was shown to be true.   Furthermore, he claimed
that although the interests of Pennsylvania had often been
injured by slavery, nevertheless Pennsylvania had remained
faithful to the compromises.[1]   This message offended the
Democrats so deeply that the house refused to order its
printing for distribution.[2]   In April the house by a strict
party vote decided to repeal the act of March 3, 1847, which
refused the use of the state jails for the detention of fugitive slaves.   The senate, however, took no action on the
bill.[3]   This act for the first time was being considered as a
party issue.

The message of the President on the admission of California was declared by the Whigs to meet with general approval in the North, but not so his views on the formation
of the new territories.   This region, it was said, had been
declared by Mexico in 1829 to be free soil, and consequently
slavery could be introduced only by a positive act of Congress or of the states to be erected there.   The policy of
" non-intervention " would keep the area free, and therefore there was no longer need to agitate for the Wilmot
Proviso.[4]   This attitude was more clearly reflected in the

[1] *House Journal,* 1850, vol. ii, pp. 419 *et seq.*

[2] *Ibid.,* vol. i, p. 727.

[3] *Ibid.,* vol. i, pp. 495, 845; *Senate Journal,* 1850, vol. i, 916.

[4] *Pittsburgh Gazette,* January 28, 1850.

Pennsylvania house of representatives, where efforts were made to repeal the resolutions of 1847 in favor of the Wilmot Proviso.[1] It was stated that if this policy should be adopted, the South would make concessions on the tariff, internal improvements, and land distribution.[2]

The attitude of the orthodox Democracy on the slavery issue was reflected in a mass meeting in Philadelphia on February 22, 1850. The meeting, sponsored by the supporters of James Buchanan, deprecated all disunion talk and agitation, and abandoned the " no extension of slavery " plank of the state convention of 1849. It resolved that " the people of the separate territories, when politically organized, . . . have then exclusively the right to prohibit or allow slavery in such territories." The Wilmot Proviso was declared to be

the same ancient, aristocratic, pernicious and pestilent political heresy, (ever repudiated and denounced by· the Democratic party of the Union), which seeks by means of an implication of power of Congress, gradually to undermine State sovereignty, destroy legislation in the respective States, consolidate the Union, and establish on the ruins of States Rights, a central sovereignty, easily controlled or managed by the few at the expense of the many.[3]

The other resolutions recommended the passage of a fugitive slave law and endeavored to assuage the South which was talking of disunion.

This position was combatted by the free-soil Democrats at a mass meeting at Philadelphia on March 13, 1850. They decried the abandoning of the party position of 1849, which they declared was the policy not only of the state

[1] *Public Ledger*, January 24, 1850.

[2] *Ibid.*, February 19, 1850.

[3] *Ibid.*, February 23, 1850.

Democracy but also of the state. John M. Read, the principal speaker, forcefully emphasized this fact. Free soil
was required for free labor, he contended, as was proven
by the absence of immigration to the South.[1]

These mass meetings were held chiefly as replies to the
call for the Nashville convention and the subsequent disunion discussion. The Whig journals of the state, relying
on the coolness and firmness of the President, refused to
become excited over the disunion agitation. One of them
said, " The chivalry of the South have dissolved the Union
any day these three months, yet it stands firm and we cannot, for the soul of us, feel it is in any more danger to-day
than it was yesterday." [2] Another of the journals claimed
that the Nashville convention, called by a " Southern junto,
who are desirous of dissolving the Union, unless they can
force the North into a cowardly compliance with their un-
righteous and unjust demands, is likely to prove a complete
failure." [3] When the convention adjourned without accomplishing anything, F. J. Grund, the Washington correspondent of the independent *Public Ledger,* called it

humbug No. 3. The first humbug was the Wilmot Proviso;
the second humbug was Col. Jeff. Davis' Proviso, (the Missouri
Compromise line, with a positive recognition of slavery south
of it), and the third is the attempt of a handful of enthusiasts
in favor of Niggerdom to present an ultimatum to the Congress
of the United States! [4]

In the meantime, the question of the admission of Cali-

[1] *Public Ledger,* March 14, 1450; Read's speech in full in *ibid.,* April
4, 1850.

[2] *Daily Commercial Journal,* March 8, 1850.

[3] *Pittsburgh Gazette,* April 5, 1850.

[4] June 12, 1850. Proceedings of the Nashville Convention in *ibid.,*
June 4-14, 1850.

fornia and the organization of the new territories was closely followed by the public as it was discussed in Congress. The Whigs of Pennsylvania resented the fact that these two questions had been joined. One of them put it, " The free State of California, with as just a right of admission as any State in the Union, is to be made the pack horse to carry slavery into the new territories, provided nature and their present inhabitants will let it go there." [1] It was again mildly asserted that the Whigs would have to insist on the Wilmot Proviso or some other compromise.[2] The continued agitation of the South Carolina leaders led one editor wearily to express the hope that there might be found a way to let her " slip quietly and peacefully out of the Union. Since the days of her Revolutionary deeds, she has been but a pest and a nuisance; and the Union could well spare her, and Texas to boot." [3] The passage of the series of bills in September was considered to settle the question of the extension of slavery in the negative.[4]

The Whigs of Pennsylvania were from the opening day of Congress eagerly watching the apparently interminable struggle over the slavery question in the hope that it would soon be ended so that the tariff might receive some attention. Constantly they pointed out the inadequacy of the existing rates, and claimed that idle mills and workingmen rioting because of reduced wages were the result of the lack of protection to industry.[5] This state of affairs was

[1] *Pittsburgh Gazette*, April 22, 1850.

[2] *Daily News*, May 27, 1850.

[3] *Daily Commercial Journal*, August 8, 1850.

[4] *Ibid.*, September 14, 1850.

[5] *Ibid.*, March 9; *Pittsburgh Gazette*, May 3; *Daily News*, May 3, 1850. The *Public Ledger*, May 18, 1850, said that of the 121 live furnaces in western Pennsylvania, with a total capacity of 96,600 tons per annum, only 59 with a capacity of 47,200 tons per annum were in blast.

attributed not so much to the low rates as to the *ad valorem* principle on which they were based.[1] Merchants, farmers, and the manufacturing class all felt the absence of protection. Overproduction, if it existed, as the Democrats claimed it did, existed according to the Whigs only in the British mills and certainly not in the American.[2] As the session dragged on, the hope of the Whigs in Pennsylvania that the tariff would be favorably altered changed to disgust that nothing was being done. An editor of western Pennsylvania thus voiced his disapproval at the continued neglect,

While our leading statesmen are willing to risk their reputation, for wisdom and consistency, by concocting unpalatable, if not disreputable, compromises, because a few dissatisfied spirits have blustered about disunion, they seem to care nothing for the desires and demands and necessities of hundreds of thousands of toiling freemen—which the present policy is fast impoverishing. . . . Is it not time for this struggle to cease, and for some useful legislation to be entered upon?[3]

The hope that the tariff might be considered at this session of Congress was crushed when the southern Whigs joined the Democrats in voting to postpone the question of

[1] *Pittsburgh Gazette,* April 9; *Daily News,* April 17, 1850.

[2] *Daily Commercial Journal,* August 7, 1850.

[3] *Pittsburgh Gazette,* May 13, 1850. On May 31, 1850, Congressman Moses Hampton, of the Allegheny district, tendered his resignation. In his letter to the Whig county convention, he said, " But we do not admit that the slave holding states are the only sufferers by a want of proper legislation for the protection of property, for I will venture to say, that the State of Pennsylvania alone has lost more in a pecuniary point of view, within the last four years, by the repeal of the tariff of 1842, than the value of all the slaves that have ever escaped from all the slave holding States, since the formation of the Union." *Daily Commercial Journal,* June 6, 1850.

amending the tariff until after the settlement of the slavery issue.[1]

The state parties, in the meantime, were making preparations for the elections of that year. The Democratic state convention met at Williamsport on May 29, 1850, and on the twenty-sixth ballot nominated W. T. Morrison for canal commissioner.[2] Prior to the assembling of the Whig state convention on June 19, the county conventions of the Whigs called for changes in the existing tariff and for no further extension of slavery.[3] Joshua Dungan was nominated by the Whigs for canal commissioner. Congress had as yet taken no final action on any of the measures before it. The convention urged speedy action on the tariff and submitted the following resolution,

The Whigs of Pennsylvania desire to present the question to the present Congress, whether their action on the subject is to be controlled by the wishes of the British Minister, or the voice of the Northern freemen of the American Union.

The Whigs declared that they were " opposed as they have ever been, to the extension of slavery," and that they stood " neither on the Baltimore Platform nor the Nash-

---

[1] *Public Ledger,* August 19, 1850; Toombs was reported to have said privately that the " reason for his vote was the opposition of some of the leading Whigs to the settlement of the slavery question on equitable terms."

[2] *Ibid.,* May 31, June 3, 1850. At this convention Cameron was accused of attempting to bribe delegates. Pamphlet, *Report of the Proceedings of the Williamsport Convention.*

[3] The York county resolutions commended the governor for his sturdy defense of the state against the attacks in the Georgia and Virginia resolutions, and they joined the Franklin county Whigs in condemning the lower house of the legislature for refusing to publish his message. This refusal was " only another indication of the willingness of that party in the North to submit to the requisitions of their Southern allies." *Pittsburgh Gazette,* June 3, 1850.

ville Platform, nor any other local or temporary structure, but . . . . on the great structure of the Constitution." [1] Their position on the slavery question was now diametrically opposed to the position of the Democrats, who in their state convention had rejected their state resolution of the year before and had endorsed the national plank of 1848.

The state election attracted little attention, as the session of Congress had been so long that only a short period of time intervened between adjournment and election day. The fact that the acts of Congress were compromises made it impossible to use them in the campaign. The rupture in Wilmot's district, which had developed in 1848 over the endorsement of Van Buren, was healed by the withdrawal both of Wilmot and of his rival and the subsequent nomination of Galusha A. Grow, who was Wilmot's law partner and had been adopted as a compromise candidate at his insistence. The views of Grow on the slavery question were as radical as those of Wilmot.[2] The majority of the Whig candidates for Congress had free-soil proclivities;[3] but the Whig state central committee in discussing the issues of the election did not introduce the slavery question. The election was declared to be of great importance because the new legislature would choose a federal Senator and reapportion the state. Efforts should be made to secure the Congressmen for the Whigs since the tariff needed revision and since the Democrats, although business was depressed, were opposing any alteration in the tariff schedule on the ground that it would be inexpedient to make changes.[4]

[1] *Public Ledger*, June 20, 21, 1850.

[2] *Ibid.*, October 8, 1850. Grow acknowledged "the constitutional power of Congress to prohibit by positive law, the extension of slavery into the territories of the nation" and recognized "the necessity for the exercise of this power." DuBois and Mathews, *Galusha A. Grow*, pp. 67, *et seq.*

[3] List of the candidates in *Public Ledger*, October 8, 1850.

[4] *Daily Commercial Journal*, September 16, 1850.

Before election day, but after the death of President Taylor, the " Rough and Ready County Convention" of Philadelphia converted itself into the " Whig County Convention," an act which clearly illustrated the recession of the Native American movement.[1] In the first congressional district the Whigs threw their influence to Levin, the Native American candidate, who had maintained considerable strength in this district. A faction of the Whigs, led by Senator Cooper and Josiah Randall, were opposing the leadership of the party by the governor. This faction nominated a Whig candidate for Congress in the first district, who diverted votes from Levin and secured the election of the Democratic candidate.[2] The Native Americans in the main supported the Whig nominees, but an independent faction polled about 250 votes.[3] Despite this opposition the Whigs as usual secured most of the offices in Philadelphia city and county.[4]

[1] *Daily News*, August 15, 1850.

[2] Wm. D. Lewis, September 21, 1850, James E. Harvey, October 14, 1850, to Thomas Corwin; Corwin Papers, Lib. of Cong. *Public Ledger,* October 1, 12, 1850.

[3] *Daily News,* October 12, 1850. Early in 1850, there occurred a new outbreak of anti-Catholicism, but this time in Pittsburgh. A certain man, by the name of Barker, was placed in jail as the result of his vehement anti-Catholic street preaching. This detention was considered to be persecution, with the result that Barker was nominated for mayor as the " Anti-Catholic and People's Candidate." Largely through the votes of the Whigs he defeated both his Whig and Democratic opponents. After being pardoned by Governor Johnston and after being released from jail, he served his term as mayor. *Pittsburgh Gazette,* January 9, 10; *Daily Commercial Journal,* January 11, 1850.

[4] Horn R. Kneass, Democrat, was returned as elected district-attorney of the county of Philadelphia. His opponent, Wm. B. Reed, appealed to the courts. The court decided that Reed had been duly elected; 2 *Pars. Eq. Cas.* 553. Judges Wm. D. Kelley and King, Democrats, as the result of this decision were rejected by their party, but Campbell, who dissented, the following year received a nomination to the

The election for state officers showed a Democratic majority of about 13,500.[1] The Whigs secured only nine of the twenty-four Congressmen, and controlled neither of the two houses of the legislature. Consequently, a Democratic Senator, Richard Brodhead, was chosen to represent the state at Washington.[2] The constitutional amendment to make the judges of the supreme court of the state elective by the people was adopted by a large majority.[3] In contrasting this election with the one of 1848, the large decrease in the number of votes cast is at once noticeable. The loss to both parties was great but was much greater for the Whigs, who were unable to hold the voters who had been attracted in 1848 by the candidacy of General Taylor.

As previously mentioned, the distribution of the federal patronage in Pennsylvania caused a division in the Whig ranks. Senator Cooper, who was dissatisfied with the reception of his suggestions to William D. Lewis about men to be appointed to subordinate positions in the customs house, attempted to block the confirmation of Lewis' nomination to the collectorship of the port of Philadelphia. The appointment had barely been made, when charges of fraud were presented against Lewis.[4] Governor Johnston, a

supreme court of the state. The following year Kelley was nominated by the Whigs to be President Judge of the county. Despite the bitter attacks of the Democrats and of a few Native Americans, he was easily elected. *Public Ledger*, October 11, 1851. Subsequently Kelley changed from a free-trader to a high protectionist.

[1] *Public Ledger*, October 24, 1850.

[2] *Ibid.*, January 2, 15, 1851.

[3] *House Journal*, 1851, vol i, p. 493; the vote for the amendment was 144,594, against it 71,995.

[4] Pamphlet by Wm. D. Lewis, *A brief Account of the Efforts of Senator Cooper . . . . to prevent the Confirmation of Wm. D. Lewis;* also, *Preliminary Reply, of Mr. Levin to Senator Cooper;* various letters in the Corwin Papers, Lib. of Cong.

supporter of Lewis, strongly opposed the efforts which were being made to secure his removal, which was being advocated, he felt, " for no other reason than the gratification of a few gentlemen who have private griefs against the present incumbents." [1] The result of the charges was an official investigation, which failed to establish any guilt on the part of Lewis.[2] The outcome of the investigation was that the state administration, even though it had strong free-soil tendencies, rather than the supporters of Senator Cooper would receive the aid of the national administration in controlling the state party Randall, one of Cooper's chief co-workers, sadly acknowledged defeat as follows,

If the administration continue to give the Free Soil party of Pennsylvania their support and patronage, time will develop what course we shall take, whether we shall raise the standard of opposition or retire and ground our arms—but in no event could we unite with Seward, Clayton, Johnston & Co. Respect to ourselves—to you—and our other friends—and the principles which you and we have so triumphantly maintained would forbid so unholy a combination.[3]

Johnston, on the other hand, had been waiting for the decision of the administration before deciding on his course of action. It was not until after Corwin's letter of April 16 exonerating Lewis had been published that he announced his intention to stand for reelection as the Whig candidate. Had he refused to be the Whig candidate, his refusal

[1] Wm. F. Johnston, April 11, 1851, to Millard Fillmore; copy in the Corwin Papers, Lib. of Cong.

[2] Letter of Thomas Corwin, Secretary of the Treasury, in the *Public Ledger*, April 18, 1851.

[3] Josiah Randall, April 30, 1851, to Webster; Webster Papers, Lib. of Cong.

would have meant the shortening of the life of the Whig party within the state.

When the Whig state convention met at Lancaster on June 24, it unanimously nominated Johnston for reelection on the first ballot.. John Strohm, whose vote in the senate in 1838 had been instrumental in ending the Buckshot War by securing the recognition of the Hopkins house, was selected as the party candidate for canal commissioner. The convention also selected candidates for the state supreme court, one of whom was Richard Coulter, a member of the existing bench. Coulter had been proposed to but not accepted by the Democratic convention to nominate judicial candidates. The resolutions, which were adopted by a vote of 92 to 27, clearly indicated that the Whig party was under the control of the free-soil element. The resolutions advocated a thoroughgoing revision of the tariff. The convention refused to endorse the recent compromises of Congress and merely " Resolved, that the adjustment measures of the last Congress shall be faithfully observed and respected by the Whigs." The twenty-seven members voting in the negative wished to endorse the compromises in unmistakably strong language. Some members of the convention, refusing to vote on the resolutions, opposed them because of their free-soil expressions. One of them, ex-Congressman Ogle, said that he was " against slavery in any shape, and especially against that slavery which three thousand abolitionists in Pennsylvania would establish in regard to politics and politicians in the State!" The convention indicated that its choice for the next presidential candidate was General Winfield Scott. In a speech immediately following his nomination, Governor Johnston, in outlining his views on the slavery question, said that he would not have voted for either the Texas Boundary Bill or the Fugitive Slave Bill but, since they were the law of the land, these two measures would have to be respected. He, however, insisted that they needed amendment.[1]

The Democrats held two conventions, the one to nominate the usual state officers and the other to select candidates for the supreme court. The first convention, which met at Reading on June 4, was completely under the control of the Buchanan forces. William Bigler was nominated for governor and Seth Clover for canal commissioner. Bigler was not a novice in state politics, having served two terms in the senate and having held a number of appointive offices. His career had been an upward struggle from obscurity and poverty to prominence and wealth. The early death of his father, caused by a fruitless effort to gain a livelihood from a wild tract in Mercer county, terminated his brief school career. He served an apprenticeship of three years on the *Centre Democrat* under his brother John, who later was chosen the first governor of California in the same year his erstwhile apprentice was elected governor of Pennsylvania. Bigler after serving his apprenticeship borrowed money to purchase a second-hand press and half-worn type. With this equipment, in 1833, he moved to Clearfield county to establish the *Clearfield Democrat*, " as he used afterwards in a jocular spirit to characterize it, an eight-by-ten Jackson paper, to counteract the influence of a seven-by-nine Whig paper which had preceded him into that mountainous region." [2]   After a few years, he sold the paper, became interested in the lumber business, and soon was one of the largest producers of timber on the West Branch of the

[1] *Public Ledger*, June 25-30, 1851. Stevens' control of the Whig party in Lancaster county was weakened. His vote in 1850 had been smaller than in 1848. This year the county convention did not elect him a delegate to the state convention. *Pittsburgh Gazette*, June 19, 1851.

[2] Armor, *Lives of the Governors of Pennsylvania*, p. 414.

Susquehanna River. The acquisition of wealth did not diminish his ardor for the Democracy, nor was the nature of his business such as to influence him to favor a protective tariff. On the slavery question, his views had shifted with those of his party, and he was in full sympathy with the action of the convention.

The resolutions urged the repeal of the state statute of March 3, 1847, which forbade the use of the state jails for the detention of fugitive slaves. The compromise measures of 1850 were fully endorsed, but on the tariff question an ambiguous resolution was adopted.[1] On June 11 a different set of delegates assembled at Harrisburg to nominate candidates to the supreme court. Amongst the five nominees was James Campbell, of Philadelphia, who was chosen despite strenuous objections.[2] A group of leading Democratic lawyers of Philadelphia declared that he was mentally incapable of performing the duties of a justice of the state supreme court, that his endorsement at the Philadelphia county primary had been secured by fraud, and that he had been endorsed in large measure because he was an Irishman and a Catholic.[3]

In the campaign of this year the Whigs attempted to make the tariff the chief issue. Constantly they referred to the depressed condition of the iron industry. They could not ignore the question of the compromises, so they generally adopted the position which had been taken by Governor Johnston that the law must be obeyed as long as it remained on the statute books but that these measures ought to be amended.[4] In the meantime, Governor Johnston was

[1] *Public Ledger*, June 5, 6, 1851.

[2] *Ibid.*, June 12, 13, 1851.

[3] *Ibid.*, May 31, 1851.

[4] *Pittsburgh Gazette*, June 19, 1851; *Pennsylvania Inquirer*, August 22, 1851. In some of the counties, where the free-soil element was

withholding his signature to a bill repealing the sections of the act of March 3, 1847, which forbade the use of the state jails for the retention of captured fugitive slaves. The Democrats were trying to make his refusal to sign the bill the issue of the campaign.[1] The Wh gs showed that this act of March 3, 1847, had passed the legislature without a roll-call and had been signed by a Democratic governor. Amongst those in the senate when the bill had passed without objection was William Bigler, now the Democratic candidate for governor. With this reply the Whigs answered the criticisms of their opponents and continued to discuss the need of tariff reform and the value of the state sinking fund, which had been inaugurated by Johnston. The Whigs were making headway with their campaign arguments, when, on September 11, occurred the Christiana riot. This event completely changed the issue and put the Whigs on the defensive.

In order to understand properly the manner in which the Christiana riot influenced the election, it will be necessary to review the enforcement of the Fugitive Slave Law of

particularly strong, the attacks on slavery by the Whigs were severe. In Beaver county they resolved, " That on the subject of slavery we maintain the position we have always occupied, looking upon it as an institution at variance with religion, the rights of man, and civil liberty, as well as subversive of the best interests of those among whom it exists; and therefore we cannot help expressing our dissatisfaction with the provisions of the fugitive slave law." *Pittsburgh Gazette,* June 27, 1851.

[1] On May 5, 1851, Bigler wrote Buchanan, " What will Gov. Johnston do with the repealing section? If he signs it, the Liberty men in the West will not touch him but will bring a man of their own into the field. If he refuses to sign it, he cannot maintain h'mself with a certain class of Whigs. This is his dilemma. *Our course is to sustain the letter and spirit of the Compromise.* If Gov. J. refuses to sign the bill now in his hands, this will be the great issue." Buchanan Mss. See also the proceedings of a Democratic meeting at which Bigler stressed this point; *Public Ledger,* August 4, 22, 1851.

1850 within the state. The law had scarcely been enacted before an exodus of negroes to the north was noticed, even those who for years had lived in certain communities near the Mason and Dixon line left their old abodes.[1] One month after the passage of the act, on October 18, 1850, the first case before a federal court came up for decision in Philadelphia before Judges Grier and Kane, who determined that the alleged fugitive slave should be tried before the United States Circuit Court and not before the commissioner. The fugitive was ordered to be released on the technical ground that ownership was not legally established by the claimant, who had failed properly to authenticate the will under which he was executor and residuary legatee. The decision seemed to indicate that the law would be strictly applied against the claimant.[2] Although the fugi-

[1] *Public Ledger*, September 25, October 2; *Pittsburgh Gazette*, September 24, 1850; *cf.* also Fred Landon, " Negro Migration to Canada," *Journal of Negro History*, January, 1920; Siebert, *Underground Railroad*, p. 249. A comparison of the census returns of 1850 and 1860 shows an increase in the negro population of the state, which is equaled by the increase in the neighborhood of Philadelphia. Around Pittsburgh and in the counties along the Maryland border, there was a marked decrease, which is balanced by the increase in the counties of the interior, particularly in those near Harrisburg.

[2] *Ex parte* Garnet, *Fed. Cases* 5243; *Public Ledger*, October 19, 1850. There had been an earlier case under the new law, which had resulted in the remanding of the negroes. Three negroes escaped from Virginia taking some horses to aid them. They were pursued by their owners and overtaken at Harrisburg. Since they could not be detained in the county jail as fugitive slaves, they were charged with larceny, and held on the order of a justice of the peace. On a writ of *habeas corpus* they were, on August 24, 1850, brought before the Dauphin county court. They were ordered to be released on the ground that the warrant of arrest did not state where the crime had been committed and that the ownership of the property alleged to have been stolen was not sufficiently averred. The court intimated that the negroes might be seized as escaped slaves. Commonwealth *v.* Wilson *et al.*, 1 *Phila. Rep.* 80. The suggestion of the court was adopted

tive in this case was freed, yet misunderstandings of the
decision prevailed. The doubt as to the fairness of procedure Judge Grier tried to remove by a public letter in
which he stated that under the law the alleged fugitive
slave was granted the same protection accorded a white
man who was threatened with extradition. For both men
the only question involved was one of identity.[1] While the
case had been in progress, threats of violence had been heard.
Judge Grier made it understood that he was determined to
carry the case through, even though it might be necessary
to call on the President for a thousand soldiers.[2]

At times, however, the apprehension of the fugitives was
prevented,[3] and opposition to the law was freely and openly
expressed, chiefly by the Whigs.[4] On November 18, 1850,

as the negroes were leaving the jail. Rioting followed during which
one of the slaves escaped. The owners, the other two slaves, and
several of the crowd were imprisoned for rioting and bound over for
an appearance at the next session of the Court of Quarter Sessions;
Public Ledger, August 25, 26, 27, 1850. On September 30, without any
excitement, the slaves were handed over to their owners under the
authority of the new law; *ibid.*, October 1, 1850. A verdict of "not
guilty" was returned in the case of the owners and assistants; Commonwealth *v.* Wm. Taylor *et al.*, 4 *Clark* (*Pa.*) 480.

[1] *Public Ledger*, October 28, 1850.

[2] *Ibid.*, October 19, 1850.

[3] The failure to capture a party of thirteen escaped negroes because
of the intervention of the citizens of Wilkes-Barre is noted; *Public
Ledger*, October 21, 1850.

[4] The *Pittsburgh Gazette,* October 20, 1850, held the law to be "mor-
ally void, although legally binding," and it resisted "not the constitutional requirement, but the unnecessary and degrading encroachment upon the rights and feelings of the people of the free States, in
enforcing its claims." Thaddeus Stevens, in a case before the United
States District Court, was reported to have urged citizens to aid
escaping slaves, to have called the law "hateful," and to have appealed
to the "higher law." For this speech he was taken to task by his
fellow counsel in the case, Wm. B. Reed; *Daily News*, October 24, 1850.
The *Daily News*, Senator Cooper's organ, upheld the law; October
23, 24, 1850.

Judge Kane of the United States District Court charged his grand jury to be on the watch for those who were obstructing the operation of the law. But, he cautioned them, " I would distinguish liberally, and I would have you to distinguish between mere extravagance of diction and the endeavor by threats or force to obstruct the execution of the laws of the country." [1]   Three days later a large Union meeting was held at Philadelphia, at which resolutions calling for the repeal of the act of March 3, 1847, and for hearty support of the compromises were adopted. This meeting, sponsored only by the Democrats and by the anti-Johnston Whigs, was of great service in the South in quieting the fear that the Fugitive Slave Law would not be enforced in Pennsylvania. [2]

The next case under the law was tried before Commissioner Ingraham at Philadelphia in December, 1850, and caused much unfavorable comment. An alleged fugitive slave, Adam Gibson, on insufficient testimony and after an imperfect hearing, was placed in the custody of the agents of the claimant to be conveyed to him in Maryland. When the negro was taken to his alleged owner, the reception of the negro was refused because he was not the runaway slave. Although many persons had been attracted to the trial of the negro, yet there had been no attempt made to block the proceedings by a rescue. On the return of the negro to Philadelphia, not only the commissioner but also the law received a vast amount of harsh criticism. [3]   In March, 1851, Price, the agent in the Gibson case, was sentenced by a state court to a term of imprisonment for eight

[1] *Public Ledger*, November 19, 1850.

[2] *Ibid.*, November 22, 1850.

[3] *Ibid.*, December 23, 24; even the *Daily News*, December 24, 1850, attacked the " new judge in Israel."

years in the Eastern Penitentary for the technical kidnaping of a child born in Pennsylvania, who had been spirited
away with its mother, an escaped slave. For being implicated in the same case, George Alberti received a ten years'
sentence.[1] The conviction and the sentencing of these two
men was used by the southern newspapers to prove to their
readers that the people of the North were unwilling to abide
by the recent compromises.[2]

After the conviction of Alberti and Price, Governor Johnston requested Governor Lowe of Maryland to extradite
J. S. Mitchel, the owner of the woman. This request was
refused.[3] In the meantime, attacks on the statute of March
3, 1847, continued, and urgent demands for its repeal were
made.[4] In a special message to the legislature Governor
Johnston defended the act and replied to the criticisms of
Governor Lowe. The dispute between Maryland and
Pennsylvania involved the question of the freedom of children born in a free state of a slave mother. The common
law, which Maryland followed, held that a child so born
was slave, while Pennsylvania by statute had declared that
the child was free. Those, who opposed the act of March
3, 1847, claimed that a great deal of misunderstanding
would be averted by its repeal. The agitation for the repeal of the act finally resulted in the passage of a bill to
accomplish this. The bill was passed just before the close

[1] Commonwealth v. Alberti et al., 2 Pars. Eq. Cas. 495; Public Ledger,
January 6, March 6, 1851. In 1850, in Cumberland county, a kidnapper
had been convicted under the act of 1847, the constitutionality of
which had been upheld, although it ran counter to the common law
principle of partus sequitur ventrem; 4 Clark (Pa.) 431.

[2] Public Ledger, September 9, 1851.

[3] Ibid., March 10, 1851; cf. message of Governor E. L. Lowe of Maryland on January 7, 1852, for his views on the trial of Alberti; Maryland Legislative Documents, 1852, pp. 33-40.

[4] Mass meeting of anti-Johnston Whigs, Philadelphia, February 27,
1851; Public Ledger, February 28, 1851.

of the legislative session, and Governor Johnston was withholding his signature, for which he was being attacked during the course of the campaign.

The chief criticism against the Fugitive Slave Law was
because of the creation of the special tribunals.[1] So intense
was the opposition to this feature of the law, particularly
after the hasty decision in the Gibson Case, that Judge
Kane of the United States District had the cases arising
within the next few months after that decision brought
from the commissioner before him on writs of *habeas
corpus.*[2] In all the cases, although there was always considerable excitement, there was no attempt at a rescue,
whether the alleged fugitive were remanded or set free.[3]

Then occurred the Christiana riot in Lancaster county on
September 11, 1851, which resulted in the death of Edward
Gorsuch, the owner of the alleged fugitives, and the wound-
ing of his son.[4] This portion of the state, lying close
to the Maryland border, was a refuge for fugitives. It
had also been the scene of several recent " kidnaping "
expeditions and feeling against the " slave-catchers " was
running high.[5] The riot was immediately seized upon by

[1] Message of Governor Johnston of January 8, 1851; *Public Ledger,*
January 9, 1851. This annual message has been omitted from the
Pennsylvania Archives.

[2] Summary of three cases in May, *The Fugitive Slave Law and its
Victims;* for other cases *cf. Public Ledger* January 25, 27, 28, February 7, 8, 10, March 8, 10, 11, 12, 13, 14, 1851.

[3] In addition to the references in the note above *cf. Public Ledger,*
December 17, 1850; February 14, March 14, April 24, July 3, 23,
August 19, 1851.

[4] Hensel, *The Christiana Riots and the Treason Trials of 1851; Public
Ledger,* September 12-18, 1851.

[5] Hensel, *op. cit.,* pp. 16, *et seq.; Public Ledger,* January 21, March 19,
1851. The people of the neighborhood in a meeting had resolved to
refuse to assist in enforcing the law and to aid all fugitives in escaping;
quoted from the *Lancaster Examiner* by the *Public Ledger,* September
18, 1851.

the Democrats as proof of their claim that the Whigs—for this was one of their strongholds—were encouraging resistance to the enforcement of the Fugitive Slave Law. The resistance had led to the murder of an individual relying on the law to recover his property.

On September 14 the leading Democrats of Philadelphia issued a call for a mass meeting to be held on the seventeenth to take action on the recent resistance to the laws and to prevent another outbreak. They also issued an open letter to the governor stating that the memorialists were "not aware that any military force has been sent to the seat of the insurrection, or that the civil authority has been strengthened by the adoption of any measures suited to the momentous crisis." The governor, who was in Philadelphia on the following day, issued a proclamation, previously prepared, offering a reward for the arrest of those guilty of the murder. In reply to the open letter, the governor denied that there was an insurrectionary movement in Lancaster county and said that he would not excite the public by marching troops into that county. Those guilty of the crime of murder and of resistance to the law would be punished. He asked for the cooperation of the memorialists, "as citizens of Pennsylvania, not only to see that the law is enforced, but to add to the confidence which we all feel in the judicial tribunals of the land, by abstaining from undue violence of language, and letting the law take its course." That evening the Whigs held a previously scheduled mass meeting, at which the governor defended his course in withholding his signature from the repealing bill. To the governor's letter and to his speech the Democrats rejoined,

The purpose of our communication has been entirely misconceived by you. The crime which had been perpetrated in our immediate neighborhood was treason, in preventing, by armed resistance, the enforcement of a law of the United States. Our purpose was to request your attention to this fact and not to censure the local police of a county, as you suppose.

They also accused the governor of tardiness in issuing his proclamation. The signers declared their belief that resistance to the law would again be attempted and that his letter would encourage this lawless design. " We understand it as a declaration of your opinion that there should be no change in the course of the State government, and that no public measures of State are required in order to prevent the recurrence of the late bloody outrage." [1] The Democrats relied exclusively on this riot in the closing days of the campaign for their election material. In addition to their correspondence with the governor, the Democrats made effective use of a letter from the Reverend Gorsuch, son of the murdered man, in which charges of neglect of duty were made against Governor Johnston.

Judge Kane of the United States District Court gave strength to the Democratic contention that treason had been committed when his charge to the grand jury on September 29 included a discussion of that crime. [2] With this crime the men, who had been arrested for being implicated in the riot, were charged. Although the trials did not come until after the election, nevertheless, the charge of the judge and the indictments were used by the Democrats as election material to prove the depravity of the Whigs. [3] The Whigs

[1] Correspondence in Hensel, *op. cit.*, pp. 145, *et seq.; Public Ledger,* September 15, 16, 17, 1851.

[2] Charge to the grand jury in 2 *Wall. Jr.* 134.

[3] For the trials *cf.* United States *v.* Hanway, 2 *Wall. Jr.* 139, in which the jury after an absence of twenty minutes returned a verdict of " not guilty" on the charge of treason. This was the leading case and the others were dismissed by writs of *nolle prosequi.* A certain indi-

vigorously denied that they were responsible for the riot and that they were a party of disorder. One of their papers put it:

The Whigs of Pennsylvania, with Governor Johnston at their head, are a Union loving, law abiding, and mob hating people and they hurl back with scorn, the base and contemptible innuendoes of their opponents. If ever the true patriots of Pennsylvania have to weep over outraged laws, violated engagements, and connivance with rapine and murder, they will find the actors in the tragedy, not among the Whigs, but in that party which has always justified wrong when it led to aggrandisement, and which is now even reeking with the blood of its Cuban victims.[1]

On October 14 the election was held with a very heavy vote being polled. The vote for governor exceeded the vote of 1848 for the same office by 29,400 votes but fell 2,500 short of the vote cast for President in the same year. Bigler received 8,455 more votes than Johnston, who in 1848 had had a majority of about 300. The increased vote of this year was distributed 18,000 to Bigler, 9,500 to Johnston, and 1,900 to Cleaver.[2] The Democrats increased their majorities in the greater number of the counties which they ordinarily carried. It was chiefly in the northern counties, comprising the area in which the influence of Wilmot was strong, that the Democrats lost votes. The free-soil men preferred Johnston to Bigler. In Lancaster

vidual, Samuel Williams, was tried for obstructing the enforcement of the Fugitive Slave Law on the ground that he brought news of the coming of Gorsuch. A verdict of "not guilty" was rendered; 5 Clark (Pa.) 155. Cf. also Public Ledger, January 13, February 6, 1852.

[1] Pittsburgh Gazette, September 22, 1851.

[2] Smull's Legislative Hand-Book, 1919, p. 720, gives the returns Bigler (Dem.) 186,489; Johnston (Whig) 178,034; Cleaver (Nat. Am.) 1,850; scattering 67.

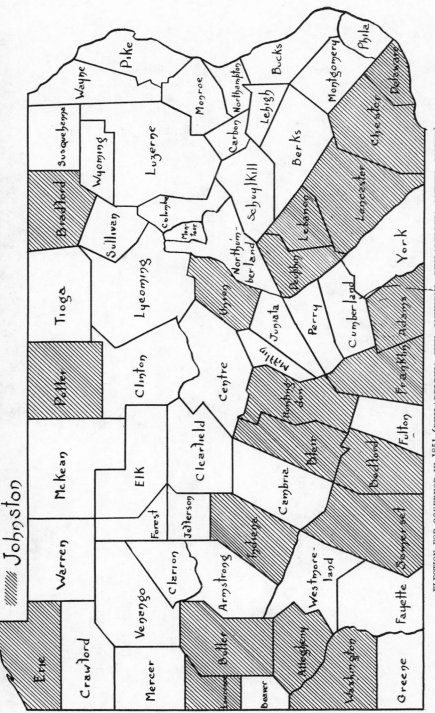

ELECTION FOR GOVERNOR IN 1851 (PHILADELPHIA CITY, JOHNSTON; PHILADELPHIA COUNTY, BIGLER)

county, where the riot occurred, and in the nearby Whig counties of Chester, Dauphin, Delaware, and Lebanon, the Whigs increased their majorities. In the nearby Democratic counties of Berks, Bucks, Montgomery, and York, the Democratic vote was increased. The returns in the rural districts indicate that the election had little effect on the customary party allegiance. In Philadelphia city and county, where the riot was particularly used by the Democrats to depict the Whigs as a party of lawlessness and where there was fear that southern trade might be lost if the Fugitive Slave Law was to be thus nullified, the Whigs lost 2,200 votes to the Democrats and to the Native Americans. The improved condition of business also cost the Whigs votes in the counties where the tariff appeal had been efficacious in securing votes from the Democrats. The mining county of Schuylkill, a Democratic region, which in 1846 and in 1848 had been carried by the Whigs on the tariff issue, now returned to the Democracy. Johnston's majority of 700 in 1848 was now converted into a minority of the same amount in this county. In the other mining counties, which were normally Democratic, the majorities against the Whigs were increased.

The Democrats elected four of the five judges of the supreme court of the state. The defeated Democratic candidate, James Campbell, lost by 3,000 votes to Richard Coulter, who received 7,000 less votes than the lowest successful Democratic judge. Coulter had been on the bench, and after having been refused a nomination by the Democrats had received one from the Whigs. The Catholicism of Campbell along with his alleged incompetency lost him 4,000 votes in Philadelphia and Allegheny counties alone.[1] The

---

[1] Official vote in the *Public Ledger,* October 31, 1851. Campbell was taken care of the following year by being appointed Postmaster-General by Pierce.

Democrats in carrying the state elected the canal commissioner, the auditor-general, and the surveyor-general. The state senate would contain sixteen Democrats, sixteen Whigs, and one Native American; the house would have fifty-five Democrats, forty Whigs, and five Native Americans. Had the Whigs and Native Americans combined on all the candidates in Philadelphia, their control of the house would have been assured.[1]

The Whig party in the South rejoiced at the defeat of Governor Johnston.[2] This rejoicing irritated the supporters of the governor within the state. One of them claimed that the southern Whigs seemed to be demented on the question of slavery, and were apparently unwilling to show any tolerance for differences of opinion. "If such an absurd course is to be pursued, there is an end of all future cooperation. What hope can southern Whigs have of Pennsylvania hereafter; when they are loud in rejoicing over the defeat of Governor Johnston, who received the votes of over 178,000 Whigs!" This rejoicing, it was noted, was not confined to Alabama and to Mississippi, but even the Whigs of Baltimore were claiming that the election of Bigler was a triumph for the national Whig administration.[3] This state of internal bickering boded no good for the coming presidential campaign.

[1] *Public Ledger*, October 24, 1851. One wing of the Native Americans had held a convention at Harrisburg on July 24, but this small body split on the question of the advisability of nominating state officers. The seceders insisted on making nominations for governor and canal commissioner but made none for the supreme court; *ibid.*, July 29, 1851. They continued the fight against an alliance with the Whigs in their county convention; *ibid.*, August 12, 1851.

[2] Cole, *The Whig Party in the South*, p. 226; message of Governor Lowe of Maryland on January 7, 1852; *Maryland Legislative Documents*, 1852, p. 40.

[3] *Pittsburgh Gazette*, November 13, 1851.

CHAPTER VI

THE WHIG PARTY MARKS TIME

1852-1853.

IN the organization of the legislature the Whigs secured the speaker of the senate because of the refusal of several Democrats to vote, but the Democrats easily maintained control of the house.[1] On January 8, 1852, immediately after the organization of the legislature, Governor Johnston returned to the senate the bill repealing the sixth section of the act of March 3, 1847. His refusal to sign the bill had been used effectively by the Democrats in the last campaign. In his veto message the governor discussed the history of the passage of the act, contending that the act was based on the interpretation of the Constitution of the United States made by the federal Supreme Court.[2] The senate could not pass the measure over the veto of the governor, whose term was about to expire. In his inaugural message of January 20, 1852, Governor Bigler urged the legislature to repeal the obnoxious sections of the act of March 3, 1847,[3] and, in compliance with his request, an act repealing the sections, which forbade the use of the state jails for the detention of fugitive slaves, was passed.[4] Before the passage of the repealing act, partly to right an

---

[1] *Public Ledger,* January 7, 8, 1852.

[2] *Pennsylvania Archives,* series iv, vol. vii, pp. 491, *et seq.*

[3] *Ibid.,* series iv, vol. vii, pp. 519, *et seq.*

[4] *Session Laws,* 1852, p. 295.

alleged wrong and partly to mollify the South, Governor Bigler pardoned George Alberti, who had been convicted of kidnaping under the statute of March 3, 1847.[1]

The effect of the defeat of the Whigs in 1851 was felt in the spring municipal elections of 1852. The election of a Democratic mayor on January 13 in the Whig city of Pittsburgh led to the warning that " this abandonment of Whig nominees, by known Whigs, *must* stop here, or the party fails utterly, for all good ends." [2]   The defeat of the Whig candidate was due to many Whigs supporting Mayor Barker, who was running for reelection on the Anti-Catholic ticket.[3]

As was the custom, the state conventions were held in March. The Democrats, despite the strenuous opposition of Simon Cameron, endorsed Buchanan for the presidency, and nominated William Seabright for canal commissioner.[4] Before the election another convention was necessitated by the death of Seabright. This convention met on September 5 and nominated William Hopkins, who had been the speaker of the successful house in the Buckshot War.[5] The Whigs in their convention reaffirmed their action of the year before and endorsed Scott for the presidency. As their candidate for canal commissioner they selected Jacob Hoffman.[6]   The control of the Whig party within the state was not wrested from the free-soil element. On the other hand, the Democrats did not waiver from their opposition to the free-soil agitation.

[1] *Keystone*, February 10, 1852.
[2] *Daily Commercial Journal*, January 14, 1852.
[3] *Public Ledger*, January 15, 1852.
[4] *Ibid.*, March 5, 6, 1852.
[5] *Ibid.*, September 6, 1852.
[6] *Ibid.*, March 26, 1852.

It was not in the state but in the national party that the breach in the Whig ranks assumed alarming proportions. A caucus of the Whig Congressmen, according to party custom, drew up and issued the call for the national convention. When the caucus met this year, an effort was made by the southern members to have the caucus assume the new duty of deciding the " principles " by which the party would be guided at the coming election. The " principles " were to be an unqualified endorsement of the compromise measures. At the first session of the caucus no action was taken. At a subsequent session the assumption of the power to declare " principles " was rejected by a vote of 46 to 21. The vote was largely on a sectional basis, although seven southerners voted against the measure and seven northerners for it. Senator Cooper of Pennsylvania was the only Whig from that state who favored the proposition. The opposition to the adoption of " principles " was led by Thaddeus Stevens and by several North Carolina Whigs.[1] After their defeat in the congressional caucus, eleven of the southern Whigs issued an address in which they pledged themselves not to support the candidate of the Whig national convention unless the Compromises of 1850 were specifically endorsed. They declared themselves ready, if necessary, to form a new party.[2] In reply to this address, the *Daily Commercial Journal* reflected the attitude of the state Whig party, in saying,

The yearly exactions and demands of the South are no longer tolerable, and our only defence and substantial reliance is, *a Northern Party*.

We can elect Scott without the aid of the South, and there never will be harmony and repose, in the relations of the two

[1] *Public Ledger,* April 12, 21, 22, 29, 1852.

[2] *Ibid.,* April 29, 1852.

wings of the party until we show these disorganizers not only that we *can* do without them, but that we mean to carry our man in spite of them.

There has been always a " *Southern* Whig Party," whilst we could boast only of "A Whig Party of the Northern States." The remedy for this state of things is a " Northern Whig Party," and the defiant attitude of the Southern Whigs suggests this as the proper time for an application of the remedy.[1]

The state Whigs were still rankling under the gloating of the southern Whigs over the defeat of Johnston a few months before.

At a caucus, held the day before the assembling of the national convention at Baltimore, the southern Whigs intimated that in return for a resolution in the convention affirming the finality of the Compromises of 1850 they would favor resolutions endorsing a protective tariff and the improvement of the rivers and harbors.[2]   The convention, before it balloted for a candidate, adopted its platform.   A tariff of specific duties was endorsed, and the appropriation of money for the improvement of rivers and harbors was advocated.   The last resolution dealt with the compromises, which were declared to be " a settlement in principle and substance of the dangerous and exciting questions which they embrace," and which would be maintained " as essential to the nationality of the Whig party and the integrity of the Union."[3]   The free-soil element of Pennsylvania, controlling the delegation of the state, selected ex-Governor Johnston as the state member of the committee on resolutions.   The vote of the state delegation for the

[1] May 3, 1852.

[2] *Public Ledger*, June 17, 1852; the friends of Webster, in particular, were said to favor these measures.

[3] Stanwood, *History of the Presidency*, vol. i, p. 252.

resolutions was twenty-one in favor and six in opposition. On the fifty-third ballot Scott was nominated for the presidency; he received twenty-six and Fillmore one of the votes from the Pennsylvania delegates. The nomination of William A. Graham of North Carolina for the vice-presidency caused no struggle.[1] The Whigs of the South, not satisfied with the resolutions, awaited Scott's letter of acceptance before taking further action. Its contents, when published on June 24, did not please them; so on July 3 they issued a manifesto in which they declared Scott to be " the favorite candidate of the Free Soil wing of the Whig party," and they regarded it " as the highest duty of the well wishers of the country everywhere, whatever else they may do, to at least withhold from him their support. This we intend to do." [2] The most ardent admirers of Scott in Pennsylvania, professing to feel no alarm over this manifesto, declared that the signers came from states which at best would give Scott no support. " We believe," declared one editor, " General Scott will never feel the opposition of these gentry, and we are not sorry that their treason is, at length, fully unmasked." [3]

Prior to the Whig convention, the Democrats had placed their candidates in nomination. Throughout the balloting the Pennsylvania delegation supported Buchanan; but it soon became evident that neither he, nor Cass, nor Douglas could be nominated. On the thirty-fourth ballot a few votes were cast for Pierce, and on the forty-ninth a break occurred in his favor and he was nominated. The Buchanan supporters were somewhat mollified by the nomination of W. R. King, one of Buchanan's most intimate friends.

[1] *Public Ledger*, June 17-22, 1852.
[2] *Ibid.*, June 30, July 8, 1852.
[3] *Daily Commercial Journal*, July 7, 1852.

for the vice-presidency.[1] After the nominations were known, the Whigs raised the cry " Who is Franklin Pierce? " They contended that Pierce was not to be blamed for his obscurity but that the Democrats were to be censured for nominating a man of such unknown qualities.[2]

On July 6 the Native Americans, who in 1848 had cooperated with the Whigs, held a national convention at Trenton. They decided to change the party name from " Native American " to " American." Daniel Webster and George C. Washington were placed before the public as their nominees.[3] Strong objections were made to these nominations particularly by the anti-Levin branch of the party.[4] The failing health of Webster removed him as a possibility, so in the election the Native Americans voted for Jacob Broom of Philadelphia and Reynell Coates of New Jersey, who were placed in nomination by the executive committee after the death of Webster and the declination of Washington.[5] In the Philadelphia districts and in four other districts of the state, the Native Americans ran congressional candidates.[6]

In August there assembled at Pittsburgh the national convention of the Free Soil Democracy. The convention nominated John P. Hale and George W. Julian. Prior to the national convention, there had been a state mass convention of the " friends of freedom " to prepare for the

[1] *Public Ledger*, June 2-7, 1852.

[2] *Daily Commercial Journal*, June 28, 1852.

[3] *Public Ledger*, July 7, 1852. In order to avoid confusing them with the Know-Nothings or Americans they will be referred to by their older designation.

[4] Letter of Peter Sken Smith in *ibid.*, August 30, 1852.

[5] *Ibid.*, October 30, 1852; C. O. Paullin, " The National Ticket of Broom and Coates, 1852," in *The American Historical Review*, vol. xxv, pp. 689-691, July, 1920.

[6] *Public Ledger* October 12, 1852.

national convention. At one of its later meetings the state
convention nominated a state ticket.[1] The convention recommended that congressional candidates be run in each
district, but only in the three districts at the headwaters of
the Ohio was this done in Pennsylvania. The vote of the
party in the state was much smaller than in 1848, particularly in Wilmot's district.[2] In the Whig counties it succeeded in retaining its small following.

The Whigs raised the question of the tariff as the big
issue of the campaign, but met with little success.[3] The
Whig cry for Pennsylvania was said to be " Scott, Graham
and a Tariff with specific Duties."[4] The stressing of the
deceit of the Democracy in 1844 had no practical effect.[5]
In both parties there was an apathy towards the campaign
which had not been in evidence in preceding presidential
elections. The *Public Ledger,* an independent paper, said,

We see here and there, especially in the great cities, almost
daily attempts to hold "mass meetings." But though these
meetings are crowded to suffocation in the newspapers, very

[1] *Public Ledger,* August 11-14, 1852.

[2] Wilmot realized that the Whig party is "now substantially a Free
Soil party and would resist any further aggression of the slave
power; but if they succeed in electing a president they would be
pro-slavery, as is the Democratic party. So long as they are out they
will be an anti-slavery party. . . . There will be an organized political
nucleus for the Free-Soil elements of the free States to fall back
upon in this contest. We Free-Soilers of the northern counties will
therefore probably vote for Pierce in this election, not because we
believe in him, but because in our judgment it is the wisest course to
prepare for the conflict which must come upon the extension of
slavery in this country." Quoted in DuBois and Matthews. *Galusha
A. Grow,* p. 94.

[3] *Daily Commercial Journal,* July 21, 23, 24, August 4; *Public
Ledger,* September 2, 1852.

[4] *Daily Commercial Journal,* June 26, 1852.

[5] *Ibid.,* August 27, 1852.

few attend them bodily. They seem to think that a metaphorical attendance will do as well for the cause, whatever it be, and much better for themselves.[1]

On October 12 the state elections were held with the Democrats receiving twenty thousand more votes than the Whigs.[2] The legislature would be divided in control due to hold-overs in the senate which would contain seventeen Whigs, fifteen Democrats, and one Native American; the house would be made up of sixty-two Democrats and thirty-eight Whigs. The Democrats elected sixteen of the twenty-five Congressmen and the Whigs nine. If the Whigs and Native Americans had combined in three of the Philadelphia districts, the fusion candidates would have been elected. In the Beaver-Lawrence-Mercer district in western Pennsylvania the Whig candidate for Congress was defeated because of the large number of votes cast for the Free Soil nominee.[3]

The Whigs claimed that their defeat in the state election was due to the " stay-at-home " vote. In the presidential election, they affirmed, they would be successful, if they could induce these men to go to the polls. Increased votes

[1] September 9, 1852.

[2] The official returns for canal commissioner are given in the *Public Ledger*, October 28, 1852; Hopkins (Dem.) 171,551; Hoffman (Whig) 151,601; Wyman (Free Soil) 3,843; McDonald (Nat. Am.) 8,187. Judge Coulter of the state supreme court had died in April. George Woodward had been appointed to fill the vacancy. Later he was nominated by the Democrats and defeated Joseph Buffington, the Whig nominee, by 172,619 to 153,715.

[3] *Ibid.*, October 16, 1852; the beginning of a reaction against the control of the free-soil element is seen in the Whig party, particularly in Lancaster county. The " Silver Greys " succeeded in ousting the " Wooly Heads "; they nominated Isaac Hiester for Congress. Stevens' activity as counsel for the defense in the trial of the Christiana rioters helped in his overthrow from leadership; *ibid.*, August 23, October 11, 1852.

had been secured in 1840 and in 1848 by party activity and
the elections had been won.   What was to prevent the same
result from being attained now? [1]   The introduction of the
temperance question in some of the local elections had
worked to the disadvantage of the Whigs, who were always
affected by the introduction of these extraneous issues. [2]   In
the presidential campaign the Democrats made free use of
the attacks on Scott by the southern Whigs. [3]   In a speech
at Greensburg Buchanan devoted himself to the question of
the advisability of raising the commanding general of the
army to the presidency.   The views of Scott, as given in a
letter of October 25, 1841, were criticized as showing his
incompetency. [4]   The course of the Whigs in endorsing
Governor Johnston's withholding his signature to the
bill repealing the act of March 3, 1847, was condemned. [5]
The Democrats by these criticisms made the Whigs abandon
the issue of the tariff of 1846 as the main question and
forced them to reply to their attacks.

The election was carried by Pierce with a majority of

[1] *Daily Commercial Journal*, October 15, 1852; address of the Allegheny County Scott Club, *ibid.*, October 22, 1852.

[2] *Ibid.*, October 13, 16, 1852.

[3] The pamphlet, *Whig Testimony against General Scott*, was widely
circulated.

[4] Moore, *Works of James Buchanan*, vol. viii, pp. 460, *et seq.* This
letter of Scott had been sent by him to various Whig leaders in the
North after the party broke with Tyler; copies in the Ewing Papers
and in the McLean Papers, Lib. of Cong. At the same time, Scott
was actively corresponding with Thaddeus Stevens, who was hoping
to restore the Anti-Masons to power under the possible leadership
of Scott; letters of Stevens to Scott, October 20, 1841, February 15,
1843, of Scott to Stevens, November 1, 4, 21, 1841, May 5, August 2,
1842; Stevens Papers, Lib. of Cong.

[5] *Daily Commercial Journal*, October 4; *Public Ledger*, October 8,
1852.

9,000 votes over his three opponents within the state. [1]
Upon the defeat of Scott, the *Daily Commercial Journal*
remarked,

For the sake of conciliating the South, the Whigs of the
North admitted into their platform of principles an element
which was distasteful to the mass of the Whigs of the North,
and, as the sequel has shown, lost to the cause northern Whig
States. The South was imperative in exacting the admission
of this element of discord; and after securing its admission,
the States of the South—the Whig States—have refused to
sustain either platform or candidate, and we are covered with
defeat. This is the point of difficulty, in submitting with good
grace and comfortable temper, to the defeat of Scott and
Graham.
For our own part, patience and our capacity of endurance
have been wholly exhausted in the labor of standing by the
South, to witness the South stand by and succor and give
victory to our opponents. We will no more of it. [2]

The statements of R. M. Riddle, editor of the paper, that
the party ought to be dissolved did not meet with hearty
approval even in the western part of the state. One of the
leading Whigs of Butler county took issue with him and
maintained that it was necessary for the Whigs to hold
to their old policies. [3] Judge H. M. Brackenridge of Allegheny county felt that the North and not the South was to
blame for the estrangement between the two sections. The
abolitionists and the free-soilers were the ones who were
threatening to break up the Whig party. This was shown

[1] *Smull's Legislative Hand-Book*, 1919, p. 715, gives the returns as
Pierce (Dem.) 198,562; Scott (Whig) 179,104; Hale (Free Soil Dem.)
8,495; Broom (Native American) 1,678.

[2] November 4, 1852.

[3] Letter of Samuel A. Purviance to R. M. Riddle, November 15, 1852;
Daily Commercial Journal, November 22, 1852.

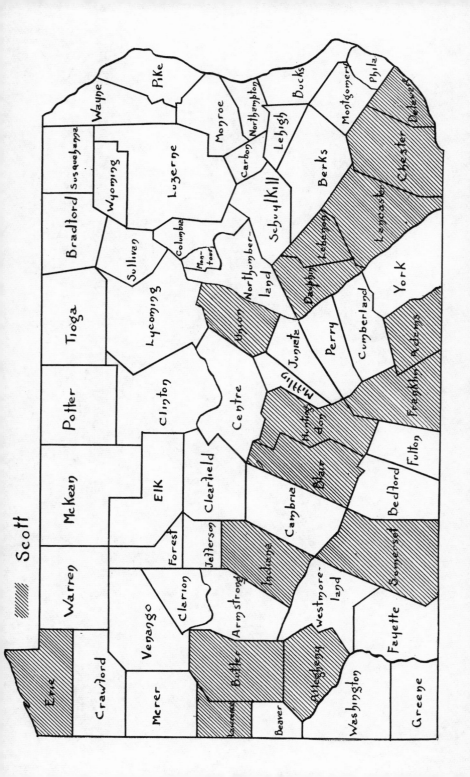

by the fact that the South had favored a protective tariff
before the passage of the Missouri Compromise Act; with
the passage of this act had begun the agitation against
slavery with the resultant objection of the South to a protective tariff.[1]   William D. Lewis, a leader of the free
soil wing in Philadelphia, wrote after the election,

We are told in the good book that " whom the Lord loveth
he chasteneth," which of course it would be impiety to doubt.
It is clear then that the Whig party must stand high in his
favor, for he has recently given it such a chastening as I hope
he may deem sufficient to purify its rebellious blood for all time.[2]

After the elections the discouragement and despair of
the Whigs was pronounced and profound.   A ray of light
pierced the darkness when the Pittsburgh Whigs defeated
the Democratic mayor who was up for reelection.[3]   Whatever doubt existed as to the continued existence of the
Whig party was removed when the Whig state central
committee, meeting at Harrisburg on February 16, issued
a call for a state convention to meet at Lancaster in March.[4]
The most significant act of the convention was the appointment of a large central committee of fifty-five, which indicated a determined effort to effect a thoroughgoing re-
vivification of the state Whig party.[5]   The spirit shown
at the convention soon slumped.   At another state convention, meeting in August at Huntingdon, for the pur-

[1] Letter to R. M. Riddle; *ibid.*, November 22, 1852.

[2] Letter of November 13, 1852, to J. M. Clayton; Clayton Papers,
Lib. of Cong.

[3] *Daily Commercial Journal,* December 30, 1852, January 10, 12, 1853.
The Anti-Catholic party had disappeared and so there was nothing
to divert Whig votes away from their candidate, R. M. Riddle.

[4] *Pennsylvania Telegraph,* February 19, 1853.

[5] *Ibid.,* March 26, June 1; *Daily News,* May 14, 1853.

pose of nominating a candidate to succeed Judge Gibson
on the supreme court, only a few counties were represented.[1]
This lack of interest and this apathy continued throughout
the campaign of 1853.[2] It could be attributed in part to the
fact that only minor officers were to be elected, but the indifference, more pronounced than usual, indicated party
disintegration.   Nevertheless, an assertion by Horace Greeley that the Whig party was dead was vigorously denied.[3]
Elections in Tennessee, Kentucky, and other southern states
were taken as denials of his claim.[4]

Without success the Whigs endeavored to raise an issue
on the question of the sale of the public works.   They had
been characterized by a leading Democrat as "a lazarre
house of corruption" and by a Whig as "an infirmary for
broken down politicians."[5]   This question had been lightly
touched upon in the first Whig convention, but was
stressed in the second.[6]   The Democrats, however, did not
oppose the demand for the sale of the public works, and,
consequently, there could be no issue raised on this question.[7]   Although the Whigs were insisting on the sale of

[1] *Pennsylvania Telegraph*, August 3, 31, 1853.

[2] *Ibid.*, October 19, 1853.

[3] *Daily News*, May 20, 26, 1853.

[4] *Evening Bulletin*, August 15, 1853.

[5] *Pennsylvania Telegraph*, April 9, 1853.

[6] *Ibid.*, August 31, 1853.

[7] The following year the act of April 27, 1854, authorized the offering
at auction of the main line of the public works; but no bids were
received. On December 20, 1855, the Pennsylvania Railroad Company
made an offer for the main line. Under the authority of the act of
May 16, 1857, which, in the main, followed the offer of the Pennsylvania Railroad Company, an auction was held on June 25, 1857, at
which the main line was purchased by the railroad. The lateral
canals were sold under authority of the act of April 21, 1858. This
ended state ownership of internal improvements other than roads.
Bishop, "State Works of Pennsylvania," in *Transactions of the Connecticut Academy of Arts and Sciences*, vol. xiii, pp. 254, *et seq.*

the public works as a means of relieving the state from its
tremendous financial burden, which had been incurred
through the construction of these works, yet they tried to
get support in certain sections of the state because they had
favored local extensions.[1] The beginning of a demand that
the tonnage tax on freight hauled by the Pennsylvania
Railroad be repealed was heard.[2]

The campaign became complicated by the appearance of
many local issues. For a time the question of a loan of
two million dollars by Philadelphia county to the Sunbury
and Erie Railroad threatened to become an issue in Philadelphia,[3] but attention was soon diverted to the movement
for the consolidation of Philadelphia city and county. Although both the Whig and the Democratic county conventions declared for consolidation, yet a ticket was formed
from the nominees of both parties, who were known to be
particularly favorable to consolidation. As was usual under
such circumstances, the result favored the Democrats.[4] In
many of the counties the temperance question assumed such
large proportions as to be alarming to the old parties. The
Whigs generally endorsed candidates, who were pledged

[1] *Pennsylvania Telegraph*, September 28, 1853.

[2] *Daily News*, March 16, 1853.

[3] The city councils had made provision for a loan of two million dollars, but since the conditions had not been met by the railroad, the loan
had not been made. The contemplated loan by the county was to take the
place of the loan by the city, which eventually made the loan and
thereby quieted the agitation over the question of the legality of the
loan by the county. The city had previously subscribed four million
dollars to the Pennsylvania Railroad, one half million to the Hemp-
field Railroad, and one half million to the Easton and Water Gap
Railroad. *Evening Bulletin*, March 4, 7, 8, 11, 14, 1853; January 9,
1854.

[4] *Daily News*, September 30, October 17; *Public Ledger*, October 15;
Evening Bulletin, October 15, 1853.

to the reform. If they failed to do this, an independent nomination would be made by the reformers. As a result of the injection of this question into county politics, the Democrats secured ten members of the lower house and two in the upper from what were ordinarily Whig districts.[1]

The election of 1853 resulted in an easy victory for the Democrats. No issue of either state or national significance was involved and the election was based on party solidarity. In fact, the Whig party was politically bankrupt. Even though the anti-free-soil branch of the state Whig party admitted that the old issues had been settled, yet they insisted that there was need of it since " the distinctive principle or feature of the Whig party is what it has ever been, a conservative opposition to the rank radicalism and Jacobinism which has ever been a distinguishing feature of Locofocoism."[2] Others of the Whig party hailed the defeat as a good omen, claiming that it portended the disappearance of partizanship, because all the old questions had been settled. One of them declared that " no cohesive principle exists any longer between partizans, except the memory of past animosities and the prospect of future spoils."[3] Although the apparent collapse of the Whig party was noted, yet no such similar breakup of the Democratic party was evidenced to cheer the Whigs. The passage of the con-

[1] *Daily News,* October 21; *Pennsylvania Telegraph,* October 19, November 16; *Westmoreland Intelligencer,* October 20, 1853. The Whigs now lost control of the senate, which contained 18 Democrats, 14 Whigs, and 1 Native American; the house contained 71 Democrats, 25 Whigs, and 4 Native Americans; *Pennsylvania Telegraph,* November 2, 1853. The vote for canal commissioner was Forsyth (Dem.) 152,867, Pownall (Whig) 117,937; Morgan (Native American) 7,764; Mitchell (Free Soil) 3,579; *Public Ledger,* October 27, 1853.

[2] *Daily News,* October 25, 1853.

[3] *Evening Bulletin,* October 15, 1853.

solidation act, signed by the governor on February 2, 1854, brought the question of the reorganization of the Whig party to the fore, at least so far as Philadelphia city and county were concerned.[1]

[1] *Session Laws*, 1854, p. 21; *Daily News*, January 12, 18, February 4, 1854.

CHAPTER VII

The Disappearance of the Whig Party

1854-1856.

In the early part of 1854 there was a recrudescence of
anti-Catholic sentiment, which was closely associated with
intense hatred of foreigners. Heretofore, candidates in
local elections had been defeated by an appeal to religious
prejudices, but now the agitation was to assume state-wide
proportions.   In the past few years there had been a number
of causes to increase the fear felt because of the alarming
number of immigrants.   In the election of 1852 assertions
were made that the Democrats put up placards urging the
Catholics to vote for Scott, with the anticipated result that
many Protestants, generally Whigs and native-born, had
rejected him but no foreign- or native-born Catholics had
been attracted to him.[1]   The opposition, partly anti-Catholic, which had prevented the elevation of Campbell to the
supreme court of the state, was deeply offended when Pierce
made him Postmaster-General.[2]   The tour of Bedini, the
nuncio of the Pope, in the latter part of 1853 and in the beginning of 1854, led to rioting in various cities of the United
States.   The anti-Catholic element occasionally condemned
the rioters, but universally condemned the nuncio as the
cause of the disorder.   In order not to offend their supporters of German ancestry, the Whigs declared that it was

[1] *Pennsylvania Telegraph,* November 10, 17, 1852.
[2] *Public Ledger,* January 4; *Evening Bulletin,* March 8, 1853.

only the Irish Catholics who did not condemn Bedini.[1] This anti-Catholic sentiment, sedulously aroused this year by the Whigs, was to prove of temporary advantage but of ultimate discomfiture to them.

The four parties within the state in their conventions made nominations for the elections, which were of importance as a governor was to be chosen. As usual, the struggle would lie between the Whigs and the Democrats, although the Native American nominations would draw some votes away from the Whigs and the nomination of David Wilmot as the gubernatorial candidate of the Free Soil Democracy would harm the orthodox Democracy. The Whigs, led by the free-soil element of their party, placed James Pollock, of Northumberland county, in nomination for the governorship; the Democrats nominated Governor Bigler for reelection. The Whig candidate stood in many ways in sharp contrast to the Democratic nominee. Pollock, president judge of the eighth district, had been graduated from Princeton with the highest honors; Bigler had a meager common-school education. Pollock had served three terms in Congress, representing a normally Democratic district; Bigler had held none but state offices. Pollock was born of native American parents of Scotch-Irish descent; Bigler's parents were of German descent. Consequently, as the Know Nothing movement developed, its adherents supported Pollock rather than Bigler.

The consideration of the Kansas-Nebraska Bill by Congress raised an issue which was eagerly seized by the Whigs.[2] Their state convention, on March 15,

Resolved, that those provisions of the Kansas and Nebraska

[1] *Evening Bulletin,* February 2, 13, 15, 1854.

[2] *Daily News,* January 30, February 17; *Pennsylvania Telegraph,* February 17, 1854.

Bill now before Congress, which affect and repeal the Missouri
Compromise, are a deliberate breach of plighted faith and
public compact, a high-handed attempt to force slavery into
a vast territory now free from it by law, a reckless renewing of
a quieted agitation, and therefore meet the stern, indignant and
unanimous condemnation of the Whig party.[1]

This question was vigorously pressed and suggestions were
made that Pollock withdraw in favor of Wilmot, but the
proposition was promptly rejected.[2]   Pollock, in reply to a
letter from opponents of the Kansas-Nebraska Bill, placed
himself in their ranks.[3]   The letter attracted the leaders
of the Free Soil Democracy, who opened a correspondence
with him.   The result was the withdrawal of the nomination of Wilmot and the pledging of their support to Pollock.[4]
This act was significant, indicating the coalescing of free-
soil sentiment into one party.   Wilmot had in 1848 bolted
the regular Democratic organization and had supported
Van Buren.   In 1851 he had supported Bigler and in 1852
Pierce, not because he favored them, but because he feared
that, if the Whig party came into power, it would cease to be
free-soil.   He was preparing for the dissolution of the
Whig party on the slavery question.   The accession of Wilmot to the support of Pollock startled many of the Whigs,

[1] *Pennsylvania Telegraph,* March 18, 1854. The Whig press was
almost unanimous in condemning the measure. Even the *Daily News,*
February 17, 1854, which in 1850 had condemned Governor Johnston
for not endorsing the compromises of that year, declared itself
emphatically against the repeal of the compromises of 1820. It
asserted that if those of 1820 were not binding, neither were those
of 1850, and that "the real friends of the measures of 1850 will be
the first to sound the tocsin for *their* repeal."

[2] *Daily News,* April 22; *Pennsylvania Telegraph,* April 29, 1854.

[3] *Pennsylvania Archives,* series iv, vol. vii, p. 784, for letter of June
19, 1854.

[4] *Westmoreland Intelligencer,* September 7, 1854.

who, recalling Wilmot's vote in favor of the Tariff Act of 1846, declared that they wanted no fusion with free traders.[1] The tariff could not, however, be raised as an issue, and emphasis during the campaign was placed on the Kansas-Nebraska measure. The Whig state central committee, under the leadership of A. G. Curtin, declared that " never, in the history of Pennsylvania, was there a clearer and stronger line drawn—never a more distinct definition of principle." [2] Bigler, however, even after his recovery from an illness which prevented him from being active in the early days of the campaign, refused to discuss the slavery question.[3] In its final address, issued on October 5, the Whig state central committee, referring to this attitude on the part of the Democratic candidate, said, " The Nebraska question—the great issue between the propagandists of slavery and the defenders of human liberty—is ignored." [4] In addition to the support of the abolitionists, Pollock was assured the support of another reform element within the state. The electors were to vote on the question of whether the state ought to adopt a stringent liquor law. The reply of Bigler to an inquiry was considered inadequate, while the answer of Pollock was deemed satisfactory; consequently Pollock was endorsed

The opposition to the Catholics and to the foreign-born was taking definite shape in the organization of secret political societies. This was an independent movement and was not connected with the remnant of the former Native American organization. In Philadelphia a celebration be-

---

[1] *Daily News,* August 25, 1854.

[2] *Ibid.,* July 20, 1854.

[3] *Evening Bulletin,* October 7, 1854.

[4] *Daily News,* October 9, 1854.

[5] *Pennsylvania Archives,* series iv, vol. vii, p. 783.

cause of the consolidation of the city and county, planned
for Washington's birthday, 1854, was postponed until March
10. In the parade were a large number of "American"
organizations, composed of native-born citizens, who had
"organized within a few years." Several delegations
of "Know Nothings," as they were called because of
their ostentatious reticence, were in line.[1] That these new
organizations were working in secret for political power and
that they were rapidly developing strength was shown in a
non-partisan election for school directors in Lancaster city
on May 3. Two men, not avowed candidates, received six
hundred votes, while the two defeated candidates, who were
Catholics, received only sixty votes.[2] A still more important indication of the strength of the movement was given
in the election for mayor of the enlarged city of Philadelphia on June 6. In this election Robert T. Conrad and a
preponderantly Whig council with other Whig officials were
elected by the votes of the Know Nothings, receiving a
majority of more than eighty-five hundred.[3] "This earth-
quake shake," wrote a Democrat to Buchanan, "alarms us
in the fate of Governor Bigler."[4]

[1] *Evening Bulletin*, March 10, 1854.

[2] *Inland Daily*, May 9; *Pennsylvania Telegraph*, May 10, 1854; Judge
A. L. Hayes to Buchanan, May 8, 1854, Buchanan Mss.

[3] *Daily News*, June 8, 1854; in its issue of May 31, 1854, this journal
contended that the Germans were going with the Democracy and had
made the contest one of "Lager Beer and Vaux versus Temperance
and Conrad." The *Evening Bulletin*, June 7, 1854, claimed that the
election was a rebuke of the state and of the national administrations
for having taken up Campbell. "The weakness on foreign questions,
the bullying on home questions, the indecencies of the Nebraska
legislation, the base resort to all sorts of demagogue tricks, the traffic
in offices to secure votes, the filibustering inclinations and the general
unfitness for the control of a great nation" have all contributed to
the merited defeat.

[4] Daniel T. Jenks, June 9, 1854; Buchanan Mss.

The Democrats sharply attacked the Whigs for organizing the Know Nothings, whose principles, particularly of religious intolerance, were shown to be contrary to those of the founder of the commonwealth. Pollock, they declared, had been initiated into the order and full details of the ceremony were printed.[1] To show the inconsistency of the movement, assertions were made that Thaddeus Stevens, leader of the former Anti-Masons, had taken the oath of secrecy and had been duly inducted into the mysteries of the society.[2] To the attacks of the Democrats the supporters of the movement replied that the Jesuits, a Catholic organization, had been the originators of secret religious societies with a political purpose.[3] The omnipresence of representatives of the " Most Holy Order of Jesus " was vividly depicted for the doubtful. According to one journal,

The help in your kitchen, and the girl in your nursery, are Jesuits. The fellow who blacks your boots is one of the same Order: but he don't like " saycret societies," and he declaims against " Know Nothings " with a volubility that defies the oral peculiarities of a Billingsgate fish woman. At the very time he is doing this, he is peering into your private affairs—telling Bishops and Priests what you eat for breakfast, dinner, and supper; how you do the business in which you are engaged; what your income is, and how you manage to live.[4]

The Democrats were determined to root out the influence of the Know Nothings within their own party. Candidates in Philadelphia were questioned as to their possible mem-

[1] Pamphlet, *To the Thinking Voter of Pennsylvania.*

[2] Forney, *Address on Religious Intolerance and Political Proscription,* p. 47; *Daily News,* September 30, 1854.

[3] *Pennsylvania Telegraph,* June 14; *Daily News,* July 25, 1854.

[4] *Pennsylvania Telegraph,* June 14, 1854.

bership in the new organization.[1] Mott, Democratic candidate for canal commissioner, was endorsed by the Know Nothings, but it was vigorously denied that he was therefore a member of that society.[2] The Whigs declared that the Know Nothings drew their members from all the old parties, and that consequently they could not justly be condemned for the movement.[3]

In the elections for Congress the issue was sharply and clearly drawn on the Kansas-Nebraska Act. In strong, normal Democratic districts the Whigs threw their influence to " Independent Democrats," who pledged themselves to work for the repeal of the measure. The Whigs as a body stood bound in opposition to the act. In Lancaster county, a stronghold of the Whigs, where two years before the " Silver Greys," so called because they favored the slaveholder, had secured control of the party organization, an independent Whig, run by the Stevens " Wooly Head " faction, which leaned towards abolition, was elected with the help of the Know Nothings.[4] In the second congressional district of Philadelphia, Joseph R. Chandler was refused a nomination for reelection because he was a Catholic.[5] The reasons openly avowed were that he had not opposed the establishment of a branch mint at New York, which was detrimental to Philadelphia, that he had voted for the subsidy to the Collins steamship line, a New York corporation, and that his actions at the Vatican during a recent visit had been unseemly.[6] The friends of Chandler placed him in nomination as an independent Whig candidate

---

[1] *Evening Bulletin,* September 12, 1854.

[2] *Daily News,* August 30, 1854.

[3] *Ibid.,* October 4, 1854.

[4] *Evening Bulletin,* October 28, 1854.

[5] *Ibid.,* September 6; *Daily News,* September 28, 1854.

[6] *Daily News,* October 2, 1854.

The Counties in Which the Know Nothing Vote the Decisive Factor

but he was easily defeated.[1]   In the fourth congressional district, also in Philadelphia, pressure was brought to bear on the Whig nominee, who withdrew in favor of the Native American candidate, Jacob Broom, presidential candidate in 1852, who was duly elected.   In the first district, although the Native American candidate withdrew, the Whig was defeated.[2]   Of the twenty-five Congressmen-elect twenty-one were anti-Nebraska men, composed of fourteen Whigs, one " Independent " Whig, one Native American, and five Democrats; this gave the administration only four Democratic supporters from the state.[3]

The general election for state officials resulted in the choice of James Pollock, Whig, for governor, of Henry S. Mott, Democrat, for canal commissioner, and of Jeremiah S. Black, Democrat, for judge of the supreme court. The total vote was approximately 370,000, of which the Democrats controlled 167,000, the Whigs 83,000, and the Know Nothings 120,000.[4]   The Know Nothing vote was well diffused throughout the state, and differed from the nativist vote of 1844 in this respect.   Although not independently organized, the Know Nothings by selecting candidates from the nominees of the major parties secured their election.   The result was a legislature of a peculiar

[1] *Evening Bulletin,* September 12, 16, 19, October 28, 1854.

[2] *Daily News,* October 9, 1854.

[3] *Evening Bulletin,* October 21, 1854.

[4] Official returns for governor in *Smull's Legislative Hand-Book,* 1919, p. 720, James Pollock (Whig and American) 203,822; William Bigler (Dem.) 166,991; B. Rush Bradford (Nat. Am.) 2,194; scattering 33. Official returns in *Evening Bulletin,* October 26, 1854, for canal commissioner, Henry S. Mott (Dem.) 274,074; George Darsie (Whig) 83,331; B. M. Spicer (Nat. Am.) 1,244; for supreme court judge, Jeremiah S. Black (Dem.) 167,010; Thomas H. Baird (Nat. Am.) 120,596; Daniel Smyser (Whig) 73,571; for prohibition 158,342, against 163,510.

complexion. There were twenty-five Democrats in the lower house, thirteen Democratic-Americans, three independent Democrats, and one Temperance-Democrat, a total of forty-two. The Whigs had fifty-three members, composed of thirty-six Whigs, fifteen Whig-Americans, and two Temperance-Whigs. There were also four Americans and one Temperance-American.[1] This legislature well illustrates the cross currents of politics in the state as the result of the advent of the Know Nothings. Certainly it cannot with justice be claimed that the Democratic defeat was due exclusively to either the Know Nothing movement or the anti-Nebraska agitation, although either one of them independently would have accomplished the overthrow of the Democrats in 1854. There was no doubt but that the Whigs were badly disorganized. The question, however, of the disposition of the 83,000 Whigs remained to be solved. The governor-elect realized that the old parties were decadent and looked to the organization of a " liberal, tolerant, high-minded and truly American party." He viewed the victory as the " vindication of great American principles, too long the sport of demagogues and too often overthrown by influences foreign to the best interests of our Country." [2]

When the legislature assembled, some of the difficulties of organizing the society, which had worked in secret, into a political party came into evidence. On February 9, 1855, a caucus of the Know Nothings or Americans, as they were now called, was held to place a candidate for the United States Senate in nomination. Ninety-one members of the

---

[1] *Evening Bulletin,* October 21, 1854. It now became customary to call the Know Nothings by the name of Americans; they will be referred to hereafter as such.

[2] Letter from James Pollock, October 30, 1854, to John M. Clayton; Clayton Papers, Lib. of Cong.

legislature, considerably more than avowed themselves
Americans, attended. The voting was by ballot and not
viva voce. On the sixth ballot one more vote than members
attending was cast, and Simon Cameron was within one
vote of having a majority. Thirty-two members then withdrew, declaring that they would not abide by the decision of
the caucus. On the next ballot Cameron received the nomination of the remainder of the caucus.[1] The nomination
was widely condemned, regardless of party affiliation. The
seceding members in an address, justifying their withdrawal, affirmed,

But what we say unto one we say unto all, invite us not in to
partake of a buzzard's feast. Ask us not to support a nomination brought about, as we believe, by the concentrated and
cohesive power of public plunder, and the superadded element
of shameless and wholesale private bribery.[2]

Inasmuch as Cameron did not control a majority of the
votes of the members of the legislature, and inasmuch as
the opposition could not concentrate on one candidate, the
election was postponed until the following year.[3]

Successful efforts to organize the Know Nothings, or the
Americans, on a national scale were made. The slavery
question, which had split the Whig party, was to have the
same effect on the newer organization. This was evidenced
when the national council assembled in June. The resolutions, which were adopted, declared in Article XII that

the National Council has deemed it the best guarantee of common justice and of future peace, to abide by and maintain the
existing laws upon the subject of Slavery, as a final and con-
clusive settlement of that subject, in spirit and in substance.

[1] *Daily News,* February 12, 15, 1855.

[2] *Pennsylvania Telegraph,* February 21, 1855.

[3] *Daily News,* March 14, 15, 1855.

And regarding it their highest duty to avow their opinions upon a subject so important, in distinct and unequivocal terms, it is hereby declared as the sense of this National Council, that Congress possesses no power, under the Constitution, to legislate upon the subject of Slavery in the States where it does or may exist, or to exclude any State from admission into the Union, because its Constitution does or does not recognize the institution of Slavery as a part of its social system; and expressly pretermitting any expression of opinion upon the power of Congress to establish or prohibit Slavery in any Territory, it is the sense of the National Council that Congress ought not to legislate upon the subject of Slavery within the Territory of the United States, and that any interference by Congress with Slavery as it exists in the District of Columbia, would be a violation of the spirit and intention of the compact by which the State of Maryland ceded the District to the United States, and a breach of the National faith.[1]

Fifteen members of the council, led by ex-Governor Johnston of Pennsylvania, withdrew, protesting against the introduction of the slavery question and maintaining that its introduction was contrary to the principles of the American party, and that, if the question were to be disposed of, the Missouri Compromise should have been endorsed.[2]   When the convention itself met, fifty-four delegates from twelve

---

[1] *Evening Bulletin,* June 15, 1855.

[2] *Pennsylvania Telegraph,* June 20, 1855; the delegates came from Pennsylvania, Illinois, New Jersey, Vermont, Delaware, and Connecticut. The Indiana delegates issued a separate protest. The same journal, on June 27, 1855, approved of the course adopted, saying, "To exact a National sentiment in favor of a sectional institution—and that institution *slavery*—is simply an absurdity. . . . Philadelphia and New York may cry 'Peace! Peace!'—but until you concede *freedom* to Kansas and Nebraska, and restore the Missouri Compromise, the masses from the interior will respond 'no peace!' Platforms may be reared as high as heaven, and numerous as the stars, but if constructed of Kansas timber, the parties occupying them would do well to dispose of their estates and appoint executors."

New England and western states withdrew because of the introduction of this question.[1] The bolters from the Philadelphia convention met at Cincinnati on November 21, 1855, according to call. A motion to expunge Article XII, however, was not adopted and no definite action was taken.[2]

The fight on Article XII was carried by ex-Governor Johnston into the Pennsylvania convention of the American party, which assembled at Reading on July 2. The convention was under the control of the free-soil element, and Article XII failed of adoption by a vote of 30 to 143. On the other hand, the strong free-soil report of the majority of the platform committee was rejected by a vote of 89 to 104, and the milder minority report was accepted by a vote of 133 to 53. The substitute for Article XII stated that the slavery question should not have been brought up in the National Council, but now that this question had been forced upon the attention of the party the state convention felt compelled to declare that the repeal of the Missouri Compromise was " an infraction of the plighted faith of the nation " and that the compromise should be restored. Seventy-three of those supporting the minority report were eastern delegates. Of those who opposed it because of its mildness thirty were western delegates and twenty-three eastern. This action of the state convention led to the withdrawal of ten Philadelphia delegates, for whom the platform was too radical. This group had been endeavoring to block the free-soil element, continued their efforts, and in the election of 1856 merged with the Democrats.[3]

The formation of the Republican party had, in the mean-

[1] *Ibid.,* June 20; *Daily News,* June 14, 1855. The bolters came from Ohio, Indiana, Illinois, Michigan, Massachusetts, New Hampshire, Vermont, Maine, Rhode Island, Connecticut, Iowa, and Wisconsin.

[2] *Pennsylvania Telegraph,* September 12, November 28, 1855.

[3] *Ibid.,* July 11; *Daily News,* July 9, August 27, 1855.

time, been under way within the state. On November 27, 1854, a local organization was effected in Wilmot's district,[1] which was followed by similar movements in other portions of the state.[2] The strength of the new party came from the dissatisfied free-soil element of the older parties. Many "old line" Whigs, however, barred by the religious proscription of the American party, distrusted the radicalism of the Republican party, and consequently attempted to fuse the local Whig organization with the Democrats, in the hope that the new parties might be overwhelmed.[3] The fusion nominees of the conservative Whigs and of the Democrats were barely defeated in the May municipal elections in Philadelphia by the combined efforts of the radical Whigs and Americans.[4]

In July, 1855, attention was strikingly attracted to the slavery question by the imprisonment of Passmore Williamson in the Moyamensing Jail, Philadelphia. Williamson was a Friend and acted as secretary of the Pennsylvania Abolition Society. He had encouraged a female slave with her two children to abandon their owner, who was on his way through the city to New York where he intended to embark for Nicaragua to take up his duties as consul. Upon the failure of Williamson to produce the escaped slaves when a writ of *alias habeas corpus* was served on him by order of Judge Kane of the United States District Court, he was adjudged guilty of contempt of court, and was imprisoned until such time as he should purge himself of the contempt. By one trial or another the case was kept

[1] *Daily News,* December 4, 1855.

[2] *Pennsylvania Telegraph,* March 21; *Evening Bulletin,* August 31, 1854.

[3] Address of the Whig committee of correspondence, *Daily News,* August 31, 1855.

[4] *Ibid.,* April 3, 10, 25, May 4, 11, 1855.

prominently before the public from July 18, the date of the escape, until November 3, when Williamson was released.[1] During the time of his imprisonment the state organization of the Republican party was being effected.[2] At the state mass convention, which met at Pittsburgh on September 5, strong anti-slavery resolutions were adopted. The candidate for canal commissioner proposed by the committee was set aside by the convention and amidst great enthusiasm Passmore Williamson was nominated. This action was strenuously opposed by Alex. K. McClure, Theophilus Fenn, and others, who hoped to nominate an individual acceptable to the less radical Whigs, who were soon to meet in state convention.[3]

In all the counties of the state a political realignment was necessary for the election of 1855. The Democrats absorbed a large number of Whigs who were alarmed at the radicalism of the new parties. In practically every county of the state the Democrats ran their ticket. In a majority of the counties the American party had assumed control of the old Whig organizations, but in former Whig strongholds the Whig party maintained an independent existence. In the western portion of the state and in the northern tier of counties, where the Liberty and Free Soil parties had existed, and in the counties around Philadelphia, where

[1] *Evening Bulletin,* July 19, 20, 21, 27, 28, August 1, 9, 29, 30, 31, September 1, 3, 8, 10, 28, 29, October 8, 9, 12, November 3, 7, 1855. United States *ex rel.* John H. Wheeler *v.* Passmore Williamson, 5 *Clark* 365,377; Passmore Williamson's Case, 26 *Penna.* 9; Williamson *v.* Lewis 39 *Penna.* 9; Hildreth, *Atrocious Judges,* pp. 389-432, "Case of Passmore Williamson."

[2] On August 8, 1855, thirty-two representatives from ten counties had assembled at Reading and issued the call for the mass convention; *Daily News,* August 13, 1855.

[3] *Ibid.,* August 29, September 8; *Evening Bulletin,* September 6, 1855.

Friends were numerous, the Republican party succeeded in organizing.[1]

The only general official to be elected this year was the canal commissioner, for which office all the parties made nominations. Of the opposition to the Democrats, the Native Americans, meeting on June 7, were the first to nominate. They were followed on July 2 by the Americans, on September 5 by the Republicans, and on September 11 by the Whigs.[2] There assembled for the Whig convention fifty-nine delegates, some of whom had been active in the Republican convention, but the remnant of the Whigs had no cohesive principle. The report of the committee on resolutions decried proscription, condemned the slavery course of the federal administration, favored the restoration of the Missouri Compromise, opposed filibustering, proposed the modification of the Fugitive Slave Law and a provision for jury trial for the alleged fugitive slave, and advocated the sale of the state-owned public works; but this report was tabled and no resolutions were adopted.[3] With four opposing party candidates in the field, it was evident that the Democrats would have no difficulty in electing their candidate, so efforts were made to effect some sort of cooperation. On September 27 the state central committees of the Whig, the American, and the Republican parties met at Harrisburg. Each committee then withdrew its party nominee, and the joint committee thereupon

[1] *Daily News,* June 2, 14, 28, 29, July 16, 20, 21, 26, 28, 31, August 3, 4, 6, 9, 11, 13, 15, 20, 22, 23, 27, 29, 30, 31, September 3, 5, 7, 8, 11, 12, 13, 17, 19, 20, 21, October 4, 5; *Evening Bulletin,* August 29, September 5; *Pennsylvania Telegraph,* July 4, 11, August 1, 8, September 5, 1855.

[2] *Daily News,* June 11, July 9, September 8; *Pennsylvania Telegraph,* July 11, September 19; *Evening Bulletin,* September 7, 12, 1855.

[3] *Pennsylvania Telegraph,* September 19; *Evening Bulletin,* September 12, 1855.

nominated Thomas Nicholson as the " Union " candidate
for canal commissioner.[1]

Although their opponents agreed on a " Union " candidate, nevertheless, the Democrats succeeded in electing
their nominee, but only by a plurality.[2] In the senate there
would be seventeen Democrats, fourteen Americans, one
Republican, and one Whig hold-over; in the house there
would be sixty-five Democrats, twenty-one Americans, nine
Republicans, five anti-Democratic fusionists, and no Whigs.[3]
The election did not indicate the strength of the Democrats, but clearly showed that the opposition had proceeded
only a short way towards cooperation. The Republicans
in particular were severely criticized by the Americans,
whom they were beginning to replace.[4] In summing up the
reasons for their failure to defeat the Democrats, one
journal said,

Our contemporaries are busily engaged in hunting for explan-
ations of our late defeat in Pennsylvania,—one attributes the
result to the Liquor League, another to the withdrawal of
Williamson,—a third to the Foreign Protestant vote,—a fourth
to disaffected Whigs,—a fifth to the anti-Nebraska position
of the Order,—a sixth to the secrecy and exclusiveness of the

[1] *Daily News,* September 20, 26, October 1, 8; *Pennsylvania Telegraph,*
October 3, 1855. George Darsie, who had been president of the Republican convention, denied that Williamson's name had been withdrawn.

[2] *Pennsylvania Telegraph,* October 24, 1855, gives the official returns:
Plumer (Dem.) 161,281; Nicholson (Union) 149,745; Williamson
(Rep.) 7,224; Martin (Amer.) 678; Cleaver (Nat. Amer.) 4,056; Hen-
derson (Whig) 2,293.

[3] *Evening Bulletin,* October 20, 1855.

[4] *Pittsburgh Times,* quoted in *Pennsylvania Telegraph,* October 10,
1855. The *Daily News,* November 10, 1855, called the Republican
party "a miserable failure" and accused it of "rushing into a wild
abolition crusade against the South."

Americans,—and the *Pennsylvanian* and the Washington *Union* to the popularity of Pierce, Campbell and the Nebraska infamy.[1]

The movement for cooperation was continued when the state legislature assembled. On February 13, 1856, the Whig, American and Republican members issued a call for a " Union Convention " to meet at Harrisburg on March 26; the delegates to this convention were to be selected in county " Union Conventions." [2]   According to the call the conventon assembled and determined to effect a thorough-going scheme of cooperation for the coming state election. This was made evident in the nice distribution of the nominations; for auditor-general Davison Phelps, an American from the western portion of the state, was nominated, for surveyor-general Bartholomew Laporte, a Republican from the northern portion, and for canal commissioner Thomas E. Cochran, an " old line " Whig from the eastern section.[3] With these nominees the " Union " organization could at the same time make sectional and political appeals. The convention practically marked the end of the Whig party as a state organization, for it lost its identity.

Efforts to throw the remaining Whig county organizations to one of the other parties continued. In the greater portion of the counties independent organizations had been abandoned for the election of 1855. In the western portion of the state the Whigs had, in the main, fused with the Americans, who were now in turn being absorbed by the Republicans.[4] In Philadelphia the Whig organization

---

[1] *Pennsylvania Telegraph,* October 10, 1855.

[2] *Carlisle Herald,* March 19, 1856.

[3] *Public Ledger,* March 27, 28; *Harrisburg Telegraph,* March 28, April 1, 1856.

[4] *Daily News,* February 25, 1856.

had been continued by those who were bitterly opposed to the proscriptive Americans. They forced out of their county convention all who were suspected of being affiliated with the American movement. In the spring of 1856 they formed an independent ticket for the municipal elections, but later withdrew it. Lack of strength and lack of interest led them on April 24 definitely to abandon their existence as a party.[1] Their support was then given to the Democrats whose ticket they helped elect.[2] This marked the end of the last local organization within the state.

Although the Whig party had disappeared as a state and as a local organization, yet its existence as a national or-

---

[1] *Ibid.*, March 10, 15, 19, 25, 28, April 1, 25, 1856. This movement in Philadelphia was led by Josiah Randall and William B. Reed, who were offended by the anti-Catholic policy of the American party. Reed on February 7, 1856, wrote to Buchanan, "I have been all my life as you know a Whig, and if I do mark my *old age* by a conversion or apostacy it will be a very disinterested one. This has come to pass mainly through the growth of this miserable business of Know Nothingism which has corrupted and destroyed the party I once belonged to. Mingled with this is a conviction, the fruit of slow reflection, that the Democratic party is now and is likely to continue the conservative party of the nation. So much for myself— about which it is hardly worth while to say so much." Reed mentioned the fact that other "old line Whigs" were adopting the same course; Buchanan Mss. In Lancaster county Isaac Hiester, who in 1852 had defeated Stevens and the "Wooly Heads" and had reestablished the "Silver Greys" in control of the county Whig organization but had again lost it in 1854 through the Know Nothing movement, now went over to the Democrats; *Harrisburg Telegraph*, March 4, 1856. Benjamin H. Brewster complained to Buchanan on October 16, 1858, that these acquisitions had all deserted by that date. "They never intended to stay. They all wanted to be captains in our common plebian ranks and as we had not commissions for them they have deserted." Buchanan Mss.

[2] The Republicans made nominations for the municipal elections in Philadelphia but they received little support. The vote for mayor was Vaux (Dem.) 29,534; Moore (Amer.) 25,445; Thomas (Rep.) 280; *Daily News*, April 11, 16, May 9, 1856.

ganization terminated only with the presidential election. The American party was the first to make its nominations. Trouble had arisen in the party because of two articles in its platform of 1855. Article VIII, dealing with the Catholic question, deeply offended the Louisiana delegation, while Article XII, dealing with the slavery question, led to the withdrawal from the organization of a large number of northerners. On February 18, 1856, the National Council met at Philadelphia and repealed the platform of 1855. In the new series of resolutions the slavery question was carefully avoided.[1] In the nominating convention, which met on February 22, 1856, the slavery question was again raised by contesting delegations from Pennsylvania. The " Edie " delegates, chosen at the Reading state convention of the year before, who were free-soil in their tendencies, were seated because of the regularity of their selection. The " Hunsecker " delegation, chosen by the bolters from the state convention, although pro-slavery, was rejected. The discussion of the resolutions led to the temporary withdrawal of a large number of southern delegates, while the nomination of Fillmore and Donelson led to the permanent withdrawal of northern delegates. A portion of the Pennsylvania delegation, led by ex-Governor Johnston, joined with other northern seceders in issuing a pronunciamento justifying their action and looking for coöperation with the Republicans. They condemned the platform of their party and insisted on the restoration of the Missouri Compromise.[2] The state council of the American party, as a result of these withdrawals, now came under the control of those who had been defeated in the state convention

[1] *Ibid.*, February 20, 21, 22; *Public Ledger*, February 20, 21, 22; *Harrisburg Telegraph*, February 22, 1856.

[2] *Daily News*, February 23, 25, 26, 27; *Public Ledger*, February 23, 25, 26, 1856.

of the year before and who were intent on mollifying the South.[1] When the council met on May 13 at Harrisburg, the seceders from the Philadelphia convention were condemned and the nominations of Fillmore and Donelson endorsed.[2]

The Republican party was completing its preparations for participation in the national elections. On February 22, 1856, a preliminary mass convention of the party was held at Pittsburgh. The expectation of some form of cooperation with the American party was not realized; for the latter party proceeded, without consulting the Republicans, to make its own nominations. Consequently, the Republicans called a nominating convention to assemble on June 17 at Philadelphia.[3] Five days before the date set for the assembling of this convention, there met at New York the seceders from the American convention, who called themselves the " North Americans." An invitation had been extended them to cooperate with the Republicans. A committee was appointed to proceed to Philadelphia, after an informal ballot had disclosed the fact that their preferences were Banks and Johnston.[4] The Republicans treated with this committee very informally. Frémont and Dayton were the Republican nominees.[5] Following this action, Banks withdrew his name as the potential candidate of the " North Americans." The committee upon its return to New York complained of the treatment which they had received, but recommended that their party endorse the Republican nominees. The convention then nominated

---

[1] *Daily News*, February 27, 1856.

[2] *Harrisburg Telegraph,* May 15, 1856.

[3] *Ibid.,* February 26, March 4, 1856.

[4] *Daily News.* June 13, 14, 16, 17, 18, 1856.

[5] *Harrisburg Telegraph,* June 19, 26, 1856.

Frémont and Johnston.[1]   Later in the campaign, on August
29, Johnston withdrew, and thereupon the support of the
"North Americans," with the exception of a small group,
was given to the Republican party.[2]

On September 17 there gathered at Baltimore a Whig
national convention for which somehow or other delegates
from twenty-one states had been selected.   They claimed
to be " old line " Whigs, who assembled to reaffirm the faith,
but many avowed Americans were in attendance.   The convention placed Fillmore and Donelson in nomination.[3]   This
action attracted little attention, although in Philadelphia a
mass meeting was held to celebrate the event.[4]   In the interior of the state the Whig remnant had joined in endorsing Frémont and Dayton as the " People's Candidates "
and were forming " Union " tickets.[5]

In the spring campaign of 1856, the Democrats of Pennsylvania indiscriminately attacked both the Americans and
the Republicans, particularly after the formation of the
state " Union " ticket.   The chief organ of the state party
said that the national American convention was " composed
of flesh, fish, fowl and small beer, the latter ingredient
forming the largest part of the *pot pourri*. . . . No part of
the assemblage knows what it wants, but the negro portion,
and they go for Nigger first, last and all the time." [6]   When

[1] *Daily News,* June 21, 1856.

[2] *Harrisburg Telegraph,* September 11, 1856; the New Jersey and five
other delegates nominated Robert F. Stockton and Kenneth Raynor,
Daily News, June 17, 18, July 10, 1856. Johnston's letter of withdrawal in *Evening Bulletin,* September 15, 1856.

[3] *Daily News,* September 18, 19, 1856.

[4] *Ibid.,* September 22, 1856.

[5] *Harrisburg Telegraph,* July 17, August 7, 14, 28, September 4, 11,
1856.

[6] *Daily Pennsylvanian,* February 21, 1856.

the Democrats carried the mayoralty election of Philadelphia in May, this journal gloried at the defeat of the " Dark Lantern Party " and at the discomfiture of the " Nigger Worshippers." [1]   When it became evident that the Americans and the Republicans were not cooperating in the national campaign, the Democrats, changing their tactics, attacked primarily the Republicans, striving to prove them as unpalatable to the Americans as to the Democrats.   If cooperation should be achieved by the Republicans and by the Americans, the Democrats might lose the state and the election; otherwise, their candidate was fairly sure of success.

In adopting the policy of attacking the Republicans most bitterly, the Democrats avoided being too offensive to the Americans.   They asserted that Frémont was a Catholic, and, despite the denials of his supporters, repeated the charges.   They pointed out how distasteful it was to see clergymen, like Henry Ward Beecher and Theodore Parker, take an active part in politics.   The formation of German Republican clubs was mentioned again and again, in the hope that their organization would disgust the ardent Americans.[2]   The Democrats not only strove to keep the Republicans and Americans apart, but renewed their efforts to capture more of the votes of the " old line " Whigs. In past elections they had secured a number from this group, by painting the Americans, who referred to their party as " Sam," as the party of proscription.   After the preliminary plans for cooperation in the presidential election had been perfected, one editor stated that " Sam has

---

[1] *Daily Pennsylvanian,* May 8, 31, 1856.

[2] *Ibid.,* September 20, 27, October 25; *Harrisburg Weekly Telegraph,* September 25, October 9, 23; *Bedford Gazette,* July 25, August 22, September 19, October 3, 10, 1856.

yielded to Sambo." [1]   Repeatedly they made the claim that
Frémont was a sectional candidate, favored abolition, and
that disunion would follow his election.[2]   The sneer of
Thaddeus Stevens, that "The cry of 'The Union is in
danger' is the argument of fools to an audience of idiots,"
was declared to be characteristic of "that bold, daring, con-
scienceless demagogue."   Many evils had descended upon
the state in the past because the opposition party had yielded
to his leadership, and now he was unfurling the banner of
disunion for them.[3]

If disunion came as a result of the election of
Frémont, as the Democrats asserted it surely would, then,
they continued, the profitable trade of Philadelphia with
the South would be lost.   In fact, the trade of some
Philadelphia merchants in that area was already being tampered with.   According to a card, published by Morris L.
Hallowell and Company, who had an extensive southern
trade in dry goods and clothing, "systematic and pertina-
cious efforts" were made in the South to divert trade away
from them "by appeals to the prejudices of buyers on the
score of *unsound* political sentiments of some of the members of our firm."   The firm held "in *especial* contempt that
class of dealers in our city who 'sell their principles with
their goods.'"   In order that there might be no mistaking
their position they concluded their card as follows:

The members of our firm, entertaining a wide difference of
views on various topics, and as many opinions on the Slavery
Question as there are members of it, are fully united on *one*
point namely: that where any one presumes to demand as a
preliminary to purchasing from us, that he shall know our

[1] *Daily Pennsylvanian*, October 4, 1856.

[2] *Ibid.*, September 6, 13, 16, October 2, 7, 1856.

[3] *Ibid.*, October 7, 1856.

opinions on Slavery, or any other mooted question in Religion
or Politics, he shall be informed . . . that he *cannot* purchase
from us for cash or upon *any* terms, until he shall have amply
apologized for the insult.[1]

Stories were assiduously circulated that if Buchanan should
be defeated, the South would refuse to pay the sixty million
dollars, which it owed to the merchants and manufacturers
of Philadelphia.[2]   That Philadelphia merchants, manufacturers, and workingmen were dependent for their prosperity
on continued amicable relations with the South, which,
in turn, were dependent upon the election of Buchanan, was
the gist of this Democratic argument.   Queries to manufacturers brought out the extent of the southern trade.   Richard Morris and Son, engine-makers, said, " The South is
decidedly our best customer; " to it they annually sent
$300,000 worth of commodities, but to the New England
states nothing.   Bailey and Brothers, jewellers, thought that
without their southern trade their sales would drop off
one-half; they sold nothing to the New England states.
Dunlap and Brothers, coach makers, claimed that their
business with the South was ten times as large as that with
New England.   They said, " Should difficulty occur with
the South, we will be compelled to close part of our factory
and discharge half of our men."   From a scrutiny of these
and other facts, the editor of the Democratic *Daily Pennsylvanian* concluded that

the main source of the great wealth and prosperity of Philadelphia, and indeed of all the Northern States, is the trade of
the slaveholding States—this it is that builds up and sustains
the cities and towns of the North—builds up and sustains our

[1] *Evening Bulletin,* August 23, 1856.
[2] *Ibid.,* September 30, 1856.

commerce and our manufactures, and gives to the real estate in and about Philadelphia its present increased value.

Will you, workingmen, mechanics, manufacturers, merchants, or property-holders, strike it down, as is proposed by Black-Republican leaders, either by a dissolution of the Union, or by endangering its peaceful continuance? or by alienation of the friendly feeling of the Southern States? Will you destroy or jeopard it that the three or four millions of negro slaves in these States may be set *free*, let *loose* upon the country, to come upon *you*, the people of Pennsylvania, to fill your cities, towns, and country, with paupers and crime, as is now exhibited in St. Domingo and Jamaica, to take the place of you, white workingmen, mechanics, and manufacturers, or to become your equals and companions? Ask the Judge Kelleys and the Speaker Banks', and all their Fremont Abolition leaders and their Fillmore aiders and abettors, these questions.[1]

The Democrats asserted that, if Buchanan should be elected, it " will have been the work of the conservative men of the country, including many of the mercantile classes." The Republicans urged the voters not to forget that Buchanan was one of the authors of the Ostend Manifesto, and that if he were true to its doctrines, war would inevitably follow. Naturally, in that event, the merchants would be the first to suffer.[2] The Republicans tried to appeal to the workingmen by reviving the stale charge that Buchanan favored a daily wage of ten cents for them.[3] Little advantage was derived from this line of attack.

The Democrats fully realized that of their two opponents Frémont was the more formidable, and constantly referred to him as " The Abolition Candidate." [4] One editor from

---

[1] October 11, 1856.

[2] *Evening Bulletin*, October 28, 1856.

[3] *Harrisburg Weekly Telegraph*, September 25, October 9, 1856.

[4] *Daily Pennsylvanian*, October 2, 7, 1856.

the western portion of the state said the true issue was,
" Is a white man as good as a black man?"[1]   The Democratic state central committee, under the leadership of
John W. Forney, declared the negro in the North was
nowhere the equal of the white man and asked, " Why
is it that Abolitionism does not begin at home and reform
these things?"[2]   The Republicans did not shirk from meeting these attacks, admitting that the " extension or non-ex-
tension [of slavery] is the sole issue," but denied that the
question of interference with it where it existed was involved.[3]

In June Buchanan had been nominated at Cincinnati
as the Democratic candidate for the presidency.   With two
opponents in a normally Democratic state, it was quite
evident that the Democrats would be victorious.   Despite the
proposal that a " Union " electoral ticket be formed, the
American party held a state convention to form a Fillmore
and Donelson electoral ticket.[4]   This proved to be the chief
obstacle in the way of thoroughgoing cooperation.   However, on October 7, 1856, the " Union " state central committee, appointed at the March convention to secure the
election of the state officers there nominated, called a convention of all the Buchanan opponents to meet on October
21.   They proposed, in their call, a plan of proportional
cooperation, whereby the voters were to vote for the same
twenty-six electors' and the twenty-seventh elector, who
was to head the list, was to be either Fillmore or Frémont
according to the preference of the voter.   In the event that
the " Union " ticket should be elected, the twenty-seventh

---

[1] *Bedford Gazette,* August 1, 1856.

[2] *Daily Pennsylvanian,* August 30, 1856.

[3] *Evening Bulletin,* November 1, 1856.

[4] *Daily News,* August 7, 1856.

elector would be lost but the other twenty-six electors were to vote for Fillmore and for Frémont according to the proportion of votes which they had received as the twenty-seventh elector.[1] Before the convention met, the state election was held and the Democrats were victorious by a small majority of two thousand.[2] This defeat acted as an incentive for the adoption of the proposed plan. The electoral ticket which was thus formed was endorsed by the Republican and the " North American " committees, but by only six, a minority, of the Fillmore and Donelson committee.[3]

The views of both the Republicans and Democratic parties were most assiduously spread throughout the state both before and after the state elections on October 14. The intensity of the campaign increased prior to the presidential election. The Democrats claimed that the Republicans in secret conclave in New York city had raised $100,000 to be used in the state.[4] They themselves apparently had a large fund at their disposal. Into each one of the twenty-eight senatorial districts of the state, they sent speakers, either from beyond the state or from some other portion of the state. For two weeks prior to the election, some sixty men were kept busy with itinerant speechmaking.[5] In no preceding campaign had the state been so thoroughly covered by any political party.

[1] *Carlisle Herald*, October 15, 1856.

[2] *Harrisburg Weekly Telegraph*, October 30, 1856; the vote for canal commissioner was George Scott (Dem.) 212,925; Thomas Cochran ("Union") 210,172.

[3] *Ibid.*, October 22, 1856.

[4] *Daily Pennsylvanian*, October 18, 1856; for the gathering of funds in other states to be used in Pennsylvania, see Rhodes, *History of the United States*, vol. ii, pp. 230-231.

[5] *Ibid.*, October 18, 1856.

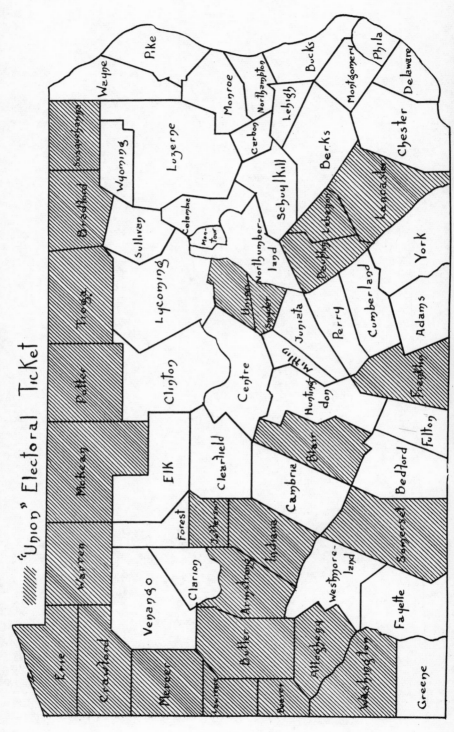

"Union" Electoral Ticket

PRESIDENTIAL ELECTION OF 1856

Amidst great excitement, the election was held on November 4. The returns indicated that Buchanan, due to the failure of some of the Americans to cooperate with the Republicans, carried the state by a comfortable plurality of 27,000. Of the popular vote he received 230,686. As the twenty-seventh elector on the "Union" ticket, Frémont received 147,286 and Fillmore 55,852 votes; but the first elector on the "Union" ticket received 203,534. For the independent American electoral ticket 26,337 votes were cast. Buchanan thus had a majority of only 815 votes. Had there been a thoroughgoing cooperation, it is probable that Buchanan would not have carried the state. In that case, he would not have had a majority of the votes of the electoral colleges, and the choice of a President would have devolved upon the national House of Representatives.[1]

[1] The state electoral returns are in *Legislative Documents*, 1857, pp. 666-677.

CHAPTER VIII

CHARACTERISTICS OF THE WHIG PARTY

THE Whig party, both in its national and in its state organizations, was peculiarly one of compromise and concession. Policies were announced, adhered to for a time, and, on the threat of internal opposition, modified and ultimately abandoned. While the shifting of parties on alleged principles is a common phenomenon of politics, yet possibly no party was ever so thoroughly committed to it as was the Whig. In a measure, it was inevitable that this should be so. Its great leader and idol, Henry Clay, had earned for himself, because of his compromising and compounding on the tariff issue in 1833, the title of " The Great Pacificator." A willingness to compromise on other issues marked his later career, culminating in the series of laws adopted in 1850, none of which definitively answered the questions which had been raised. With Clay and other leaders willing to abandon avowed principles and unwilling to adhere to definitely announced policies, the party wandering after the will-o'-the-wisp of immediate gain finally lost all.

The existence of the Whig party was not, however, without some advantage to the country. Its policy of political opportunism afforded ample time for the divergent sentiments in the sections to crystallize, showed the futility of efforts to compromise on fundamental principles, and proved the incompatibility of membership which was not founded on homogeneity. For, the accessions, which came to the Whig party as the result of its compromising, prevented

236

the party from becoming homogeneous, which in turn forced it on to other compromises. At the elections for the presidency in 1844 and in 1852, at which the party endeavored to enunciate principles, the Whigs suffered defeat. In its two successful elections, the candidates, made palatable by a certain amount of military glory, were nominated without platforms.

Within the state, the lack of homogeneity and its accompanying evils were strikingly in evidence. At the formation of the party, the National Republicans, who had a strong following only in and around Philadelphia, converted themselves into the Whig party, accomplishing the transformation largely throughout a mere change of name. The Anti-Masons, who had more supporters in the state than the National Republicans, controlled the opposition to the Democracy in the interior counties. By holding themselves aloof and by not joining the new Whig organization, they compelled the Whigs to be pretentiously conciliatory to them, and thus secured the direction of the opposition to the Democracy for the entire state until after the Buckshot War. Consequently, the Whigs during this period found themselves committed to a policy with which they were not in sympathy. Only the collapse of political Anti-Masonry relieved the Whigs from their embarrassing situation; but the sentiment for Anti-Masonry persisted and sporadically continued to vex the Whigs. Political like-mindedness, the basic principle of all effective party organization, was consequently missing amongst the Whigs. Another political element, coming early to the Whigs, but not numerically as important as the Anti-Masons, was from the " Convention Democrats." Although numerically few, yet they exercised, temporarily at least, an influence on the Whigs out of proportion to their strength. But in the long run they lost their power, because, on account of their small numbers, the possibility of their withdrawal from the party caused no great alarm to the Whigs.[1]

The lack of homogeneity is possibily best seen in the readiness with which defections occurred from the ranks of the Whigs. The sudden spread of the Native American movement in 1844, particularly in Philadelphia city and county, caused the Whigs great concern, for the new party was composed largely of former Whigs and the movement was symptomatic of what might recur at any moment. The defeat of Clay and the remarkable strength of the Native Americans left the Whigs so badly disorganized that disintegration of the party threatened for a time in the early part of 1845. The failure of the Native American movement to assume national proportions led to its gradual decadence within the state, removed the possibility of its achieving even an effective state organization, and left a mere local party, but strong enough, if not cooperating with the Whigs, to prevent them from carrying the elections. Efforts to win back the former Whigs through coalition and then amalgamation were made, but without a great deal of success. The nomination of Taylor in 1848 made it possible for the Native Americans to cooperate with the Whigs without feeling that they were abandoning their party. Many Native Americans and a few Taylor Democrats were thus definitely won to the party. A number of irreconcilable Native Americans by maintaining an independent organization after the election of Taylor and by refusing to cooperate caused the defeat of Whig candidates, and constantly through their existence threatened a revival of active Native Americanism.

With the appearance of the Know Nothing movement in 1854, the Whig party, as a national organization, was well

---

[1] For a keen analysis of the Whig party in another state, see Fox, *The Decline of Aristocracy in the Politics of New York*, pp. 409, et seq.

on its way to decay. The readiness with which Whigs went off and joined the new organization precluded the possibility of a rejuvention of the Whig national party. The blighting effect was first evidenced in the state party. As a state organization, the Whigs had weathered the stormy defeats in the gubernatorial election of 1851 and in the presidential election of 1852. In the former election, Free Soil Democrats had supported Johnston, but the following year refused their votes to Scott. After the latter election, statements that the party was dead abounded; but the state organization, weakened as it was, nevertheless showed some signs of vitality in the election for canal commissioner in 1853. Prospects for a revival of the party were fairly bright in 1854, but were soon lost to view because of the dazzling brilliancy of the Know Nothing movement. Unmistakable evidence was now at hand that the Whig party could not recover its lost glory, and that within a short period of time the party would completely disappear.

The instability of the Whig constituency, in part acquired and held as the result of frequent compromising and vacillating, was its chief element of weakness. At any moment, disaffection might lead large or small groups out of the party. The Native American and the Know Nothing movements illustrate the danger from this source. The Liberty party in the forties and the Temperance movement in the fifties carried away in local elections a number of Whigs. A problem, consequently, constantly facing the Whigs was how to prevent the disaffection and how to win back the disaffected. At times the efforts of the Whigs were successful. But the shifting of the members of the party almost en masse to the Know Nothings left only a feeble minority of the Whigs, making futile efforts to maintain the old organization. The absence of common definite political principles had worked itself out to its logical conclusion. The

Whig party of the state in its effort to absorb so many heterogeneous elements had constantly been suffering from acute political indigestion, which had regularly caused it discomfort and ultimately brought it to an untimely end.

Throughout its career, the Whig party was a minority party in the state, but a minority party of sufficient strength to cause the opposition considerable alarm. Rarely did it succeed in carrying an election. Two of its five electoral tickets, the one in 1840 by a majority of less than 350, and the other in 1848 by a majority of 2,400 and a plurality of 13,500, were elected. Of their gubernatorial candidates, the Whigs succeeded in electing only William F. Johnston, in 1848, and that by a narrow majority of 225. Ritner, the Anti-Masonic candidate in 1835, was supported by the Whigs and was elected as the result of the split in the Democratic party. The election of James Pollock in 1854, the Whig nominee, was made possible only because of the support of the Know Nothings and was by no means an indication of Whig vitality. The political upheaval in 1846 made the election of a Whig canal commissioner a certainty, just as the election of 1848 made the choice of a United States Senator by the Whig legislature an actuality. The weakness of the party made impossible the appearance of a powerful office-holding Whig, capable of using the patronage to build up a strong political machine. For a time, Governor Johnston offered some hope, but his leadership was immediately threatened by Senator Cooper and the free-soil tendencies of the governor alienated sympathizers with the South. The southerners themselves tried to prevent the use of the federal patronage to strengthen the position of the governor. His defeat for reelection in 1851 eliminated the strongest leader the party had developed in Pennsylvania and left it with a discredited head.

At the formation of the Whig party, there seemed to be

presented an issue which would sharply divide Whigs from Democrats. The hostility of President Jackson to the Bank of the United States and the means used by him to crush it lent themselves readily to political agitation. Although enthusiasm for the bank was connected with cries of " executive usurpation," nevertheless progress, sufficient to carry the election, was not made. The election of Ritner in the following year prevented the elimination of the banking question, for the bank received a state charter. At best, it was hoped that this would be a mere temporary expedient, and, at worst, not wholly undesirable; for, if the Whigs should be successful in the presidential election of 1836 or of 1840, the state charter might be converted into a national one. Two features of the act granting the state charter proved to be extremely disadvantageous to the state. The repeal of the direct taxes, intended to be nothing more than a beautiful gesture to attract attention to the Whig-Anti-Masonic coalition, resulted in the temporary financial bankruptcy of the state. The lavish expenditure of the money received for the charter secured the needed votes to obtain the passage of the bill, but did not bring the hoped-for permanent support. The act, however, pledged the state to construct extensions of the public works which burdened it by their unprofitableness. The continued existence of the dreaded money monopoly, now a state corporation, did not tend to assuage the fears of the people of the interior of the state. The business depression beginning in 1837 and the numerous suspensions of the banks kept the question of finance prominently in the foreground for a number of years. The Whigs attempted to avoid responsibility for the plight in which their policy had put the state. It was only after the final failure of the Bank of the United States and the recovery of the country from the industrial depression that other issues demanded more attention.

In the early forties, the question which, so far as the state was concerned, attracted most attention was the tariff. Between the two parties there was no line of demarcation on this issue. The Tariff Bill of 1842, although not conceding all that the ardent protectionists demanded, did not receive an adverse vote from a Pennsylvania Congressman in its passage through the house. In the election of 1844 both parties claimed to be the ardent friends and guardians of this measure. Widely separated positions were taken on the question of the annexation of Texas, with the Democrats favoring and the Whigs opposing it. The admission of Texas was an accomplished fact before the tariff received consideration. When the bill of 1846 passed the Senate, the two Senators from Texas made the passage of the bill possible by their votes. No extensive argument was required to convince the Whigs of the state that the tariff had been tampered with on the insistence of the slave-owners that less protection was needed. For a time, even the Democrats, stunned by the passage of the bill, joined in the retaliatory action of the state against slavery. They participated in the passage of the act of March 3, 1847, forbidding the use of the state jails for the detention of captured fugitive slaves, and in adopting resolutions endorsing the Wilmot Proviso. By the election of 1848 the Democrats of the state had partially recovered from their panic and willingly followed the national party in the pro-slavery principles which it enunciated. The national Whig party failed to adopt a platform for this election; consequently it was possible for the state parties to take individual lines of departure. In Pennsylvania, the Whig party, continuing its opposition to the extension of slavery, was completely under the control of the free-soil element. Although all the elements of decay were present in the national Whig party in the election of 1848, yet they did not become fully manifest until the succeeding election. By that time, it was evident that the state parties had wandered so far apart that no common meeting ground could be agreed upon, and that the scattering of the membership must follow. The efforts of the American party to frame a platform acceptable to the divergent elements were likewise unsuccessful. With the appearance of the Republican party and its adoption of understandable principles, new life was infused into the opposition to the Democracy.

One naturally expects to find the wealthy merchants and manufacturers rallying to the Whig standard. Thomas P. Cope, whose commercial ventures were made in all parts of the globe and who founded one of the first regular lines of packets between the United States and Europe, and John Price Wetherill, who left "a large fortune, probably near a million," made in manufacturing, assume positions of leadership in the ranks of the party in Philadelphia. The leaders of the Philadelphia Bar, John Sergeant and Horace Binney, closely associated with the mercantile and the vested interest classes, occasionally found time to leave their lucrative practice and accept political office. That the Whigs were in control of the banking interests of the state was the conclusion reached by an analysis of the officials of these institutions made by a Democratic journal. The majority of the manufacturers of iron took their stand in the Whig ranks; occasionally, however, due to the avowed protective tariff principles of the Democracy, a manufacturer, who started life as a Democrat, did not abandon his party upon the acquisition of wealth. In the thinly settled mountainous districts, the halting policy of the Democracy on the tariff question was early and consistently condemned. One of their journals criticized Governor Wolf, a Democrat, as follows:

See his annual message to the Legislature in favor of Henry Clay's "American System," the " Protective Tariff," so called, which extorted from the working people $35,000,000 a year, and lavished a great part of it upon favorites, and the rank aristocracy of the cities, under the name of protection.[1]

In 1846, a Democrat from this section was the only one of the Representatives from the state who dared vote for the Tariff Bill of 1846. Despite his vote, or possibly because of it, he was triumphantly reelected.

The evaluation of the property in the counties of the state for the purposes of taxation gives interesting information on the prosperity of the Whig counties. The data for 1851, when there were sixty-four counties, seventeen of which were normally Whig, is somewhat fuller than that for other periods.[2] Philadelphia city, in addition to the seventeen counties, was regularly carried by the Whigs and the county by the Democrats, where the Whigs, however, always showed considerable strength. The statistics for the county and the city are unfortunately not separated. Although Philadelphia city and county contained less than eighteen per cent of the population, yet they possessed almost twenty-eight per cent of the evaluated .property of the state. Omitting Philadelphia city and county and arranging the other counties of the state according to population, it is seen that fifteen of the first thirty-three counties are normally Whig. If they are arranged according to the evaluation of their property thirteen of the first thirty-three are Whig. A difference is noted, for in the second classification the Whig counties are nearer the head of the list. The seventeen Whig counties—Philadelphia city and county are omitted—contained somewhat more that thirty-

[1] *Democratic State Journal,* May 11, 1835, quoting *Wilkesbarre Farmer.*

[2] *House Journal,* 1852, vol. ii, pp. 136-137.

five per cent of the population but a trifle less than forty-three per cent of the wealth. If Philadelphia city and county are included, the Whig counties contained somewhat over fifty-eight per cent of the population and over eighty-one per cent of the wealth. The Whigs were thus in control of the more prosperous counties of the state. In the more prosperous of the normal Democratic counties, with the exception of Berks, the Whigs possessed a strong following, at times well over forty per cent of the voters. Fertile Berks, settled by Germans, was the fourth county of the state in population and in wealth. The voters had been won over early by the Democratic-Republican party, later worshipped Andrew Jackson, and the imperturbable " Pennsylvania Dutch " farmers never failed to roll up large Democratic majorities. The voters, due to the absence of a sectarian appeal, had been untouched by the Anti-Masonic movement and consequently remained true to their Democratic faith. The conclusion is almost inevitable that although the Whig party did not include all the people of wealth in the state, yet the vast majority of those possessing vested interests felt that the Whig party offered them more protection than did the opposition party.

From the foundation of the Whig party, the Democrats claimed that the policy of their opponents was to favor the wealthier classes. One of their journals at the capital asserted,

The Whig, resting government on wealth, lays the foundation of a monied aristocracy; Democracy, resting government on the intelligence and morality of the masses, establishes the supremacy of the people, and opens the way to the principality of virtue.[1]

At its foundation, the Whig Party, particularly in the

[1] *Democratic State Journal*, December 8, 1835.

counties of the interior, claimed for itself true democratic
principles, in some instances, as has been seen, asserting
that the party was based on the foundations laid by Jefferson.
During the first decade of its existence, these claims gradually disappeared. The statement of the *Pennsylvania Telegraph*, that " Whig policy is democratic without being revolutionary; conservative in opposition to agrarian," [1] may
be taken as a typical view of themselves during the second
decade. The tendency to stress the fact that the party was
conservative appeared more strongly with the passage of
time. When the death rattle was in the throat of the
Whig party, one of the more conservative of the Whig
journals said, in reply to the assertions that the Whig party
was dead,

Indeed, not only is the Whig party still alive, but, in one sense
at least, it can never die. A party composed of similar materials to that which rallied around Clay and Webster must
always exist in this country under one name or another. For
it is the representative of the more highly educated, the more
prudent, and the wealthier classes, combined, if you will, with
the more aristocratic. Thousands, who start life as Democrats, end by deserting to this party, because, with age, the
illusions of youth disappear, and faith grows cold.

The editor thought that the Whigs had been in the minority
because the country was young, but as it grew older the
Whigs would predominate.[2] Hardly had these predictions
been made, when many of the conservative " old line "
Whigs, alarmed at the radicalism of the new American and
the newer Republican parties and realizing that their old
organization had passed on to its political reward, found
refuge in the ranks of the Democrats because they considered it the only conservative party.

[1] August 3, 1847.
[2] *Evening Bulletin*, August 15, 1853.

I. CRITICAL BIBLIOGRAPHY [1]

MANUSCRIPTS

Papers of Nicholas Biddle; Library of Congress. Valuable for the political activities of the bank officers and agents.

Papers of Nicholas Biddle; Historical Society of Pennsylvania. Concerned primarily with the business of the bank.

Papers of James Buchanan; Hist. Soc. of Penna. A large and valuable collection of letters from the leading Democrats of the state and many drafts of letters from Buchanan.

Papers of Lewis S. Coryell; Hist. Soc. of Penna. Letters from many anti-Buchanan Democrats.

Papers of Edward McPherson; Lib. of Cong. A few letters from Whigs which are of value.

Papers of William McPherson; Hist. Soc. of Penna. Chiefly letters to Joseph Wallace, for a time chairman of the state Anti-Masonic party, which show the trend of that party during the period 1832 to 1844.

Papers of Joseph Ritner; State Library of Pennsylvania. Chiefly petitions, of little value.

Papers of John Sergeant; Hist. Soc. of Penna. Nothing of value for this period.

Society Collection; Hist. Soc. of Penna. Isolated letters of considerable value.

Papers of Thaddeus Stevens; Lib. of Cong. Contain some material of value.

Papers of Governor George Wolf; State Lib. of Penna. Chiefly petitions and memorials of no great value.

Papers of Governor George Wolf; Hist. Soc. of Penna. A few Democratic letters of value.

PUBLISHED WORKS AND CORRESPONDENCE

Kelley, William D., *Speeches, Addresses and Letters on Industrial and Financial Questions.* Philadelphia, 1872. The introduction is the most valuable portion of the volume.

[1] The critical bibliography is limited to Pennsylvania material, inasmuch as many bibliographies on the general field are available. A non-critical bibliography of other cited material is added.

McGrane, Reginald C., editor, *The Correspondence of Nicholas Biddle dealing with National Affairs, 1807-1844.* Boston, 1919. Very valuable for the activity of the bank officials in the early years of the party.

Moore, John Bassett, editor, *The Works of James Buchanan comprising his Speeches, State Papers, and Private Correspondence.* 12 vols. Philadelphia, 1908-1911. Extremely valuable for the light thrown on the Whig party by the activities and views of the leader of their opponents.

DOCUMENTS

Laws of Pennsylvania, 1834-1856. Harrisburg, 1834-1856.

Journals of the Senate of Pennsylvania, 1834-1856. Harrisburg, 1834-1856.

Journals of the House of Representatives of Pennsylvania. Harrisburg, 1834-1856.

Executive Documents of the Legislature of Pennsylvania, 1843-1856. Harrisburg, 1843-1856.

Legislative Documents of Pennsylvania, 1854-1856. Harrisburg, 1854-1856.

Pennsylvania Archives, series iv, "Papers of the Governors." 12 vols. Harrisburg, 1900-1902. The collection is incomplete and unsatisfactory.

Proceedings and Debates of the Convention of the Commonwealth of Pennsylvania to propose Amendments to the Constitution, commenced and held at Harrisburg, on the second day of May, 1837. 14 vols. Harrisburg, 1837-1839.

Journal of the Convention of the State of Pennsylvania to propose Amendments to the Constitution. 2 vols. Harrisburg, 1837-1838.

Minutes of the Committee of the Whole, of the Convention of the State of Pennsylvania, to propose Amendments to the Constitution. Bound with the *Journal of the Convention.*

Clark, John A., *Pennsylvania Law Journal Reports, containing Cases decided by the Federal and State Courts of Pennsylvania.* 5 vols. Philadelphia, 1872-73. Volumes iv and v contain cases on the constitutionality of the Act of March 3, 1847, and others involving interference with the enforcement of the Fugitive Slave Law.

The Federal Cases, comprising Cases argued and determined in the Circuit and District Courts of the United States, from the earliest times to the beginning of the Federal Reporter. Case No. 5243, a Pennsylvania case, is the first one arising under the Fugitive Slave Law. 31 vols. St. Paul, 1894-98.

Parsons, A. V., *Select Cases in Equity and at Law, argued and determined in the Court of Common Pleas of the First Judicial Dis-*

trict of Pennsylvania from 1842-51. 2 vols. Philadelphia, 1888. Contains the proceedings in the trial of George Alberti for kidnaping.

Reports of the Supreme Court of Pennsylvania. Volumes xxvi and xxxix contain cases arising out of the detention of Passmore Williamson.

Reports of the Supreme Court of the United States. 16 *Peters* for Prigg *v.* Pennsylvania.

Wallace, Henry E., *Philadelphia Reports, or Legal Intelligencer condensed; containing the Decisions published in the Legal Intelligencers.* Volume i (Philadelphia, 1856) for the trial of escaped negroes at Harrisburg.

Wallace, John William, *Cases in the Circuit Court of the United States for the Third Circuit.* 3 vols. Philadelphia, 1849-71. The treason trials, arising out of the Christiana riot, are in volume ii.

Smull's Legislative Hand-Book and Manual of the State of Pennsylvania, 1919. Harrisburg, 1919.

NEWSPAPERS [1]

A. INDEPENDENT

Public Ledger, Philadelphia. 1836-1857; Hist. Soc. of Penna.; State Lib.; N. Y. Pub. Lib.

The Register of Pennsylvania, devoted to the Preservation of Facts and Documents, and every other Kind of Useful Information respecting the State of Pennsylvania, edited by Samuel Hazard, Philadelphia, 1828-1835.

Hazard's United States Commercial and Statistical Register, containing Documents, Facts, and other Useful Information, illustrative of the History and Resources of the American Union, and of each State, Philadelphia. 1839-1842.

Morning Chronicle, Pittsburgh. 1842-1856; Pittsburgh Carnegie Lib.

Anthracite Gazette and Schuylkill County Advocate, Pottsville. May-Dec., 1847; Lib. of Cong.

B. ANTI-MASONIC, WHIG, AND AMERICAN

Butler County Whig, Butler. 1846-1851, N. Y. Hist. Soc.; 1846-1855, Pitt. Car. Lib.

Carlisle Herald, Carlisle. 1852-1856, Lib. of Cong.

Franklin Whig, Chambersburg. 1835-1840, State Lib.

Franklin Repository, Chambersburg. 1834-1840, State Lib.

---

[1] The arrangement is alphabetical according to the place of publication.

Repository and Whig, Chambersburg. 1842, State Lib.; 1854, Hist. Soc. of Penna.

Germantown Telegraph, Germantown. 1834-1856, Hist. Soc. of Penna.

Westmoreland Intelligencer, Greensburg. 1850-1856, State Lib.

Daily American, Harrisburg. Dec. 1850-May 1851, State Lib.

Clay Bugle, Harrisburg. Jan.-Oct., 1844, State Lib.

Harrisburg Chronicle, Harrisburg. 1834-1840, State Lib.

Old Warrior, Harrisburg. 1844, State Lib.

Pennsylvania Intelligencer, Harrisburg. 1834-1844, State Lib.

Pennsylvania Telegraph, Harrisburg. 1834-1856, State Lib.; 1851-1853, Lib. of Cong.

Whig State Journal, Harrisburg. 1851-1853, State Lib.

The Watchman, Harrisburg. June-Oct., 1841. State Lib.

Inland Daily, Lancaster. 1854, State Lib.

Lancaster Examiner and Herald, Lancaster. Jan.-June, 1847, Lib. of Cong.

Lancaster Union and Tribune, Lancaster. 1847, Lib. of Cong.

Lebanon Courier, Lebanon. 1850-1856, Hist. Soc. of Penna.

Daily Chronicle, Philadelphia. 1840-1843, 1845-1846, Hist. Soc. of Penna.

Daily Forum, Philadelphia. A few numbers, 1843-1844, N. Y. Pub. Lib.

Evening Bulletin, Philadelphia. 1847-1848, Lib. of Cong.; 1850-1856, State Lib.

National Gazette, Philadelphia. 1834-1841, State Lib.; Lib. of Cong.

North American, Philadelphia. 1839-1856, Hist. Soc. of Penna.; 1840-1856, Lib. of Cong.; 1847-1855, State Lib.; 1855-1856, N. Y. Pub. Lib.

Pennsylvania Inquirer, Philadelphia. 1833-1834, State Lib.; 1834, 1840-1846, 1850, 1852, Hist. Soc. of Penna.; 1845-1852, Lib. of Cong.

Daily News, Philadelphia. 1849-1850, 1853-1856, Lib. of Cong.

United States Gazette, Philadelphia. 1834-1838, 1840-1841, 1844-1847, State Lib.; 1842-1844, Lib. of Cong.

Daily Commercial Journal, Pittsburgh. 1845-1850, 1852-1853, Lib. of Cong.

Pittsburgh Daily Dispatch, Pittsburgh. 1847-1850, 1855-1856, Pitt. Car. Lib.

Pittsburgh Daily Gazette, Pittsburgh. 1834-1856, Pitt. Car. Lib.; 1849-1851, Lib. of Cong.

Pittsburgh Evening Telegraph, Pittsburgh. 1847-1848, Pitt. Car. Lib.

Pittsburgh Mercury, Pittsburgh. 1835-1842, Pitt. Car. Lib.

Miners' Journal, Pottsville. 1841-1850, Hist. Soc. of Penna.; 1842-1843, 1845-1856, Lib. of Cong.

C. DEMOCRATIC

Der Friedensbote, Allentown. 1834-1843. Hist. Soc. of Penna.
Der Lecha Patriot, Allentown. 1841-1856, Hist. Soc. of Penna.
Lehigh Reporter, Allentown. 1846-1848, Hist. Soc. of Penna.
Bedford Gazette, Bedford. 1834-1856, State Lib.
Perry County Democrat, Bloomfield. 1841-1847, Hist. Soc. of Penna.
Perry County Standard, Bloomfield. 1844-1846, Hist. Soc. of Penna.
American Volunteer, Carlisle. 1835-1851, State Lib.; 1846-1848, 1852-1856, Lib. of Cong.
Upland Union, Chester. 1834-1843, State Lib.
Doylestown Democrat and Bucks County Gazette, Doylestown. 1847 State Lib.
Easton Daily Express, Easton. 1856, Hist. Soc. of Penna.
Republican Compiler, Gettysburg. 1847-1848, Lib. of Cong.
Greensburg Democrat, Greensburg. 1854-1856, State Lib.
American Herald, Greensburg. 1854-1856, State Lib.
Democratic State Journal, Harrisburg. 1835-1837, State Lib.
Democratic Union, Harrisburg. 1843-1849, State Lib.; 1843-1845, Hist. Soc. of Penna.; 1845-1848, Lib. of Cong.
Harrisburg Argus, Harrisburg. 1845-1848, Lib. of Cong.
Die Harrisburger-Morgenröthe, Harrisburg. 1834-1840, State Lib.
The Keystone, Harrisburg. 1836-1843, 1848-1856, State Lib.; 1839-1843, Lib. of Cong.
Morning Herald and Harrisburg Daily Herald, Harrisburg. 1853-1856, State Lib.
Pennsylvania Reporter, Harrisburg. 1834-1846, State Lib.; 1836-1843, Hist. Soc. of Penna.; 1837-1840, Lib. of Cong.
Pennsylvania Staats Zeitung, Harrisburg. 1843-1848, State Lib.
State Capital Gazette, Harrisburg. 1839-1843, State Lib.
Lancaster Intelligencer, Lancaster. 1834-1852, State Lib.; 1847-1848, Lib. of Cong.
Lancasterian and Chronicle of the Times, Lancaster. 1848-1855, State Lib.
Lebanon Advertiser, Lebanon. 1849-1856, State Lib.
Lewisburg Chronicle, Lewisburg. 1851-1856, Hist. Soc. of Penna.
The Advocate, Lewistown. 1840-1843, State Lib.
Lewistown Republican and Mifflin County Workingmen's Advocate, Lewistown. 1840-1844, State Lib.
Manayunk Courier, Manayunk. 1848, Hist. Soc. of Penna.
Marietta Advocate and Farmers' and Mechanics' Intelligencer, Marietta. 1834-1835, State Lib.
Crawford Democrat and Northwestern Advertiser, Meadville. 1835-1847, State Lib.

Crawford Messenger, Meadville. 1834-1835, State Lib.

Juniata Register, Mifflintown. 1849-1851, State Lib.

Tuscorora Register and Juniata County Inquirer, Mifflintown. 1852-1855, State Lib.

Norristown Register, Norristown. 1843-1849, 1854-1856, Hist. Soc. of Penna.; 1847-1848, Lib. of Cong.

Norristown Watchman, Norristown. 1849-1851, Hist. Soc. of Penna.

American Advocate, Philadelphia. 1844-1845, N. Y. Pub. Lib.

American Courier, Philadelphia. 1847-1852, Lib. of Cong.

American Sentinel, Philadelphia. 1840-1847, State Lib.; 1845-1846, Lib. of Cong.

Daily Keystone and People's Journal, Philadelphia. 1845-1847, Lib. of Cong.

Daily Register, Philadelphia. 1851, Hist. Soc. of Penna.

Democratic Argus, Philadelphia. 1843-1844, Hist. Soc. of Penna.

The Pennsylvanian, Philadelphia. 1834-1856, Lib. of Cong.; Hist. Soc. of Penna.; 1846-1856, State Lib.

Spirit of the Times, Philadelphia. 1838-1845, 1847-1849, State Lib., 1842, 1844-1845, Hist. Soc. of Penna.; 1845-1848, Lib. of Cong.

Der Freiheits Freund, Pittsburgh. 1844-1856, Pitt. Car. Lib.

The Morning Ariel, Pittsburgh. 1845, Lib. of Cong.

Pittsburgh Post, Pittsburgh. 1842-1856, Pitt. Car. Lib.; 1845, 1847-1848, 1853-1856, Lib. of Cong.

Pottsville Emporium, Pottsville. 1847-1848, Lib. of Cong.

Alt Berks, Reading. 1841-1844, Hist. Soc. of Penna.

Democratic Press, Reading. 1835-1840, State Lib.

Der Liberale Beobachter, Reading. 1839-1856, Hist. Soc. of Penna.

Reading Gazette, Reading. 1843-1848, State Lib.

Bradford Reporter, Towanda. 1845-1847, 1850-1852, State Lib.

The American Republican and Chester County Democrat, West Chester. 1847-1848, Lib. of Cong.

Luzerne Democrat, Wilkes-Barre. 1847-1848, Lib. of Cong.

Republican Farmer and Democratic Journal, Wilkes-Barre. 1835-1847, State Lib.

York Gazette, York. 1847-1848, Lib. of Cong.

D. NATIVE AMERICAN

American Press and Republican, Lancaster. 1846-1848, Lib. of Cong.

Native American, Philadelphia. 1844, N. Y. Hist. Soc.

Native Eagle, Philadelphia. A few numbers in 1845-1846, N. Y. Pub. Lib.

The Sun, Philadelphia. 1846-1847, 1851-1852, Hist. Soc. of Penna.; 1849-1850, Lib. of Cong.

PAMPHLETS AND SPEECHES [1]

Meredith, William M., *An Oration delivered by request before the Whigs of Philadelphia, on the fourth of July, 1834.* Philadelphia, 1834.

Proceedings of a Convention of the Delegates from the Citizens of Pennsylvania, opposed to Executive Usurpation and Abuse, which assembled at Harrisburg, May 27, 1834. Harrisburg, 1834.

Proceedings of the Democratic State Convention, which assembled at Lewistown, on Wednesday, May 6, 1835. Harrisburg 1835.

Proceedings of the Democratic Republican Convention of Young Men of the State of Pennsylvania, held at Harrisburg, July 4, 1836. Harrisburg, 1836.

Opinion of the Hon. John Fox, President Judge of the Judicial District composed of the Counties of Bucks and Montgomery, against the Exercise of Negro Suffrage in Pennsylvania. Harrisburg, 1838.

Appeal of Forty Thousand Citizens, threatened with Disfranchisement, to the People of Pennsylvania. Philadelphia, 1838.

Burden, Jesse R., *Remarks of Dr. J. R. Burden, of Philadelphia Co., in the Senate of Pennsylvania, on the Abolition Question, February, 1838. Also his Valeditory Address as Speaker of the Senate, April, 1838.* Philadelphia, 1838.

Sergeant, John, *Speech of John Sergeant on the Judicial Tenure, delivered in the Convention of Pennsylvania on the 7th and 8th November, 1837.* Philadelphia, 1838.

Proceedings of the Whigs of Chester County, favourable to a distinct Organization of the Whig Party. West Chester, 1838.

Proceedings of a Convention of Democratic Young Men, Delegates from the Citizens of Pennsylvania, in favour of the Re-election of Joseph Ritner, and opposed to Martin Van Buren and the Sub-Treasury. Assembled at Reading, June 4, 1838. Reading, 1838.

A candid Statement of the Philadelphia County Ticket. (Harrisburg, 1839.)

Penrose, Charles B., *Address of the Hon. Charles B. Penrose, Speaker of the Senate; and the Speeches of Messrs. Fraley (City), Williams, Pearson, and Penrose, delivered in the Senate of Pennsylvania, on the Subject of the Insurrection at Harrisburg, at the Meeting of the Legislature in December, 1838.* Harrisburg, 1839.

The Buckshot War; or the last Kick of Anti-Masonry. A Burlesque Medley—poetic, prosaic, humorous, satirical, etc., by Peleg Sturtevant. Harrisburg, 1839.

Address of the Democratic Whig Association of the City and County

---

[1] Arranged chronologically.

of Philadelphia, to the People of Pennsylvania. April, 1839. Philadelphia, 1839.

Proceedings of the Democratic Whig State Convention; held in Chambersburg, Pa., on the 13th and 14th of June, 1839. Chambersburg, 1839.

The Democratic Medley, or Sayings and Doings, with the History of one Day, to which it added the Whigs' Light-House, and a Trip through the Custom-House and Post-Office. Calculated for the Meridian of Philadelphia, by a Member of the Democratic Party. Philadelphia, (1839).

Address of Citizens of Bradford County, formerly opposed to Martin Van Buren, showing why they now prefer him to Gen. Harrison. Towanda, 1840.

Proceedings of the Democratic State Convention. (Harrisburg, 1840.)

Miner, Charles, *An Address, delivered at the Democratic Whig Festival, at Wilkes-Barre, Penn., December 4, 1840. In honour of the Election of Gen. Wm. Henry Harrison.* Wilkes-Barre, 1841.

To the Democratic Party of Pennsylvania on the next Presidential Election, by Anthony Wayne. Philadelphia, 1841.

Hare, Robert, *A brief Exposition of the Injury done to the Community, and especially to the Poor, by the Prohibition of Bills under Five Dollars, while such Bills are permitted to circulate in adjoining States. In a Letter to William B. Reed, Esq., also a subsequent Letter, on the late Failure to resume Specie Payments. To which is annexed a Scheme for a National Currency.* Philadelphia, 1841.

Ritner, Joseph, *Vindication of General Washington from the Stigma of Adherence to Secret Societies by Joseph Ritner. . . . . Together with a letter to Daniel Webster and his Reply.* Boston, 1841.

The Life of General Markle. Philadelphia, 1844.

Das Leben Generals Joseph Markle. Philadelphia, 1844.

Address of the Democratic Hickory Club, for the City and County of Philadelphia, recommending Martin Van Buren as the Presidential Candidate for 1844. Also the Letter of Mr. Van Buren to the State Convention of Indiana. (Philadelphia, 1844.)

A few Remarks in behalf of the Tariff and Currency, with a brief Comparison of the Merits of the two Candidates for the Presidency, by a Mechanic. Philadelphia, 1844.

One Thousand Dollars Reward! To be paid if the Quotations are not those of Polk on the Tariff. Philadelphia, (1844).

A few plain Facts, addressed to the People of Pennsylvania, by a Citizen of Pennsylvania. Philadelphia, 1844.

Report of the Discussion at Pottsville, August 10, 1844, between J. G. Clarkson and F. W. Hughes, on the course of Henry Clay and J. K. Polk, relative to the Protective System, etc. Philadelphia, 1844.

Causes of the Kensington Riots explained, in a Series of Letters to the Hon. Daniel O'Connell, by a Pennsylvanian—a Dutchman. Philadelphia, 1845.

A full and complete Account of the late awful Riots in Philadelphia. Philadelphia, (1844).

The full Particulars of the late Riots, with a View of the Burning of the Catholic Churches, St. Michael's and St. Augustine's. Philadelphia, (1844).

A brief View of the Origin and Object of the Native American Party; by a Native American. Philadelphia, 1844.

Preamble and By-Laws of the Native American Central Executive Committee of the City of Philadelphia. Philadelphia, 1844.

Address of the American Republicans of the City of Philadelphia to the Native and Naturalized Citizens of the United States. Philadelphia, 1844.

Moore, Justus E., *The Warning of Thomas Jefferson: or a brief Exposition of the Dangers to be apprehended to our civil and religious Liberties, from Presbyterianism.* Philadelphia, 1844.

Arguments proving the Inconsistency and Impolicy of granting to Foreigners the Right of Voting; abstracted from a Pamphlet published in the Year 1810; by a Disciple of the Washington School. Philadelphia, 1844.

Pumroy, John N., *A Defence of our Naturalization Laws, with a friendly Warning to Members of the Native American Party.* Philadelphia, 1844.

Street Talk about a Ordinance of Councils, Passed the 11th July, 1844, organizing a Military Force for the Government of Philadelphia. Philadelphia, 1844.

Proceedings of the Native American State Convention held at Harrisburg February 22, 1845. Philadelphia, 1845.

An Address to the Mechanics and Laboring Men, who are native born Citizens of the United States, with Reasons why they ought to withhold their Support from Men who seek foreign Aid. Together with the Principles of the Native American Party, as adopted by the National Convention on the 4th of July, 1845. (Philadelphia, 1845.)

Declaration of Principles, of the Native American Convention, assembled at Philadelphia, July 4, 1845. (Philadelphia, 1845.)

Orr, Hector, *The Native American: a Gift for the People.* Philadelphia, 1845.

Whig Anti-Subscription Council Ticket. To the Whig Voters of the City of Philadelphia. Broadside. Philadelphia, (1846).

A Letter to John Jones, John Smith, and James Black, Esqs., on the Subject of the Right of the City of Philadelphia to subscribe for

Stock in the Pennsylvania Railroad Company; by John Doe, Esq. Philadelphia, 1846.

Address of the Committee opposed to Subscription. (Philadelphia, 1846.)

Council Ticket favourable to the Pennsylvania Railroad. Broadside. (Philadelphia, 1846.)

Proceedings of the Meeting of the City and County of Philadelphia in relation to the great Pennsylvania Rail Road, from Philadelphia via Harrisburg to Pittsburgh, with the Address of the Committee, to the People of Pennsylvania. Philadelphia, 1846.

Binney, Horace, *Opinion of Horace Binney upon the Right of the City Councils to subscribe for Stock in the Pennsylvania Rail-Road Company.* Philadelphia, 1846.

Wharton, Thomas I., *A Letter to Robert Toland and Isaac Elliott, Esqr's. on the Subject of the Right and Power of the City of Philadelphia to subscribe for Stock in the Pennsylvania Railroad Company.* Philadelphia, 1846.

The Pennsylvania Railroad Address of the Committee of Seven to the Citizens of Philadelphia and of Pennsylvania appointed at a Town Meeting, held at Philadelphia, on the 28th of April, 1846. (Philadelphia), 1846.

The Casting Vote of Vice-President Dallas on the Tariff of 1846. Philadelphia, 1846.

The Anti-Slavery Alphabet. Philadelphia, 1847.

Great Speech of the Hon. G. M. Dallas, upon the leading Topics of the Day, delivered at Pittsburgh, Pa., with a brief biographical Sketch, etc. Philadelphia, 1847.

Constitution and By-Laws of the Washington Female Native American Association of Southwark, instituted November, 1844. Philadelphia, 1848.

Great Whig Demonstration in favour of the Nomination of Gen. Taylor to the Presidency. The Buena Vista Festival. at Philadelphia, February 22, 1848. (Washington, 1848.)

Rough and Ready Rhymes: a Democratic Epic. Poem in Cantos; by T. Thistle. Philadelphia, 1848.

To the People of Pennsylvania...Every Citizen, who cherishes and values the Prosperity and Permanency of his Country and her Institutions, as he values his own and his Children's Prosperity and Happiness, Read! Pause!! Reflect!!! (Philadelphia, 1848.)

DeWitt, W. R., *A Discourse on the Life and Character of Francis R. Shunk, late Governor of Pennsylvania, delivered August 9, 1848.* Harrisburg, 1848.

Native American Hall Co. of Cedar Ward: Constitution and By-Laws, 1845. Philadelphia, 1849.

Leisler, Jacob, *Letters to the People of Pennsylvania on the Political Principles of the Free Soil Party.* Philadelphia,, 1850.

Bribery and Corruption!! Report of the Proceedings of the Williamsport Convention embracing the spirited Debates, given graphically; Testimony in relation to the Attempt to bribe two of the Delegates; and other interesting Particulars of the Occasion. Philadelphia, 1850.

Proceedings of the great Union Meeting held in the large Saloon of the Chinese Museum, Philadelphia, on the 21st of November, 1850, under a Call signed by upwards of five thousand Citizens, whose names are appended to the Proceedings. Philadelphia, 1850.

Lewis, Wm. D., *A brief Account of the Efforts of Senator Cooper, of Pennsylvania, and Charles Gibbons, and their Associates, to prevent the Confirmation of William D. Lewis, Collector of the Customs for the District of Philadelphia, as also of their Attempts, since his Confirmation, to procure his Removal from Office.* Philadelphia, 1851.

Reply of Charles Gibbons to the Pamphlet of William D. Lewis. Philadelphia, 1851.

In the Matter of the Charges against the Collector and Surveyor of the Port of Philadelphia: Reply of Charles Gibbons to the Argument of David Paul Brown. (Philadelphia, 1851.)

Preliminary Reply of Mr. Levin to Senator Cooper. Broadside. (Philadelphia, 1851.)

General Pierce and the Catholics. Philadelphia, 1852.

Five Years Abstract of Transactions of the Pennsylvania Society for Promoting the Abolition of Slavery, the Relief of Free Negroes unlawfully held in Bondage, and for improving the Condition of the African Race. Philadelphia, 1853.

Will the Interests of Pennsylvania be advanced, or the Revenue increased, by continuing the Tonnage Tax upon the Pennsylvania Railroad? Is a Tax upon the through Tonnage constitutional? (Philadelphia, 1854.)

Emigration, Emigrants, and Know-Nothings; by a Foreigner. Philadelphia, 1854.

A few Words to the thinking and judicious Voters of Pennsylvania. (Philadelphia, 1854.)

The Modern Battle of the Kegs; by the Poet Laureate of the Know-Nothings. Philadelphia, 1854.

Encroachments of the Roman Catholic Hierarchy on the civil and religious Liberties of People in Europe, Asia, Africa, and America. Philadelphia, (1854).

To the Democratic Members of the Legislature of Pennsylvania. (Philadelphia, 1854.)

The Ritual of the Order of Know-Nothings with the Initiation Oaths taken by James Pollock, now Governor of Pennsylvania. (Philadelphia, 1855.)

Laurens, J. Wayne, *The Crisis: or the Enemies of America unmasked.* Philadelphia, 1855.

Denig, John, *The Know Nothing Manual, or, Book for America no. 1, in which the Native American Platform and Principles as adopted by the Know Nothings are set forth and defended ... . . .together with Dissertations on Romanism.* Harrisburg, 1855.

Forney, John Wien, *Address on religious Intolerance and political Proscription, delivered at Lancaster, Pa., on the Evening of the 24th of September.* Washington, 1855.

Narrative of the Facts in the Case of Passmore Williamson. Philadelphia, 1855.

The great Fraud by which Pennsylvania is sought to be abolitionized in October and November. The Abolition State Ticket and the Abolition Electoral Fillmore Ticket. (Philadelphia, 1856.)

Randall, Josiah, *Speech of Josiah Randall, Esq., of Philadelphia, delivered at Chambersburg, August 6, 1856, at the request of the Democratic State Convention, of Pennsylvania.* In the *Democratic Hand-Book for 1856.*

An Appeal for the Union by a Philadelphia Whig. (Philadelphia, 1856.)

Mr. Buchanan's Low Wage Doctrine. Philadelphia, (1856).

Address of the State Central Democratic Committee to the People of Pennsylvania. (Philadelphia, 1856.)

Proceedings of the Pennsylvania Democratic State Convention held at Harrisburg, March 4, 1856. Philadelphia, 1856.

Reed, William B., *Appeal to Pennsylvania. A Speech of Wm. B. Reed delivered at a meeting of Friends of Buchanan and Breckenridge at Somerset, Pa., September 24, 1856.* (Philadelphia, 1856.)

History of the Rise, Progress and Downfall of Know-Nothingism in Lancaster Co.; by two expelled Members. Lancaster, 1856.

Case of Passmore Williamson. Philadelphia, 1856.

WORKS BY CONTEMPORARIES

Forney, John W., *Anecdotes of Public Men.* 2 vols. New York, 1873. Sketches originally published in the newspapers; contains characterizations of some value.

Harris, Alexander, *A Review of the Political Conflict in America, from the Commencement of the Anti-Slavery Agitation to the Close of Southern Reconstruction; comprising also a Résumé of the Career of Thaddeus Stevens: being a Survey of the Struggle of Parties, which destroyed the Republic and virtually monar-*

chized its Government. New York, 1876. Material on the early career of Stevens is of value.

Hildreth, Richard, *Atrocious Judges.* New York, 1856. The appendix contains the proceedings in the case of Passmore Williamson.

Lee, John Hancock, *The Origin and Progress of the American Party in Politics.* Philadelphia, 1855. A publication intended to make converts for the cause.

McClure, A. K., *Old Time Notes of Pennsylvania.* 2 vols. Philadelphia, 1905. Of considerable value for the closing years of the Whig party.

McClure, A. K., *Our Presidents and How We Make Them.* New York, 1902. Popular presentation based on recollection.

McClure, A. K., *Recollections of Half a Century.* Salem, 1902. Disconnected sketches, a few of which are of value for this study.

Parke, John E., *Recollections of Seventy Years and Historical Gleanings of Allegheny, Pennsylvania.* Boston, 1886. Some material on social conditions.

Sargent, Nathan, *Public Men and Events from the Commencement of Mr. Monroe's Administration, in 1817, to the Close of Mr. Fillmore's Administration, in 1853.* 2 vols. Philadelphia, 1875. The recollections of a veteran Whig correspondent at Washington; of more value for national than for state politics.

Smedley, R. C., *History of the Underground Railroad in Chester and the Neighboring Counties of Pennsylvania.* Lancaster, 1883. The activities of the abolitionists in southeastern Pennsylvania are described; an account of the Christiana riot by a man of the vicinity.

BIOGRAPHIES

Armor, William C., *Lives of the Governors of Pennsylvania with the incidental History of the State, from 1609 to 1872.* Philadelphia, 1872. Brief sketches of value.

Binney, Charles Chauncey, *The Life of Horace Binney with Selections from his Letters.* Philadelphia, 1903. Biography of a lawyer occasionally politically active.

Callender, E. B., *Thaddeus Stevens: Commoner.* Boston, 1882. The pioneer biography; contains some source quotations on his early political career.

Clayton, Mary Black, *Reminiscences of Jeremiah Sullivan Black.* St. Louis, 1887. Little of value for this period.

Curtis, George Ticknor, *Life of James Buchanan.* 2 vols. New York, 1883. An effort to depict Buchanan as a statesman, with little attention to him as a politician.

DuBois, James T., and Mathews, Gertrude S., *Galusha A. Grow,*

Father of the Homestead Law. Boston, 1917. Valuable for light thrown on political conditions in the northern tier of counties.

Egle, William H., *Andrew Gregg Curtin, his Life and Services.* Philadelphia, 1895. Concerned with later career of subject.

Harris, Alex., *A Biographical History of Lancaster County: being a History of early Settlers and eminent Men of the County; and also much other unpublished historical Information, chiefly of a local Character.* Lancaster, 1872. Contains an article on Stevens by one of his law students.

Jones, Charles Henry, *The Life and Public Services of J. Glancey Jones.* 2 vols. Philadelphia, 1910. The career of an ardent Buchanan supporter of Berks county, the stronghold of the Democratic party.

Konkle, Burton Alva, *The Life of Chief Justice Ellis Lewis, 1798-1871, of the First Elective Supreme Court of Pennsylvania.* Philadelphia, 1907. Throws no light on the political situation.

Konkle, Burton Alva, *Life and Speeches of Thomas Williams, Orator, Statesman and Jurist, 1806-1872.* 2 vols. Philadelphia, 1905. Contains a little material of value for this study.

Meigs, William M., *The Life of Charles Jared Ingersoll.* Philadelphia, 1897. The biography of a leading Democrat of Philadelphia.

McCall, Samuel W., *Thaddeus Stevens.* Boston, 1899. Weak on the early career of Stevens.

Savidge, Eugene Coleman, *Life of Benjamin Harris Brewster with Discourses and Addresses.* Philadelphia, 1891. Throws some light on the activities of the Democrats during this period.

Simpson, Henry, *The Lives of Eminent Philadelphians, now deceased, collected from original and authentic Sources.* Philadelphia, 1859. Good brief sketches.

Woodburn, James Albert, *The Life of Thaddeus Stevens, A Study in American Political History, especially in the Period of the Civil War and Reconstruction.* Indianapolis, 1913. The best biography of Stevens, but containing little on the early period of his life.

CRITICAL WORKS ON PENNSYLVANIA

Bartlett, Marguerite G., *The Chief Phases of Pennsylvania Politics in the Jacksonian Period.* Allentown, 1919. Contains some material on the constitutional convention of 1837-1838.

Bishop, Alvard Longley, "The State Works of Pennsylvania," in the *Transactions of the Connecticut Academy of Arts and Sciences,* vol. xiii, November, 1907. An excellent treatment of the subject.

Hensel, W. U., *The Christiana Riot and the Treason Trials of 1851. An Historical Sketch.* Lancaster, 1911. A painstaking study of the disturbances; contains some of the source material.

McCarthy, Charles, "The Anti-Masonic Party: a Study of Political Anti-Masonry in the United States, 1827-1840." In the *Annual Report of the American Historical Association*, 1902, vol. i, pp. 365-574. Washington, 1903. A masterly study of one branch of the future Whig party.

Scharf, J. Thomas, and Wescott, Thompson, *History of Philadelphia, 1609-1884.* 3 vols. Philadelphia, 1884. Contains much valuable material on Philadelphia politics.

Swank, James M., *Progressive Pennsylvania. A Record of the remarkable Industrial Development of the Keystone State, and with some Account of its early and its later Transportation Systems, its early Settlers, and its prominent Men.* Philadelphia, 1908. Excellent for its information on the industries of the state.

Turner, Edward R., *The Negro in Pennsylvania. Slavery—Servitude —Freedom. 1639-1861.* Washington, 1911. Throws light on the status of the negro.

Worthington, A. B., "Historical Sketch of the Finances of Pennsylvania, in the *Proceedings of the American Economic Association*, May, 1887. An excellent summary of the financial legislation of the state.

II. BIBLIOGRAPHY OF CITED MATERIAL, OTHER THAN THAT OF PENNSYLVANIA

MANUSCRIPTS

Miscellaneous Manuscript Collection of the New York Historical Society. Contains a few isolated letters of value.

Papers of John M. Clayton; Library of Congress. A number of letters of importance.

Papers of Thomas Corwin; Lib. of Cong. Of value in connection with the dispute over William D. Lewis and the collectorship of the port of Philadelphia.

Papers of John J. Crittenden; Lib. of Cong. Contain some letters from the conservative Whigs of the state.

Papers of Thomas Ewing; Lib. of Cong. Of little value for this study.

Papers of John McLean; Lib. of Cong. Of considerable value for the anti-slavery branch of the Whig party in the state, particularly from the western portion.

Papers of James K. Polk; Lib. of Cong. Of value for his campaign, but, in the main, the material can be better obtained from the Buchanan Papers.

Papers of Daniel Webster; Lib. of Cong. A number of important letters from Anti-Masonic Whigs.

COLLECTED WORKS, DIARIES AND CORRESPONDENCE

Adams, Charles Francis (editor), *Memoirs of John Quincy Adams, comprising portions of his Diary from 1795 to 1848.* 12 vols. Philadelphia, 1874-1877.

"Correspondence of John C. Calhoun," *Report of the American Historical Association, 1899,* vol. ii. Washington, 1900.

Colton, Calvin (editor), *The Private Correspondence of Henry Clay.* New York, 1855.

Diary of James K. Polk. 4 vols. Chicago, 1910.

Writings and Speeches of Daniel Webster (National Edition). 18 vols. Boston, 1903.

DOCUMENTS

House Journal, 26th Congress, 1st Session. Washington, 1840.

Maryland Legislative Documents, 1852. Annapolis, 1852.

Reports of the House of Representatives, 26th Congress, 1st Session. Washington, 1840.

Richardson, James D., *Compilation of the Messages and Papers of the Presidents, 1789-1897.* Washington, 1896-1899.

Senate Executive Journal, vol. viii. Washington, 1887.

NEWSPAPERS

Niles' Weekly Register, Baltimore; 1833-1849.

Richmond Enquirer, Richmond; 1847.

ACCOUNTS BY CONTEMPORARIES

Barnes, Thurlow Weed, *Memoirs of Thurlow Weed.* Boston, 1884.

Elliott, R. S., *Notes taken from Sixty Years.* St. Louis, 1883.

Greeley, Horace, *Recollections of a Busy Life.* New York, 1872.

May, Samuel, Jr., *The Fugitive Slave Law and its Victims.* New York, 1861.

Weed, Harriet A. (editor), *Autobiography of Thurlow Weed.* Boston, 1883.

Wise, Henry A., *Seven Decades of the Union.* Philadelphia, 1876.

BIOGRAPHIES

Kennedy, John P., *Memoirs of the Life of William Wirt.* 2 vols. Philadelphia, 1849.

Sargent, Epes, *Life and Public Services of Henry Clay.* New York, 1848.

Seward, Frederick W., *William H. Seward: an Autobiography from 1801 to 1834, with a Memoir of his Life, and Selections from his Letters.* 3 vols. New York. 1891.

Tyler, L. G., *Letters and Times of the Tylers.* 2 vols. Richmond, 1884.

OTHER WORKS

Catterall, Ralph C. H., *The Second Bank of the United States.* Chicago, 1903.

Cole, Arthur Charles, *The Whig Party in the South.* Washington, 1913.

Fox, Dixon Ryan, *The Decline of Aristocracy in the Politics of New York.* New York, 1919.

Landon, Fred, "Negro Migration to Canada," *Journal of Negro History,* January, 1920.

McMaster, John Bach, *History of the People of the United States.* 8 vols. New York, 1883-1912.

Olbrich, Emil, *The Development of Sentiment on Negro Suffrage to 1860.* Madison, 1912.

Paullin. C. O., "The National Ticket of Broom and Coates, 1852," *The American Historical Review,* vol. xxv, July, 1920.

Rhodes, James Ford, *The History of the United States.* 8 vols. New York, 1892-1919.

Siebert, Wilbur H., *The Underground Railroad.* New York, 1898.

Stanwood, Edward, *History of the Presidency.* 2 vols. Boston, 1912.

INDEX

Adams, Charles Francis, 151
Alberti, George, 185-6, 194
Allegheny county, 107, 154
Allison, J. S., 148, 152
American party: see Know Nothings
Anthracite furnaces, 100
Anti-Masonic party, organized, 11; refuse to cooperate with the National Republicans, 12; maintain independent organization, 16; reject fusion with the Whigs, 18; state convention, 1835, 18-19; nominate Harrison for presidency, 1836, 29; oppose national convention, 29; policy in constitutional convention, 35-41; control coalition with the Whigs, 20, 29, 41, 56, 237; control broken, 54-55; Buckshot War, 49-55; state convention, 1838, 57-58; activity in Whig national convention, 1839, 60-61; address in 1840, 63-64; resent sneers of Whigs, 68-69; attempts to revive party, 1843, 90-91; persistency of party sentiment, 94, and note

Bailey and Brothers, 231
Baltimore and Ohio Railroad, 131-32
Bank Act of 1836, 23-28; of 1840, 62-63; of 1841, 69-72; of 1842, 76-77
Bank of Pennsylvania, 76
Bank officials, politics of, 38
Bank of the United States, Jackson's opposition to, 13; question of, 1834, 15-18; obtains state charter, 23-26; suspends specie payment, 62, 69; provision for resuscitation, 70; liquidation, 72; officials accused

of bribery, 74; Handy Bribery Investigation, 77-79; effect of failure of, on Whig party, 79
Banks, John, 69, 74
Banks, Nathaniel P., 227
Barker, Mayor of Pittsburgh, 176n., 194
Bedini, Cardinal, 208-9
Beecher, Henry Ward, 229
Berks county, 139, 245
Best, Valentine, 167
Biddle, Nicholas, 23, 70
Bigler, John, 180
Bigler, William, Democratic nominee for governor, 1851, 180; elected, 190-192; signs bill repealing Act of March 3, 1847, 193; pardons Alberti, 194; gubernatorial candidate, 1854, 210-11; defeated, 215
Binney, Horace, 31n., 243
Birney, James G., 111
Black, Jeremiah S., 215
Bonuses, paid by the banks, 25-27
Brackenridge, H. M., 202
Brewster, Benjamin H., 225n.
"Borers", activity of, in bank bribery, 77-79
Brodhead, Daniel M., 77-79
Brodhead, Richard, 177
Broom, Jacob, 198, 215
Brown, David Paul, 31n.
Buchanan, James, "Ten Cent Jimmie", 64; withdraws as presidential candidate, 1843, 92; activity in campaign of 1844, 103; recommended for secretaryship of state by the electoral college, 114-5; tariff of 1846, 121; a former Federalist, 137n.; on slavery in new territory, 139; opposition to leadership by, 143, 194; endorsed for presidency, 1852, 194; not nominated, 197;